INTERNATIONAL STUDENTS IN NEW ZEALAND
THE MAKING OF POLICY SINCE 1950

INTERNATIONAL STUDENTS IN NEW ZEALAND

THE MAKING OF POLICY SINCE 1950

Nicholas Tarling

New Zealand Asia Institute
The University of Auckland

New Zealand Asia Institute
Te Roopu Aotearoa Ahia
58 Symonds St
The University of Auckland
P O Box 92 019
Auckland
New Zealand

www.auckland.ac.nz/nzai

ISBN 0-476-00588-4

National Library of New Zealand Cataloguing-in-Publication Data

Tarling, Nicholas.
International students in New Zealand : the making of policy since
1950 / Nicholas Tarling.
Includes bibliographical references.
ISBN 0-476-00588-4
1. Students, Foreign—Government policy—New Zealand.
2. Students, Foreign—New Zealand—History. I. New Zealand Asia
Institute (University of Auckland) II. Title.
371.826910993—dc 22

Cover and text designed by Egan-Reid Limited
Typeset by Egan-Reid Ltd, www.egan-reid.com
Printed in New Zealand

CONTENTS

PREFACE

The movement of international students is a very marked feature of the life of universities and other educational institutions in the early twentieth-first century, but it has been too little studied. Much of what has been done tends, moreover, to focus on the 'market', on selling places to foreign students, particularly from Asia, and on what are often seen as their learning difficulties. The New Zealand Asia Institute has decided, with the support of the Vice-Chancellor, Dr John Hood, to undertake additional studies, partly in order better to understand what has happened, and partly with a view to shaping the future.

The initial focus is on international students in New Zealand. It is, however, intended to range more widely, in order to put the New Zealand situation in a larger context, and to pursue and encourage comparative studies in respect of other countries. The present book represents a first step. It offers an account of the making of New Zealand's policy towards international students since the inauguration of the Colombo Plan in 1950.

The work is largely based on official materials, printed and primary. The author is grateful for permission to utilise material from the archives of the University of Auckland, the University Grants Committee, and the Vice-Chancellors Committee, and for the help he received from the National Archives and from Mrs Werren in the VCC office.

He is also indebted to two hard-working research assistants, Charlotte Hughes and Henry Acland, and to a number of people who have read and commented on all or parts of the manuscript, including Roger Peddie, Grant Wills, Jack Caldwell, Mike Murtagh, and Andrew Butcher. He is particularly grateful to James Kember, former Director of the Institute, for his participatory support and encouragement. To him the book is dedicated.

Auckland, 2004

CHAPTER ONE

THE COLOMBO PLAN

The 'Colombo Plan' was actual but also symbolic. In New Zealand, it came to stand, and in popular perception still stands, for a particular collection of attitudes and practices in international education. One of them is aid on the part of developed countries for the undeveloped, in particular in technical and practical education. Another is the emphasis on the bilateral relationship. A third, partly related to that, is the increasing sense in which the relationship becomes personal and mutual. Associated with that, fourthly, is a feeling that New Zealand is itself learning from the relationship, and, more concretely, benefiting short- and long-term from the contacts that are established, through the presence of New Zealand experts in other CP countries, and in particular through the presence of Colombo Plan students in New Zealand. Yet these features represent a shaping of the original plan, inflected by New Zealand's own attitudes and policies, that both stressed some aspects of it and downplayed others.

Initially the Plan was not so exclusively focused on students – or on 'technical assistance' – as popular memory suggests, or as is implied by the emphasis of the celebratory volume, *The Colombo Plan at 50 A New Zealand Perspective.*[1] It was perhaps natural that a small country, with limited resources and problems with foreign exchange, should not focus on capital projects. But, as Bryce Harland points out [ibid., pp. 9-10], it was soon involved in a number of them, and some officials believed that they should have a larger part in the aid programme. Harland also suggests that international aid was 'new to most New Zealanders' when the CP

---

[1]   Wellington: MFAT, n.d.

began. [p. 8] The educational aid extended to the Trust Territory of Samoa in 1945, extended to Niue and the Cooks the following year, was, of course, not 'international' aid. Sending Samoans to New Zealand second-ary schools, and to university or teachers college, may have formed something of a precedent, however, though the 'South Pacific' retained an aid priority throughout the period.

'Colombo Plan' is also a phrase used in respect of a period in the history of 'international' students in New Zealand: it at once comes to the lips of those who discuss or attempt to recall the 1950s and 1960s. Yet the number of students who were entering the New Zealand education system not under that Plan or indeed any other soon exceeded the numbers who were. In some sense they were the advance guard of today's 'private international students'. In other ways they differed. They paid domestic fees. And the attitudes and policies to them were affected by the attitudes and policies developed in respect of aided students. The policies were, as a result, much conflicted. Not until the wholesale reforms of the second Lange government did the current system displace the old. Not until quite recent years did the admission of large numbers of students from the People's Republic of China in turn give real effect to those reforms.

The attitudes associated with the Plan – dormant, perhaps, though not dead, nor quite irrelevant, though overlaid – initially belonged to the Cold War years. Behind the idealism that it both showed and generated, lay a realism, clearly evident from the start. Indeed the Commonwealth Foreign Ministers who met in Colombo in January 1950 had a larger project in mind, of which what became the CP was in fact only part. That project originated with the British, and with their perception of South and Southeast Asia in the late 1940s. India, Pakistan and Burma had gained their independence in 1947-8. The Dutch 'police actions' in Indonesia had failed. Even the French had promised that Vietnam should be 'free'. But could these newly independent states survive in the Cold War world? Stalin had set up the Cominform and adopted the Zhdanov line, and Mao was leading the CCP to victory in China. Communism had to be fought not only by supporting nationalist claims to independence, but by promoting economic and social development. The British had another aim as well. That was to involve the US in the defence of South and Southeast Asia. It had burned its fingers in China, and had no wish to take on additional burdens. But, if it could be shown that the Asian countries were aiding each other, the Americans might be more disposed to help, while their help might be more acceptable to India, the major country concerned, if part of a larger scheme that emphasised mutuality and, initially at least, downplayed defence.

Stymied in Europe by Marshall Aid and NATO, Russia, Ernest Bevin, the British Foreign Secretary, told his colleagues, was turning its attention to Asia. The answer was not a pact like NATO: 'the right policy was for the like-minded countries with interests in the East to keep in close contact and be ready to help each other in resisting any attempts to hinder peaceful development on democratic lines. He recognised the close inter-dependence of East and West and stressed the great need for the expansion of capital development and food production in the less developed countries. He hoped a policy of financial help without domination could be adopted towards these countries.'[2] On other issues they discussed at Colombo – notably the recognition of Communist China and of the Bao Dai regime in Vietnam – the Commonwealth Foreign Ministers differed. But Bevin's suggestion took hold, perhaps the more effectively because the British did not openly take the initiative, but left it to others. Those were Percy Spender of Australia and J. R. Jayawardene of Ceylon, who, after consulting the New Zealand delegation led by F. W. Doidge, offered a joint paper.

The joint memorandum suggested that a consultative committee for South and Southeast Asia should receive from governments an indication of the broad lines of action they considered feasible; examine methods of coordinating development activities in South and Southeast Asia with other interested countries and regional and international organisations; examine the measures to be taken if possible for stabilising price levels of basic products; consider a plan for the economic development of the underdeveloped countries of the area and an organisation for carrying it out within a specific period; and make recommendations to governments on these subjects.[3]

In reporting to the British cabinet the Foreign Secretary suggested that the Colombo meeting, the first of its kind to be held in Asia, 'demonstrated to a heartening degree the extent of co-operation which can be developed between East and West through the agency of the Commonwealth'. There was 'a remarkable unaninimity of view as to the menace of Communism and as to the necessity of improving the standard of life and the social welfare of the peoples of South and Southeast Asia in order to combat this menace'. The proposal on economic policy was 'widely written up as the only concrete achievement of the Meeting', and Ceylon and Australia competed for the credit. 'More soberly considered, the proposal holds out the promise of useful activity, and might help to enlist United States assistance in the area.'[4]

---

[2] q. N. Tarling, *Britain, Southeast Asia and the Onset of the Cold War*, Cambridge UP, 1998, p. 336.

[3] FMM (50) 6, 12.1.50. CAB 133/78, National Archives, London.

[4] CP (50) 18, 22.2.50. CAB 129/38.

For the British the Colombo Plan – Hunter Wade of the New Zealand delegation claimed paternity of the name, designed to avoid conflict between the claims of Spender and Jayawardene[5] – was part of a larger strategy, designed to bring the non-Communist powers together and interest the US in their fate. Some six months later, the situation was drastically changed by the outbreak of the Korean war. The Plan lost its larger strategic purpose, though among the measures the US took in reaction was to agree to support it. Instead it became, as a member of the UK Commonwealth Relations Office put it, a 'slogan' under cover of which Canada, Australia and New Zealand 'make contributions which, without such cover, they might not be able to make'; technical aid was recorded and systematically categorised; and aid from the West was brought together and could be contrasted with what was done by Russia and China.[6] It was not merely 'popular' in South and Southeast Asia, a British Treasury official suggested in 1959, 'but has now acquired some kind of emotional response, and the same is true of many Western countries'.[7]

It focused on economic cooperation, including both capital investment in projects and technical assistance. Increasingly it emphasised – certainly so far as New Zealand was concerned – the latter, which included the despatch of experts to developing countries and the reception of students from them. 'Today, in New Zealand at least, the Colombo Plan is remembered mainly as a plan for bringing Asian students to New Zealand rather than as a wide-ranging effort to support the development of Asian countries.'[8] For a small country, with its own hard-currency problems, that indeed was a realistic option. Alongside the Colombo Plan scholars, and soon outnumbering them, were private students, generally from the same countries, paying their own way, but subsidised, though not formally 'aided', inasmuch as they were charged the low-level domestic tuition fees. Often they are subsumed in current parlance in the phrase 'Colombo Plan', though they were not sent on the formal endorsement of their governments, and the largest single group were Malaysian Chinese, unable to enter universities in their own country.

Together the two groups began to make an impact which the makers of the Plan had scarcely contemplated. There was now an Asian presence on New Zealand campuses, and New Zealanders, enjoined by their government, offered the students their hospitality. Here indeed was a novelty for

[5]   *The Colombo Plan at 50*, pp. 9-10.
[6]   Report by Rumbold, 31.12.56. DO 35/5472, National Archives, London.
[7]   Draft, The Future of the Colombo Plan, in Jenkyns/Costar, 1.7.59. DO 35/8783.
[8]   *The Colombo Plan at 50*, p. 12.

an isolated country, whose immigration policies focused on Europe, and whose non-indigenous population was sustained by what was in effect a White New Zealand policy. But, though their numbers grew, they remained small, and they were not expected to stay once their training was complete. They were objects of interest, sympathy and curiosity, not of resentment or fear.

The technical assistance scheme had been set up at the first meeting of the Commonwealth Consultative Committee on the Colombo Plan, held in Sydney in May 1950, when the governments agreed to contribute a maximum of GBP 8m over three years. A council for technical cooperation was to focus on training personnel in countries where facilities were available, on sending experts, instructors and advisory missions, on providing equipment for training or use by technical experts in the region. There was an 'acute shortage of trained men', the 'inevitable result of the endeavours being made to break with traditional methods and to introduce new techniques. ... The Governments of the countries in the area are making every effort to train their own people, by developing their own training facilities, and, with the cooperation of other Governments, by sending students overseas, and by recruiting experts from abroad'.[9]

In March 1951 New Zealand agreed to provide NZP 1m a year for the first three years for economic development, and to provide training, experts and equipment to the value of NZP400k. 50 fellowships and scholarships were approved in 1951, mainly for India, Pakistan and Ceylon.[10] In 1952, however, the Minister noted that of the 60 CP trainees in New Zealand, 13 came from Malaya, 5 from Sarawak, and 3 from North Borneo.[11] He also noted the demands on departments, educational institutions, local bodies, and private firms, both for training facilities and release of experts. 'He was happy to state that the Government was receiving active support from wide sections of the community in making the stay of trainees both worthwhile and pleasant.' The government was grateful to many who were extending private hospitality to the students: 'there was no better way in which to acquaint people from Asia with the great store of good will towards them which existed in New Zealand.'[12]

At the preliminary meeting of officials held before the Consultative Committee met in Singapore in 1955, the New Zealanders declared that

---

[9] The Colombo Plan ..., Report by the Commonwealth Consultative Committee, 9-10.50. Appendices to the Journal of the House of Representatives [AJHR], 1950, A-17, pp. 52, 54.

[10] *External Affairs Review* [EAR], 2.5 (May 1952), p. 23.

[11] Statement, 4.10.52. EAR 2.11 (November 1952), p. 2.

[12] ibid., p. 3.

they were pleased with their capital aid projects, but thought that the 212 trainees so far sent were 'far too few', and they hoped that many more would come. Government and people had been 'most grateful for the contacts with the people of Asia which have resulted from the operation of the Colombo Plan. We are an isolated country. ... We are a young country which can benefit, and indeed has benefited greatly, from our growing knowledge and understanding of the culture and heritage of the people of this area.[13] 'Many strands of personal friendhip so formed can be woven into a permanent material that may prove of great protective value in the years ahead', T.L. Macdonald, now Minister of External Affairs, told the meeting itself on 20 October.[14]

Commenting at Harewood on the 1956 arrivals – 54 Asian students from 8 countries – Macdonald expanded on his predecessor's theme. New Zealand shared the view expressed at the Singapore meeting that increased emphasis should be put on technical assistance and wanted to play its part. The Minister was sure all New Zealanders would join him in welcoming them. 'We are glad to have them with us, and look forward to making their better acquaintance. They can do much to help us learn more about their countries. For our part, we hope that we shall be able to help them equip themselves for the great tasks of economic development which await them in their own countries.'[15]

In 1956 the Consultative Committee met in Wellington and was chaired by Macdonald. He took up the theme yet again. He was struck, he said, by the success of the technical cooperation side of the CP's work. 'The students from other countries come here, live for a while, and learn our customs and get to know our way of life. We know that when they go back to their own countries in South East Asia, they carry with them a knowledge of New Zealand, and in that way they are able to let their own folk know what our feelings are towards the people in South East Asia.' New Zealand experts sent to Southeast Asia also built friendships: 'they have met the people up there in terms of equality, helping the good name of New Zealand in those areas'.[16]

Significant progress had been made in the six years since the programme began, the meeting recognised, but 'all that has been accomplished is scarcely more than a beginning, and the scale and complexity of the problems to be solved is very great indeed'. New Zealand had supported a number of capital assistance projects, but had decided 'to give greater

[13]   Attachment 8 to Minutes, 6th meeting, 4.10.55. DO 35/5729.
[14]   DO 35/5731.
[15]   EAR, 6.2 (February 1956), pp. 7-8.
[16]   Statement, 5.11.56. EAR, 6.11 (November 1956), pp. 14-15.

emphasis to technical assistance (the provision of advisers and consultants, and of training in New Zealand)', and 'the number of people from Asian countries who were studying in New Zealand doubled during the year'. Several Government departments 'gave invaluable cooperation ..., and the programme under which the Colombo Plan students come to New Zealand could not have been as successful without the help of a large number of private organisations and very many individuals throughout the country'.[17]

There were 206 CP students and trainees in New Zealand at the end of March 1957, compared with 99 the previous year. 156 students had arrived during the year, more than half the total number who had come since the Plan began. The countries from which the new students came, now predominantly Southeast Asian, were Burma, 20; Ceylon, 5; India, 2; Indonesia, 41; Malaya, 42; North Borneo, 15; Pakistan, 4; Philippines, 3; Sarawak, 7; Singapore, 9; Thailand, 7. The courses they took ranged widely: administration, 3; agriculture, 21; arts, 6; commerce, 4; dentistry, 4; education and teaching, 55; engineering, 20; health, 15; communications, 4; mining, 12; law, 1; science, 10; social welfare, 1. 67 were taking university courses.[18]

Between 1950 and 1957 468 students had received training. Burma, 40; Ceylon, 70; India, 58; Indonesia, 63; Malaya, 114; Nepal, 2; North Borneo, 25; Pakistan, 59; Philippines, 3; Sarawak, 13; Singapore, 10; Thailand, 11. The major fields of study had been engineering, 94; education, 91; and health, 65.[19] In total 5622 students had received advanced training under the Colombo Plan, while the US had financed another 5000.[20]

For the first five years New Zealand had made separate appropriations for capital and technical assistance. That practice was discontinued in 1956/7, and a combined appropriation of NZP 1.1m p.a. was made. That was reduced to NZP 750k in 1957-8. That year there were 213 CP students in New Zealand, 'a record number'. Expenditure on technical assistance, including some equipment, was NZP263,170.[21]

Early in 1959 there were 250 CP students in New Zealand, including the first from Vietnam. The conference in Seattle in November 1958 had emphasised that 'in underdeveloped countries a shortage of skilled people is proving more frustrating than limits of capital resources'. As large a

[17]   Annual Report of DEA, 1956-7. AJHR 1957, A.1, p. 42.
[18]   ibid., p. 44.
[19]   The Colombo Plan: A review. EAR, 7.11 (November 1957), p. 7.
[20]   ibid., p. 1.
[21]   Report of DEA for year ended 31.3.58. AJHR 1958, A.1, pp. 28, 29.

contribution as possible was therefore made in this field, including the provision of well trained and selected experts.[22]

'A good deal of our Colombo Plan money is wasted', Frank Corner told Alister McIntosh. 'A lot of expensive equipment has merely rusted away. Much of it hasn't made any impact on the area in the way of creating friendly feeling for us.' He thought individual contacts produced the best results. 'One of the most effective things we could do is to take more students from Malaya and South East Asian countries into our universities. But our universities are over-crowded. Therefore work out an agreement with the Universities that we will divert Colombo Plan money to them for the expansion of their teaching and residence facilities on condition that they take an agreed number of S.E. Asian students. An amount of money which is insignificant when thrown into Asia could be much more significant – and produce better results – when handed out to N.Z. universties.'[23] The idea clearly influenced what New Zealand did. There was a drawback: the aid would not be clearly going to other countries.

The Colombo Plan, External Affairs observed as its tenth anniversary came round, had 'provided a setting for the practical and dynamic expression of one of the central elements of New Zealand's external policy – its desire for friendly relations with Asian countries and its willingness to assist them in their strivings for improved conditions of life and opportunity'. The Yogyakarta conference of 1959 extended the Plan to 1966, and no doubt it would continue for many years beyond that. It was timely 'to review experience and to determine steps which may be necessary to ensure that New Zealand's future aid programme falls into a coherent and balanced pattern giving the best scope for the contribution of special abilities and skills towards Asian development.'

Among its conclusions, External Affairs thought the most important was 'that technical assistance, by way of sending New Zealand experts to Asia or bringing Asian students to New Zealand, represents the most effective use, pound for pound, of the money New Zealand is able to make available to assist the development of South and South-East Asia. Exchanges of this type have not only had a proportionately large effect on current and future development in the underdeveloped countries, but have helped to build up much good will and understanding'. The government had directed 'that steps should be taken to increase New Zealand's capacity to provide technical assistance particularly by bringing Asian students and

---

[22] Report of DEA for year ended 31.3.59. AJHR 1959, A.1, p. 33.
[23] Corner/McIntosh, 6.12.57 in Ian McGibbon, ed., *Unofficial Channels*, Wellington: VUW P, 1999, p. 241.

trainees to New Zealand'. A number of proposals were being developed, one of the first the establishment of an English Language Institute at VUW. That was designed to provide training for CP students in New Zealand held back by 'a lack of facility in English'. It would also provide training in the teaching of English as a second language for Asian teachers brought to New Zealand under the Plan, and for New Zealand teachers sent to Asia. Other proposals included the enlargement of halls of residence at New Zealand university colleges to provide additional hostel accommodation for Colombo Plan students.[24]

That year, 1959-60, 65 Colombo Plan students came to New Zealand: Sarawak, 12; North Borneo, 9; Thailand, 8; Burma, 8; Ceylon, 7; Malaya, 6; Indonesia, 5; Philippines, 3; Singapore, 2; Vietnam, 2; Nepal, 1. 721 students had come to NZ since the start of the Plan. Their main fields were education, 127; engineering, 134; medical and health, 119; and food and agriculture and forestry, 112. The medical and health category included dental nurses, rather than doctors. Business/Commerce students were notably absent. But in those days that field was unattractive to New Zealand students, too, and enjoyed rather low prestige in the universities. And Information Science was still in the future.

The External Affairs Department explained the shift that had taken place. At first most awards had been given for practical courses of comparatively short duration in agriculture, health and engineering to trainees primarily from three Asian Commonwealth countries that were founder members of the scheme, India, Pakistan and Ceylon. More recently there had been 'a great increase' in students coming from Southeast Asia, especially Malaya and British Borneo. 'In most of these countries, university facilities are not yet sufficient to meet the demand for higher education and considerable numbers of students – more than one third of those who have so far arrived in New Zealand – have therefore been nominated for university courses', mostly in engineering, agriculture and science.[25]

New Zealand's appropriation to the Colombo Plan for the 1959-60 year was back at NZP1m. That brought its total contribution since 1951 to NZP9, 315,000. The prime minister, Walter Nash, emphasised that Western countries had 'a serious obligation to assist' the countries of Asia and Africa to 'create new standards of life and opportunity' on the basis, not of dictation or compulsion, but of cooperation and mutual benefit. The Colombo Plan, External Affairs observed, provided such a

---

[24]   Report of DEA for year ending 31.3.60. AJHR 1960, A.1, pp. 20-1.
[25]   The Colombo Plan... EAR, 10.5 (May 1960), p. 4.

relationship, and could be expected to remain 'central and dominant' in New Zealand's external aid programmes.[26]

Early in 1961 Keith Holyoake, now prime minister, also minister of external affairs, welcomed the new batch of Colombo Plan students – 137 in all – and again said that the presence of such students, and that of others under other plans, 'greatly helped New Zealanders to understand their ways of life and the problems faced by their Governments'. 'At the same time', continued Mr Holyoake, 'by working and living side by side with New Zealanders, by visiting our homes and by seeing our country, they are coming to understand us. Mutual respect and sympathy built up by such personal contacts is the best foundation for good international relations.'[27]

The following month the 800th CP student arrived in New Zealand. She was one of a group of 28 English language teachers from Indonesia, who were to take a year's course at the new English Language Institute at VUW. 'While in New Zealand the group, all of whom have previously been members of English language courses in Indonesia staffed by New Zealand teachers, will extend their knowledge of English and of language-teaching techniques.' 800 was a small number in relation to the needs of the area, but their effect would be considerable, the Prime Minister added. Appropriately the 800th student was associated with 'one of New Zealand's best-known technical assistance programmes – the English language teaching project in Indonesia whose economic progress depends so much on mastering and applying the scientific and technical knowledge that is available through the medium of the English language'.[28] English language teaching was not then a business, but a government-supported programme, designed as aid in itself, and also intended to make other forms of aid more effective.

The government also took steps to improve accommodation for Colombo Plan students,such as Warwick House in Christchurch.[29] In April 1961 Holyoake announced that the government would finance a hostel building at OU so that more Asian students could be brought to New Zealand under the Plan. Bringing students and trainees to New Zealand, he again said, was 'one of the most useful and productive kinds of help that New Zealand could give'. The country was small, but 'we have a useful combination of a high level of technical skill and a down-to-earth

---

26 Report, p. 23.
27 EAR, 11.2 (February 1961), p. 22.
28 Statement, 1.3.61. EAR, 11.3 (March 1961), p. 20.
29 DEA Report for year ended 31.3.61. AJHR 1961, A.1, p. 30.

approach to practical problems'. In addition, technical assistance built up 'the relationship of knowledge and understanding ... that our position in this part of the world makes so necessary for our future'. In the hostels Asian students would be accommodated alongside New Zealand students. Day-to-day contacts made technical assistance more valuable. 'Living with people of different outlook and background is also of much value to New Zealand students.'[30]

The tenth anniversary, 1 July 1961, was Colombo Plan Day. In a statement on the occasion, the Prime Minister repeated the themes that had become usual: New Zealand's emphasis on education and training; the element of partnership and exchange; 'the opportunity to learn from countries whose cultural inheritance is in many ways richer and more varied than ours'; the prospect of continued cooperation.[31] He gave a reception for about 130 students from Wellington and Palmerston, along with New Zealand experts returned from overseas. Many of the students were in national dress, making the scene around Parliament unusually colourful. The Colombo Plan was 'so completely accepted as a part of New Zealand's regular activity that in many respects the presence in this country of some hundreds of Colombo Plan students' normally 'passed unnoticed'.[32] The total New Zealand had appropriated to date was NZP10 315 000, of which NZP1 750 000 had been spent on technical assistance. It had received 898 students, as compared wth Canada, 1374, Australia, 3084, and the UK, 3257.[33]

Over 100 CP students stayed in New Zealand homes during the August university vacation of 1961. 'This hospitality resulted largely from offers received by the Department of External Affairs from voluntary organisations including Jaycees, Rotary, Federation of University Women, United Nations Association, and the National Council of Churches, as well as from individual people. In addition, some were guests in the homes of fellow New Zealand students whom they had met in the course of their studies.' The Prime Minister expressed his appreciation. New Zealanders were helping to make the sojourn of the students 'both fruitful and enjoyable. It is through personal contributions of this nature that the ties of friendship and cooperation between New Zealand and the countries of South-East Asia are strengthened in the most lasting way, and a real community of international understanding is achieved.'[34]

---

[30]   Statement, 27.4.61. EAR, 11.4 (April 1961), pp. 25-6.
[31]   Statement, 1.7.61. EAR, 11.7 (July 961), pp. 32-3.
[32]   New Zealand's Part... ibid., p. 16.
[33]   ibid., pp. 18, 20.
[34]   Statement, 6.9.61. EAR, 11.9 (Sepetmber 1961), p. 21.

Such remarks recur, but that does not make them merely ritual; perhaps the reverse. The government was promoting as well as celebrating a policy, and was enjoying some success. The ideas it pushed took quite strong roots, still with a hold in the 1980s, both in the community at large and in the universities as well, extending, moreover, to the self-funding students as well as the formally aided. At the time, indeed, it was simpler to think in terms of aid and goodwill, while at the same time rather strenuously trying to avoid a patronising tone by stressing mutuality. The ideas took root and rather stood in the way of changes later governments sought to promote. Only in the 1990s did a more purely commercial approach prevail, accompanied by little more than lip service to the idea of 'internationalisation'. The shift in the attitude to 'home-stays' was also apparent.

The growth in the numbers of Colombo Plan students posed 'a problem of accommodation'. External Affairs attempted to encourage home-stays, but they had another purpose, too. 'In the spirit of the Colombo Plan we have much more to offer than our fine educational facilities. The knowledge and wisdom which our teachers can impart will have a much more lasting effect if these students can be introduced into our family homes where they can gain an insight into the responsibilities of good citizenship. Only in the environment of family life can our visitors truly appreciate the full meaning of community responsibilities.'[35] The response to the Prime Minister's appeal for accommodation was, he said a fortnight later, 'most gratifying and heart-warming'. 160 Wellington and Hutt families had offered to take a student. To those who lived too far away for their offer to be accepted, Holyoake commended 'the idea of weekend or holiday hospitality'.[36]

In 1963 the appeal was extended to Auckland and Christchurch. In those cities, it was recognised that some New Zealand students had trouble in getting satisfactory board. In making a special appeal for overseas students, Holyoake said, the government was seeking cooperation from 'people interested in New Zealand's international relations and who would not normally consider taking boarders'. That year 78 Colombo Plan students would come from Malaysia and Singapore, and from Thailand, 42; Indonesia, 36; Vietnam, 15; The Philippines, 8; India, 4; Pakistan, Nepal and Ceylon, 2 or 3 each.[37]

The prolonged crisis in the Congo, along with the 'winds of change', had helped to turn Commonwealth attention to Africa. At the CPM

---

[35] Statement, 13.10.62. EAR, 12.10 (October 1962), p. 38.
[36] Statement, 27.10.62. ibid., pp. 39-40.
[37] EAR, 13.2 (February 1963), p. 13.

meeting in London in May 1960, 'suggestions were ... made for a plan of economic assistance to the Commonwealth countries of Africa', supplementing UN and other aid programmes. In September the Commonwealth Economic Consultative Committee decided to set up the Special Commonwealth Aid to Africa Plan (SCAAP), rather on the Colombo Plan model, with aid on a bilateral basis. On a smaller scale, it would emphasise technical assistance. New Zealand decided to contribute NZP100k annually, funding up to 40 African students in New Zealand and 10 New Zealand experts in Africa. Learning from its Colombo Plan experience, it focused on university courses. Two Nigerians were the first to come: they were to study history at Otago.[38] The scheme would help emerging countries to overcome the challenges of development, enhance Commonwealth ties, and provide an opportunity to strengthen personal contacts.[39]

African students were included in the totals offered in Holyoake's 1963 statement. Under the Colombo Plan and SCAAP, that year altogether 225 new students from 20 countries were coming to New Zealand. 100 would be going to universities, 22 into Sixth Form to qualify for University Entrance, and 53 would be attending non-university courses or doing special work. Under SCAAP, the numbers were Kenya, 13; Tanganyika, 13; Uganda, 5; and one each from Nigeria, Sierra Leone, and Southern Rhodesia. The university students would include 31 engineers, 24 agriculture students, 20 arts students, 'destined either for teaching or for careers in administration', and 13 science students. The non-university students would take courses in physiotherapy, radiography, nursing, teaching the deaf, trade school instruction, stenography, library work, valuation, physical education, and 'the operation of a slaughterhouse'. Students from North Borneo, Thailand and Indonesia were going to ELI at VUW.

Two hundred Colombo Plan students came to New Zealand in 1963/4, bringing the total in the country to 465: 41 came from Indonesia, 36 from Sabah (North Borneo), 27 from Thailand, 20 from Sarawak, 16 from Malaya, 16 from Singapore, 13 from Vietnam, 8 from India, 8 from the Philippines, 5 from Ceylon, 3 from Nepal, 3 from Pakistan, 2 from Burma.[40] The grand total rose to 524 in 1964/5. The largest groups were from Peninsular Malaysia, 84; Thailand, 72; Sabah, 69; Sarawak, 64; Vietnam, 52; and Indonesia, 35.[41]

The 'campaign' to find homes for Colombo Plan and SCAAP students

---

[38] EAR, 11.4 (April 1961), pp. 13-14.
[39] Statement by Eyre, 24.3.61. EAR, 11.3 (March 1961), p. 26.
[40] Report of DEA for year ended 31.3.64. AJHR 1964, A.1. p. 35.
[41] Report of DEA for year ended 31.3.65. AJHR 1965, A.1, p. 41.

had received 'an excellent response' in Auckland, Wellington and Christchurch, the Prime Minister declared in March 1963: 140 homes had been offered in Auckland, 75 in Christchurch. 'Homes have also been found ... for a number of private students from Asia and the Pacific islands.' Holyoake 'expressed his appreciation of the assistance gven by the newspapers, and thanked all groups and voluntary workers who had been helping the Department of External Affairs to get the students settled in'.[42] In addition the government increased its expenditure on hostel accommodation. Over the period up to 1970, that included extensions to Arana Hall in Dunedin, Colombo Halls at MU and CU, additional beds at LC, expansion to Weir House at VUW, and a substantial contribution to International House at AU.[43]

If one included all the students in New Zealand on New Zealand government programmes, on UN scholarships, and own government funded, 'and also those who are here privately at their own expense', there were about 1900 overseas students in New Zealand, the Prime Minister said in June 1965. About 500 of them were in Auckland. He acknowledged the cooperation of Aucklanders in looking after overseas students. Some years before about 80 clubs and societies had formed the Overseas Students Bureau to help cope with offers of accommodation, arrange functions, and assist students in other ways. Some Rotary Clubs had set up an office to help them find vacation work. But it could no longer all be done on a voluntary basis. The groups had come together to form a new International Students' Hospitality organisation, and the government had appointed a Liaison Officer (Overseas Students), who would also act as its secretary [A.R. Uden]. The members of the committee included representatives of clubs and societies in the Auckland area, including the Pan-Pacific Women's Association, the Federation of University Women, Rotary and Lions. Also among them were Alma Simmonds, Welfare Counsellor assisting the DEA in the supervision of Colombo Plan and SCAAP students, for some years secretary of the Bureau, and A. H. McNaughton, senior lecturer in Education at AU, DEA's Academic Counsellor in Auckland.[44]

Technical assistance, DEA had reiterated, represented 'the most economical use of the funds allocated by the Government for use under the Colombo Plan'.[45] Up to March 1963, C.G. F. Simkin calculated, capital

---

[42] EAR, 13.3 (March 1963), p. 23.
[43] First Report of Conroller and Auditor-General, 31.3.70. AJHR 1970, B.1 Pt 2, p. 43.
[44] Statement by PM, 11.6.65. EAR, 15.6 (June 1965), p. 31.
[45] Report for year ended 31.3.63. AJHR 1963, A.1, p. 35.

grants formed 72% of New Zealand's total Colombo Plan aid, but in 1963-6 it formed only 52%, partly as a result of 'New Zealand's apparently chronic difficulty over foreign exchange'.[46] The positive attitude to technical assistance expressed in public was not always echoed within External Affairs. The exchange argument was perhaps decisive.

Treasury was opposed to any increase in Colombo Plan expenditure beyond 1.5m pounds p.a., Bryce Harland noted in March 1965. The cost of training in New Zealand would reach about NZP450k in 1965-6; experts cost 240k; continuing capital aid, mostly on the Indus, some 200k. In addition some 1m was to be spent on university buildings. Bringing in more students would require more expenditure on buildings and 'thus ... increase our vulnerability to criticism overseas': a reference, it seems, to the suggestion New Zealand was in fact spending much of its aid at home, conserving foreign exchange, while boosting its own economic activity. 'There is also the question of the effect on our universities etc. of bringing in substantially more foreign students at a time when the number of New Zealanders wishing to attend is growing more rapidly than the ability of Government to provide facilities. This is, of course, a point of interest to the Treasury.' Training in New Zealand was valuable, Harland thought, but not 'the most important requirement'. 'From a strictly economic view', money was better spent in the area – on a training college rather than scholarships, for example – or on other capital projects. The benefit of bringing people to New Zealand was 'largely of a long-term character', while capital aid, dispersed on substantial projects, produced fairly quick political returns, perhaps greatest indeed – he added, perhaps a little cynically – at the time of announcement.[47]

A colleague pointed to the 'hidden' factor in training 2000 students (or 600 Colombo Plan students) in New Zealand: 'the high cost of providing education facilities'. It was easy, he added, to overestimate the effect of training in terms of the subsequent influence of the students in their own countries: 'New Zealand is well down the list of student priorities'. In Indonesia a returned student was often 'discarded', his qualification unrecognised. Training abroad was 'regarded suspiciously by some Colombo Plan countries. It could be regarded as a device for avoiding using overseas reserves and for stimulating the internal economy.'[48]

In February 1966 the Prime Minister commented on the academic success of Colombo Plan students, perhaps as a result of the discussion within DEA. About 70 Colombo Plan and SCAAP students had completed

---

[46] *Far Eastern Economic Review,* 64.15, 6-12.4.69.
[47] Minute, 15.3.65. PM 118/29/11, MFAT, Wellington.
[48] Minute, 8.4.65. ibid.

bachelor or master courses in 1965. Of 15 Colombo Plan students who had completed BE at Canterbury, 8 had secured first-class honours, including 3 from Malaysia, three from Singapore, 1 from Thailand and 1 from Vietnam. That represented one-third of the first-class results in BE Hons that year at Canterbury. 8 Colombo Plan students and 3 African had completed masters degrees in New Zealand in 1965, and three, all from Malaysia, had graduated PhD. 53 students had completed bachelors degrees, and seven bachelors honours degrees. Several had the ability to go on to postgraduate work. DEA would 'look at exceptional cases, but the needs of the Asian countries from which they came were such that these countries generally wanted them back so that more candidates could be sent in their stead for undergraduate training'.[49]

The 2000th trainee under the CP arrived at Rongotai on 7 June 1966. He was to undertake training with the Government Printer. 'The Prime Minister said that the occasion served to emphasise that much of the training under the Colombo Plan was being provided by Government Departments and by other public institutions like the hospitals.'[50]

Another statement by the Prime Minister marked Colombo Plan Day, 1 July, in 1967. 'Present economic difficulties would not prevent New Zealand's continuing to devote a proportion of her resources towards raising living standards in Asia', he said. 'New Zealanders would never turn their backs on the needs and aspirations of their Asian neighbours and ignore their problems. On the contrary the Government has repeatedly demonstrated New Zealand's growing involvement in Asian affairs. New Zealand's participation in the Colombo Plan is convincing evidence of concern with the progress and prosperity of her Asian neighbours.' Since the plan began New Zealand had spent more than NZP14.5m on Colombo Plan aid, 'a sizable contribution from a small country with its own developmental problems'. Over 2 200 students had come to New Zealand, and 330 New Zealand experts had gone to Colombo Plan countries. 'This two-way traffic has done much to establish an atmosphere of understanding and respect between Asians and New Zealanders.' The Colombo Plan was 'an essential element in New Zealand's external policy towards its Asian neighbours'.[51]

Would it not be less costly and more efficient to train students in their own countries than in New Zealand? Bert Walker, the member for St Albans, asked on 1 September. The Prime Minister agreed, adding that New Zealand had done 'a great deal' to help in providing institutions in

---

[49] Statement, 22.2.66. EAR, 16.2 (February 1966), pp. 31-2.
[50] Statement, 8.6.66. EAR, 16.6 (June 1966), p. 24.
[51] Statement, 1.7.67. EAR, 17.7 (July 1967), pp. 21-2.

Asia and specialist staff. Outside assistance was, however, still essential. 'The Asian countries have no choice but to continue for many years yet to send large numbers of their students to institutions in Colombo Plan donor countries. The bringing of students to New Zealand has certain special advantages in developing knowledge of New Zealand and creating personal links and ties with New Zealand on the part of young men and women who, we hope and believe will, in time, have an important and influential role to play in their own countries.'[52]

Dan Riddiford, member for Wellington Central, asked whether, given New Zealand's relative remoteness from Africa and proximity to South-east Asia, it would not be preferable to increase aid to the latter rather than aid the former. Holyoake said that was 'the actual fact'. The aid to Africa was 'a relatively small contribution'.[53] There had been 182 awardees. Most had studied for New Zealand university degrees and diplomas, the most popular subject being agriculture. [Kenya, 45, Tanzania, 34; Nigeria, 25; Uganda, 22; Zambia, 20; Ghana, 18; Rhodesia, 14; Malawi, 12; Sierra Leone, 12; Mauritius, 9; The Gambia, 8; Botswana, 1; Lesotho, 1.] There had been a number of projects in Africa, too, such as aid in setting up the Malawi Correspondence School on the New Zealand model.

An article in the *External Affairs Review* also sought to meet the kind of question Riddiford raised. The resources New Zealand could devote to Africa were small. 'There is, too, growing awareness in New Zealand of the needs of South-east Asia and the South Pacific, and an increasing sense of involvement in the fortunes in [of?] these areas. Nevertheless, New Zealand has not tied itself to a purely regional approach. It continues to place great importance on the United Nations and the Commonwealth, both of which are universal in their scope. New Zealand experience has proved relevant and valuable even in distant continents, and the provision of aid has lent weight to associations which might otherwise have seemed exclusively political or traditional.' That had proved particularly so in Commonwealth Africa.

In future years training in New Zealand would be the focus, given the lack of facilities in Africa. 'Certainly New Zealanders have benefited from the presence among them of the many Africans who have already come from the Commonwealth countries; and generally speaking, the African students and trainees appear to adapt themselves very well to the New Zealand environment.'[54]

[52]   EAR, 17.9 (Sepetmber 1967), p. 45.

[53]   ibid., p. 46.

[54]   'New Zealand Aid to Commonwealth Africa.' EAR, 17.11 (Novemer 1968), pp. 12-19.

The devaluation of the New Zealand dollar late in 1967 had an impact on capital commitments, but also on technical assistance: air fares cost more, for example. In 1968 there were 493 Colombo Plan students in New Zealand, 191 from Malaysia, 83 from Vietnam, 60 from Thailand, 47 from Sinagpore, and 36 from Indonesia.[55] The following year the grand total was 505. Not all by any means were undergraduates. Of the 230 who came that year, 72 (about half of them Malaysians) did pre-university or undergraduate training, 35 did non-university courses, 56 were at ELI, and 67 came for ad hoc courses.[56] There was a trend away from under-graduate training, Foreign Affairs observed.[57]

New Zealand had contributed to the UN and Commonwealth schemes as well as to the Colombo Plan. It supported the UN Technical Assistance Programme. During the years 1951-5, the Second Committee was told on 21 October 1955, 108 students had come to New Zealand, sent by the WHO, the UN Technical Assistance Administration, FAO, and UNESCO.[58] New Zealand also offered fellowships under the UNESCO scheme for six months' study in such fields as social services, infant welfare, vocational guidance, and state housing. Five were offered in 1949, 2 to China [ROC], 1 to the Philippines, 1 to Malaya or Singapore, 1 to Burma.[59] Six per annum were offered in subsequent years, covering other countries, including Thailand, Indonesia, Sarawak and North Borneo.[60] 'For a number of years the Seddon Memorial Technical College, Auckland, has offered a special training course for trade school teachers from Malaya, Ceylon and Pakistan. Some forty of these teachers have completed this course and the demand continues unabated.'[61]

New Zealand also, of course, took part in the Commonwealth Scholarship and Fellowship Plan, developed at the Commonwealth Education Conference held at Oxford in 1959. The Prime Minister, Walter Nash, welcomed the first fellows in August 1960, one from Canada, who was to do doctoral studies at Canterbury, and a reader in politics from an Indian university, who was to be attached to Asian Studies at VUW.[62]

---

[55] Report of DEA for year ended 31.3.68. AJHR 1968, A.1, p. 38.

[56] Report of DEA for year ended 31.3.69. AJHR 1969, A.1, p. 40.

[57] Report of MFA for year ended 31.3.71, AJHR 1971, A.1, p. 69.

[58] EAR, 5.10 (October 1955), pp. 15-16.

[59] Report of DEA for year ended 31.3.49. AJHR 1949, A.1, p. 77.

[60] Report of DEA for year ended 31.3.50. AJHR 1950, A.1, p. 68; 31.3.51, p. 59; 1.4.52, p. 59.

[61] Report of Minister of Education for year ended 31.12.55. AJHR, 1956, E.1, p. 39.

[62] EAR, 10.8 (August 1960), pp. 18-19.

The scheme, first suggested at the Commonwealth Trade and Economic Conference in Montreal in 1958, had economic growth in mind, and for that it was assumed to be necessary to promote education. It was also thought that 'a Commonwealth scheme would assist in furthering mutual understanding and goodwill and in adding to Commonwealth unity'. At the Oxford meeting, provision was made for the award of 1000 academic scholarships p.a., and, largely on C.E. Beeby's initiative, 'it was agreed that the academic side of the scheme should be complemented by a "mutual aid" programme to cover all other aspects of educational development'. New Zealand offered NZP65k pa, including 30k for scholarships and 35k for mutual aid. There were 10 two-year postgraduate scholarships each year, 3 one-year adminstrative scholarships, and 3 one-year prestige fellowhips. Inn addition to students from the 'old Commonwealth', students from Kenya, Southern Rhodesia, Pakistan, Singapore and India were reported to be in New Zealand in 1961/2. 33 New Zealand graduates were studying mainly in the UK, Australia and Canada.[63]

Such schemes built on what New Zealand had already been doing, largely but not exclusively in Commonwealth countries. That was inspired by a wish to promote development and stability and thus counter communism, and it won popular support, partly through the appeal of the Commonwealth connexion and the Government's successful promotion of the Colombo Plan, which became almost a byword for educational aid, in particular through the award of scholarships.

There is, however, yet another context, indeed one of longer standing. New Zealand was committed to the Commonwealth and to Southeast Asia. It was also committed to the South Pacific, in some parts of which it had direct political responsibilities. Those, too, were being partly met by the movement of students. Though it could not all be formally termed 'international', it was seen as a form of aid, and both the concept and the practice might be seen, for both government and public, as precursor and preparation for the growth of aid in other areas in the 1950s and 1960s, though that was quite revolutionary in scale and scope. The South Pacific was to remain a long-term commitment, surviving further revolutions in overseas student policy.

In the Trust Territory of [Western] Samoa the educational policy of the Department of Territories in the 1950s aimed at a sound primary education for all; manual, technical and agricultural training for senior students; higher [i.e. post-primary] education for selected students, who

---

[63] 'The Commonwealth Education Scheme'. EAR, 12.5 (May 1962), pp. 3-5.

would receive a sound secondary education to prepare them for clerical or administrative positions, higher specialist training, or entrance to a university; and adult education, to promote responsible citizenship, increased efficiency, and fruitful use of leisure.[64]

A long-term educational aim was 'to develop a sound and adequate system of secondary education, as successful self-government requires that the executive positions should be held by well-educated Samoans. Such an education would probably mean obtaining fluency in English as well as Samoan.' Until facilities in Samoa were sufficiently advanced, the government was giving competitive scholarships for attendance at New Zealand secondary schools, and from them some students went on to commercial training, trade apprenticeships and higher education.[65]

Sending Samoans on scholarships to New Zealand secondary schools began in 1945, and from 1946 the practice extended to Niue and the Cook Islands. By 1950 the total had reached 88, 61 from Samoa, 19 from the Cooks, 8 from Niue. Five of the students were at university or teachers college, 11 were in employment or practical training, 23 had returned, 65 were still at school.[66] By 1955 the grand total was 156, 102 from Samoa, 41 from the Cooks, 13 from Niue. 21 were at university or training college. The cumulated expenditure was NZP 150 156.[67]

'[W]ith the opening of Samoa College in Western Samoa and Tereora College in the Cook Islands a gradual shift towards scholarships for higher education is to be expected', the Department of Island Territories reported in 1956. 'It is clear that notwithstanding steady improvements in educational standards in the islands the scholarship scheme will continue to form an important part of New Zealand's educational policy in the territories.'[68] That year DIT also undertook at the request of governments concerned to supervise the study and welfare of students from Fiji, Tonga, Gilbert and Ellice Islands, and the British Solomon Islands Protectorate, some 117 in total. The overall number of students for which it was responsible reached 400.[69]

The aim of the scholarship scheme, DIT reflected in its 1960 report, was to train a selected elite as soon as possible for leadership in the professions, in the public service, and in government generally in the

---

[64]   DIT Report on W. Samoa for 1955. AJHR 1956, A.4, p. 140.

[65]   ibid., p. 142.

[66]   DIT Report fo year ended 31.3.50. AJHR 1950, A.5, p. 9.

[67]   DIT Rport for year ended 31.3.55. AJHR 1955, A.5, pp. 13-15.

[68]   DIT Report for year ended 31.3.56. AJHR 1956, A.5, p. 13.

[69]   Report of Minister of Education, 31.12.56. AJHR 1957, E.1, p. 46.

islands. Provision in the islands had improved. But experience showed that brighter students who might go on to university study were handicapped unless they did their post-primary education in an English-speaking background. The scholarship scheme was therefore to continue. So far the grand total of awards was 279, 151 to Samoans, 92 to Cook Islanders, and 36 to Niueans. 50 had gone to or were at university or teachers college.[70]

Though these commitments were in some sense precedental, aid for international students was essentially a novelty. Idea and practice took hold, and the Colombo Plan, in significance both emblematic and actual, continued to be celebrated and invoked. But – an even greater novelty – many 'non-aided' international students were coming to New Zealand, establishing personal and international links, but, though coming from the same countries as the 'aided', not always in entire accord with official policies.

[70] DIT Report for year ended 31.3.60. AJHR 1960, A.5, pp. 14-15.

CHAPTER TWO

OSAC

By no means all the students who entered New Zealand from overseas in this phase came under the Colombo Plan with which it is associated or even under other forms of aid or scholarship schemes. An increasing number, and later a majority, came as 'private overseas students', a category that normally included those funded by their own governments, but also those, much more numerous, funded by themselves or by their families. In some sense this group is better seen as the precursor of today's international students than those roughly described as 'Colombo Plan'. But it is true that they had an advantage. Though they were not formally 'aided', they were in fact subsidised. They paid not the 'full-cost fees' now levied, but the low fees then charged to domestic students. It is this group above all that contemporary visitors to Southeast Asia are likely to encounter and to find grateful for their experience.

How the practice grew up is not very clear, though it is clear that it was not part of a plan, even one as flexible as the Colombo Plan. It seems at first to have been left to the initiative of the applicants, prompted by their perception of their own needs and frustrations, learning of the opportunity from Colombo Plan students by word of mouth, perhaps, certainly not by 'marketing', and then from their peers or siblings in Australia or New Zealand, or from New Zealanders in Southeast Asia in commerce or in military service. Here was an economic option, with few bureaucratic controls in the way, and even something of a welcome from the receiving institutions, and indeed from the public, accustomed by now to think that New Zealand had a role to play in assisting its less fortunate neighbours. To some extent the informality of the arrangement seems indeed to have been promoted by its semi-formal nature: it was after all a kind of aid, though not formally so defined, and most of the students came from countries that were part of the Commonwealth to which New Zealand belonged.

Within the institutions, if not outside, there was, too, a sense in which New Zealand was giving an opportunity denied at home, to Chinese in Malaysia, to Indians in Fiji, something government-to-government programmes like the Colombo Plan could not do. There was also some feeling that formal aid was too directed, and that private students, with their own choice of subject, might be making sound choices for their countries as well as themselves. The informality of the arrangement had its drawback, however. The way a Plan was implemented could be changed: the shift in New Zealand's interpretation of the Colombo Plan is a case in point. But in the absence of a Plan, changes could be more abrupt, even arbitrary, limited only by public opinion or political pressure.

The perhaps somewhat paternalist sympathy and the goodwill that the Colombo Plan evoked and developed were extended to categories of students it hardly covered: in that sense characterising the period with the words 'Colombo Plan' is justified. Overall numbers were relatively small, by contrast to those of today's full fee-payers. Given the then patterns of migration, also very different from today's, the students were seen as a distinctive addition to New Zealand society as well as to its universities.

There were push factors as well as pull factors, then as now. Indeed – perhaps, again, as now – the former may have been stronger than the latter, as the unplanned nature of the phenomenon perhaps suggests. The largest group of students came from the countries included in Malaysia after 1963, as came to be the case with the Colombo Plan students, too. There tertiary provision was very limited. When Malaya became independent in 1957, there were 1134 Federation students at the University of Malaya [then in Singapore], and 1669 overseas.[1] Though those returns did not cover 'ethnicity', the new government was clearly anxious to increase Malay participation in education. That was reflected in its response to the Colombo Plan. Most of the private students in New Zealand were ethnic Chinese, attracted not only by low costs, but also by the further economy offered by timing. The New Zealand academic year started in late February, soon after the Cambridge overseas examination results became available. If you went to New Zealand or Australia, you could start university immediately, rather than waiting for the October opening of the academic year in the northern hemisphere.

The subjects in which the students were mainly interested were

---

[1]   Annual Report for the Federation of Malaya, 1957, pp. 263-4.

Engineering and Commerce, with Science and Economics in Arts something of a fallback. At this time Engineering was confined to two 'special schools', one at CU, one, much more recently created, at AU. It was there that places were most difficult to secure, partly because of the limited size of the schools and partly because of the demand from New Zealand students. Opportunities in Commerce were more readily secured. Its teaching was cheaper and easier to provide, and domestic demand had yet to boom. Coming largely from Commonwealth countries, the students were not seeking courses in English. There was no 'industry' at this point, either in teaching English or in tertiary education, and no one would have thought to use the term. When increasing numbers came to be seen as a problem, the answer was seen in raising entrance qualifications and imposing quotas rather than in pricing. A language requirement was seen in substantial part, not as a necessary qualification, but as a means of restriction, though not officially so stated.

Not aided, nor eligible for the scholarships and bursaries open to domestic students, the private students were subsidised. All the universities, successors to the colleges of the University of New Zealand of earlier decades, were state-funded, and Government met the bulk of their expenditure, on the basis of quinquennial grants negotiated by and administered through the University Grants Committee, set up in 1961. Student fees provided a further source of funding, but they were set at a low level. Paying them, overseas students were still heavily subsidised.

The other remarkable, perhaps unique, feature of the university system was 'open entry'. Those qualified for entry to university had a right to go to university, a provision politically impossible to abandon, and only economically feasible – even when the economy was stronger than it was from the late 1960s – provided that not everyone exercised their right. The only constraint was in respect of the 'special schools', where provision was especially expensive, and where universities, with UGC approval, could be allowed to limit numbers and impose selection criteria. In other words the guarantee of a place did not guarantee a place in whatever course a student chose, but it came pretty near.

Coupled with 'open entry' was 'common entry'. The same qualification for entry was required at each of the university institutions, and it was set by the Universities Entrance Board, also set up in 1961. The basic qualification a student gained who left secondary school at the end of the lower Sixth Form was 'UE', which could be secured by examination, but more frequently was gained by 'accrediting'. The UEB also had the task of offering an entrance qualification equivalent to UE based on other examinations or qualifications, i.e. ad eundem. Only the much smaller task of granting entrance to those who already had some tertiary credits was left to the universities themselves: they, rather than UEB, were seen to have the capacity to assess the amount of credit to be given in respect of their courses.

Overseas students fell into all three of these categories. Some came through Sixth Form at a New Zealand secondary school, gaining UE. Fewer came in with tertiary credits assessed by the universities. The bulk came ad eundem at entrance level, UEB granting them the equivalent qualification on the basis of examination achievement in Australia or Malaysia or elsewhere.

If therefore there were relatively few bureaucratic obstacles in the face of overseas students, nor were the academic hurdles were very high, except, of course, in the 'special schools', some of which, like Medicine, were not indeed not open to them at all. Their numbers did not, however, rapidly increase till the later 1960s, when New Zealand had been made relatively more attractive because the US, the UK, and Australia had made themselves less attractive, while the push factors had intensified.

In 1963, however, the Minister for Immigration had set up an interdepartmental committee – with representatives from Education, External Affairs and Labour – to review student policy and prepare recommendations. There was, it argued, a case for a permanent committee, which would act as 'an advisory body on policy, welfare and procedures'; report on 'the capacity of the New Zealand educational system to provide educational facilities for overseas students'; and '[d]etermine the number of students to be admitted to the various institutions and courses and the academic qualifications they should possess'. The Department of Education should screen individual applications and also advise the Secretary of Labour when a student was not making satisfactory progress.[2] The Interdepartmental Committee [IDC] was set up, but it seems to have met rather irregularly in the following years. An important concern of the Department of Labour was with getting students who were not doing well to leave. That remained an issue, indeed, and the Ombudsman was involved in a case in 1968. University regulations on satisfactory progress were less rigorous and more leniently enforced than those of the Immigration Division.[3]

Reviewing Government expenditure in April 1968, Cabinet declined a substantial reduction in Colombo Plan aid. It invited External Affairs, however, 'to review the level of the demands made on New Zealand

---

[2] Draft, n.d. H.O. 22/1/149-2. PM 118/21/1. MFAT Box 3481, National Archives, Wellington.

[3] Report of the Ombudsman for year ended 31.3.69. AJHR 1969, A.6, pp. 53-5.

educational facilities by overseas students'. Was the use of university and other facilities imposing an 'excessive pressure' on them or would it do so in the next few years?[4] The officials' response pointed to the increase in the number of private students. 'It is believed that the present burden of some 1500 private students and about 1,000 on government aid programmes does not impose undue strain on New Zealand educational resources. ... Clearly the situation will need to be watched.' But many educational authorities believed 'that the presence of a group of overseas students is very useful in broadening the outlook of New Zealand students as well as of the public'. Some effort had been made 'both to control the numbers ... and to improve the success rate by rigorous selection on academic grounds'. New Zealand universities had tightened up their requirements for academic progress for overseas students, and the Labour Department 'observed similar or slightly higher standards'. The memorandum included part of a report from the high commission in Kuala Lumpur, indicating the number of permits sought and issued. Most of those declined were academically underqualified.[5]

The universities and UEB had indeed taken some steps towards imposing a specific English requirement, in part to enhance students' chances of success, but in part also to constrain their numbers. In July 1966 CU told UEB that, because students could not understand the lectures they were given, it was requiring candidates entering with credits to satisfy the Professorial Board as to their competence in written and spoken English. It was suggested that candidates at entrance level should be warned that success in study would depend on the ability to understand English and that the universities could not supply special tuition.[6]

Influenced by a letter from the High Commissioner in Singapore, J.H. Weir, the Vice-Chancellors Committee [VCC] agreed in March 1967 that the universities should introduce the TOEFL test for overseas students who were seeking admission with credits. Weir had pointed to a rapid increase in applications, which he thought would increase further when the Australian universities' test of English came into effect. That was counted by the secretary of the VCC among the measures taken 'to stem the flow to Australia', themselves following similar measures [including TOEFL] in the US. The chairman of the UEB was authorised to make arrangements in respect of ad eundem students at entrance level.[7] The

---

[4] A.R. Perry Cabinet Secy/MEA, n.d. CM 68/12/5/S. MFAT Box 3495.

[5] Memo for Minister, n.d. ibid.

[6] UEB minutes, 7-8.9.66, addendum to memo by Morris, 10.7.80. UGC Box 166, National Archives, Wellington.

[7] UEB minutes, 7-8.9.66.

outcome was to be the development of special test, LATOS, by the New Zealand Council of Educational Research, TOEFL having been criticised, especially by MFA officials, for 'its American bias'.[8] It was first sat in 1970. There was also concern about the language competence of students admitted after only one year in a New Zealand sixth form.[9] It was later decided that such overseas students would also sit LATOS.[10]

In June 1969 the chairman told the UGC that the proportion of private students was increasing and that that 'might cause difficulties if growing accommodation shortage led to additional restrictions in enrolments by qualified New Zealanders'. It was possible that UEB would raise the qualifications required for admission ad eundem at entrance level to bring them more into line with those in Australia and the UK. That UEB did in September 1969, in respect of students who might apply in 1971, setting out what was required in the Cambridge Higher School Certificate and the General Certificate of Education.[11]

The UGC annual report for 1969 took up the chairman's comment and suggested that the universities might have to restrict overseas enrolments. They 'may well be compelled to consider how far they can go in admitting private overseas students if qualified New Zealand candidates have to be refused places. The New Zealand taxpayer meets most of the cost of supporting the universities and it would not be unreasonable for him to insist that, if what he pays for is in short supply, it should be made available to his own children before being offered to overseas students who wish to come here at their own expense and without any official sponsorship. It need hardly be pointed out that these students and their families contribute virtually nothing as taxpayers towards the cost of our universities.'[12]

In 1965 there were 20 269 students at New Zealand universities and 1 019 overseas students including the aided, 5.02% of the total. In 1967 the totals were 24 431, 1 346, 5.50%. In 1970 31 500, 2 229, 7.07%. In Canterbury and Auckland, the number of overseas students increased more than in the other universities both absolutely and in percentage terms. The percentage of Malaysian students to other overseas students rose from 21.48% in 1965 to 52.26% in 1970. Private overseas students formed 70.79% of the total in 1970. Private Southeast Asian students formed 77.91% of the total Southeast Asian students; 75.91% of the total private overseas students; 53.74% of the total overseas students. 19.45%

---

[8] Memo by Morris, 10.7.80.
[9] UEB minutes, 21-22.5.69.
[10] UEB minutes, 27-28.4.71.
[11] UEB minutes, 3-4.9.69.
[12] Reports of UGC and university institutions..., 1969. AJHR 1970, E.3, p. 15.

of first-year overseas students in 1970 were taking BCA, BCom, Accounts Prof; 19.06% B Sc, and 35.66% Intermediate [for Engineering]. 25% of first-year students entered in 1970 with UE and 55% ad eundem.[13] First-year overseas students numbered 312 in 1965; 340 in 1966; 405 in 1967; 473 in 1968; 600 in 1969; 779 in 1970.[14]

At institutional level there were signs of 'strain'. The issue was first raised at the VCC in December 1965, when CU found it necessary to restrict entry into Engineering. In March 1966 the Committee decided that the regulation of entry was a question for individual universities, 'and not an area which the Committee should consider'. Late in 1969 CU raised the matter again. It had to impose limitations on entry in Engineering, Fine Arts and Forestry, partly because of restrictions elsewhere, partly because of the accelerated influx of overseas students. The University would also have to consider whether to restrict overseas students not merely in special schools. 'One of the limiting factors ... is the problem of finding private board': CU could no longer guarantee board to ad eundem students. The Professorial Board considered that any CU policy should be part of a national policy,[15] and CU put the matter to the VCC in December. '[W]idespread newspaper and public comment' followed.[16]

Canterbury's reference to restrictions elsewhere were references to Auckland. That was not only the site of the only other Engineering school. It had also decided to restrict its overall size to 10 000 students,[17] meaning that it could add no more than 500 a year over the next three years, and it had decided that no more than 5% of its undergraduate students could be from overseas. Their numbers had increased substantially in recent years, owing, the Academic Registrar said, to quotas in Australia, and it would not be possible to take any from Malaysia or Singapore in 1970. The restriction, D.W. Pullar rather coolly added, was 'purely an Auckland problem at the moment, and simply involved the diversion of students from these countries to other New Zealand universities'.[18]

At Victoria's December Council meeting the Acting VC, Ian Campbell, said it would become a national problem. 'Eventually there had got to be a political decision, and a fairly high level one.' If there were to be any restriction at VUW, he hoped it would be 'almost exclusively on academic

---

[13] Hampton/Stewart, 27.7.70, and enclosure. VCC Box 12, NZVCC archive.

[14] Chairman's Report, OSAC 1. UGC Box 166.

[15] Phillips/Hampton, 28.11.69. VCC Box 13.

[16] Enclosure in Hampton/Stewart, 27.7.70.

[17] N. Tarling, *Auckland The Modern University*, Auckland: The University of Auckland, 1999, pp. 29, 31-2.

[18] *Evening Post* [EP], 10.12.69.

grounds'. The student representative, W. Logan, suggested that it was necessary to be prepared with the means of exclusion in case it should be needed, rather than, like AU, waiting till the problem was 'on top of us'. One method, he suggested, 'might be to charge overseas students the full cost of a university education, including some proportion of building costs'. The Council decided to investigate the general question.[19]

N.C Phillips, Vice-Chancellor of CU, returned to the charge in the New Year. He thought the VCC should approach the UGC and the Government for 'a more rigorous and rational control over the admission of overseas students' to universities and secondary schools. All the universities needed to consider how many they could accept, given university and living accommodation.[20] At Otago the VC, R.M. Williams, noted the striking increase in students from Southeast Asia, especially in Science and Commerce. It was, he added, difficult to place students in private board. 'There are disadvantages in their congregating in flats as separate racial groups since it limits their contacts with New Zealand.' Halls of residence were probably the most suitable accommodation, 'but the result is an excess of overseas students in halls. There could be a case for requiring private overseas students to pay a special fee towards accommodation, to be used to provide more halls.' Willams thought the VCC should consider recommending that students not normally resident in New Zealand should pay 'more or less economic fees', e.g. four times the present level.[21]

Charging an 'economic' fee was not generally supported at the VCC. Urgent action on the question was, however, required, and the Committee agreed to seek a meeting with the UGC and Government departments.[22] The sense of urgency is not entirely easy to explain. Presumably the increase in numbers could be covered in the next quinquennial grant, though not indeed until then. Other limits were alleged, however, including accommodation, and the special schools were costly. And there was the Auckland question. The Committee again discussed the question in May, along with critical comments from NZUSA, which planned to call a conference.[23]

In preparation for the meeting with the UGC and the government departments, the Vice-Chancellors exchanged fuller accounts of their respective policies. The Canterbury Council had announced in May that in 1971 it would not admit more than 150 first-time overseas students, no

[19] ibid., 17.12.69.
[20] Phillips/Hampton, 20.2.70. VCC Box 13.
[21] Williams/Hampton, 23.2.70. ibid.
[22] Minutes, 13.3.70. M (70) 1 Pt 1, item 5. ibid.
[23] Minutes, 15.5.70, item 3. Memo in Hampton/Stewart, 27.7.70. VCC Box 12.

more than 100 to Science classes, and no more than 20 into Eng First Prof.[24] The Vice-Chancellor regretted the move, he told the press. Generally overseas students 'made good academic progress, and by adding variety to the student population were an asset to the university'. They had 'much to teach New Zealanders', and by educating and training them the university was 'making its best contribution towards helping developing countries'. New admissions had, however, risen from 46 in 1965 to 145 in 1969 and 308 in 1970. 'The university could not continue at this rate without a serious deterioration in standards of teaching and research, because of the pressure on its resources and because of its responsibility to find places for qualified New Zealanders', the Vice-Chancellor said. The university had taken account of limits imposed by living accommodation, teaching accommodation, staff, materials and equipment.[25] Canterbury also supplied details of its 1970 enrolment. In 1965 there had been 196 overseas students, 4.4% of the roll; in 1969 395, 6.3%; now it was 643, 9.5%. 481 were from the Malaysia region; 514 were supported by private means; 575 were accommodated privately. 372 were in Science classes, including 202 in Eng Int. 301 were first-year students.[26]

Pursuing its overall limit at a time of growth, AU had decided to limit the percentage of undergraduate overseas students, 'not out of any desire to discriminate against students from any country, but simply because the University could foresee that it would have to turn away many New Zealand students unless those from overseas were limited'. In 1969 the students already numbered 569, and it was decided to reduce the number gradually to 500 in 1972. In Engineering the percentage was already over 20%, and that was to reduce to 10-15%. Southeast Asian numbers had risen 'very sharply' in 1969, so it was also decided to hold enrolments from each area to the average percentage of enrolments for the area 1965-9. Quotas for 1971 would include 36% for Malaysia, 9% Singapore, 5% Vietnam, 7% other parts of Asia, 25% Fiji, 12% other South Pacific territories, 2% Africa, 4% other countries. Where selection was required in an area, preference would be given to sponsored students. Otherwise it would be based on academic merit.[27]

At Otago a small number of sponsored students were admitted into faculties where New Zealanders had to compete, Medicine, Dentistry, Pharmacy, and Survey. In Arts, Science, Law, Commerce, Home Science and Physical Education, private overseas students were normally admitted

[24] Turbott/MFA, 22.5.70. ibid.
[25] *The Press* [Press], 16.5.70.
[26] Memorandum by Turbott, 22.7.70. VCC Box 12.
[27] Memoranda by Musgrove, 2.6.70; Pullar, 28.7.70. ibid.

if they had the requirements of the UEB – either NZUE or admission ad eundem at entrance level – or had been given credits by OU and passed TOEFL. Senate considered that overseas students should not form more than 10% of EFTS, and that students from the Pacific islands should be given priority unless that inhibited the growth of USP. The main focus was on Science and Commerce. The limit there might be 15-20%.[28]

The roll at OU in 1970 was 5234 and overseas students numbered 395, 7.5%. 278 came from Southeast Asia, 76 from the Pacific, 13 from Africa. The first-year roll was 1383, with 121 overseas students, 8.7%. To achieve 10% overall – necessary to ensure that 'the total roll ... does not exceed that for which funds have been provided' – about 130 could be admitted in 1971, including 60 in Science and 40 in Commerce. The University also wished to ensure that overseas students were 'properly housed without excluding New Zealanders'. 1203 out of 4280 full-time students were in halls (26.2%); 168 out of 376 overseas students (44.7%). 'Since it is impossible to obtain private board for overseas students and undesirable that they congregate in racial groups, the University recognises that it is desirable to accommodate overseas students in halls of residence', but several hundred New Zealanders were declined. 'If the New Zealand Government decided to charge overseas students higher course fees the additional income might be used to provide extra places in the halls of residence for overseas students. Alternatively a contribution could be required from overseas students towards the capital cost of halls.[29]

Lincoln's policy was designed to achieve 'a spread of students from many countries', and to admit as many as could be enrolled 'without unduly handicapping staff and New Zealand students'. The College admitted students sponsored by the Colombo Plan and on Commonwealth and Malaysian government scholarships; students who had been to New Zealand secondary schools and passed UE; and students from other countries where schools taught or used English, including Australia, the UK, Fiji, Chile, Uruguay and some in Africa. A few years earlier the College had accepted a small number of private students from Malaysia and Singapore, but that policy had been changed 'since the sharp rise developed in numbers of local applicants', and none were now admitted. 'It is very doubtful that any relaxation of this decision can apply in the current quinquennium.'[30] The percentage of overseas students had fallen from 16% in 1965 to 8.7% in 1970, 81 out of 1054.[31]

---

[28]   Memorandum, sent by Williams, 19.6.70. ibid.

[29]   Memorandum, 7.70. ibid.

[30]   Burns/Hampton, 14.7.70. ibid.

[31]   Memorandum by Hunt, 3.8.70. ibid.

At Massey there were 2721 internal students, 168 overseas, 6.25%. 87 were in Agricultural Science, 14.8% of the roll, 49 under the Colombo Plan or similar schemes, 38 private. No overall policy had been set, but the University planned to maintain current levels, taking sponsored students, and making places available to private students according to country of origin and acdemic ability.[32]

No overall quotas had been established at VUW, but 'pressure of increasing numbers' was 'compelling the University to give thought to the possibility of introducing quotas or other restrictions. In common with all other unversities in New Zealand we desire to share our resources with people less well endowed with facilities for higher education, but we are also aware of the desirability of maintaining a balance between their numbers and our own people, and will introduce restrictions with some reluctance.' Like Otago, Victoria recognised a special obligation to the Pacific, but it would be affected by the establishment of the University of the South Pacific [USP]. Like the South Island universities, it was concerned over student accommodation. Until 1969 its Student Accommodation Service could offer a guarantee to all first year students, but the rise in numbers, and the worsening position on accommodation, meant that in 1970 it could issue only 118 guarantees in response to 229 applications from private students.[33]

Waikato had found 'no need to exclude students on the grounds of insufficiency of accommodation or of teachers'.[34] The Professorial Board believed there should be a national policy, in which perhaps UEB might play a role. The policy would give first priority to New Zealand and government-sponsored students; second priority to 'quotas of private overseas students in accordance with the known national foreign aid policy and/or on a basis of merit, irrespective of the country of origin'; the remainder of places in particular courses being 'allocated to privately-financed students from countries not included in the known aid areas on the basis of a specified quota from the particular countries concerned'.[35]

The VCC had discussed the issue again on 17 July. Was it necessary to amend the individual Unversity Acts to empower the universities to control entry? The Labour Department could exercise control when students sought entry permits to attend secondary schools or require a further permit if a student wished to go on to university. The universities might control entry if permits were issued only on condition that university

[32] Weir/Hampton, 2.7.70. Memorandum by Stewart, 30.7.70. ibid.
[33] Memorandum by I.D. Campell, 30.7.70. ibid.
[34] Memorandum by Llewellyn, 3.8.70. ibid.
[35] Kingsbury/Hampton, 31.7.70. ibid.

guarantees of accommodation had been obtained. 'Members expressed alarm at the present high overall percentage of overseas students to total students (more than 7%).' Not all thought that fixing percentages would be satisfactory: some felt that numbers had to be fixed. One way of regulating entrance from New Zealand schools might be a requirement that the UE examination must be taken, but UEB would be reluctant to deny accrediting. A Malaysian student found it cheaper to travel to New Zealand to take an Engineering degree than to take such a degree in Malaysia. 'Although not receiving general support, a view was expressed that fees for overseas students should be increased to an economic level.' Unless numbers were controlled, at least one university would have to seek more buildings and staff in 1971 'some time ahead of such development if New Zealand student growth alone were the determining factor'. As a 'corollary' to that, 'it was suggested that the position may already have been reached in some faculties where New Zealand students were being denied entry in favour of better academically qualified overseas students'.[36]

On the mechanics of limitation, Waikato had suggested a role for UEB. Auckland drew on its experience in attempting to limit its overall numbers. The universities, the Academic Registrar suggested, had a large measure of control in respect of students who were admitted ad eundem at entrance level by the UEB or with credits by the universities themselves, since such students had to apply for a place. The Act ruled, however, that every student who secured UE was entitled to matriculate. Once the government had through granting a study permit admitted a student into a secondary school for the purpose of gaining UE, it had built up a commitment which might 'in the long run prove an embarrassment to the Universities as a whole'. The Acts allowed a university to decline enrolment 'on the grounds of either insufficiency of accommodation or insufficiency of teachers'. Then it must pass a regulation or statute excluding a class of students. Auckland was seeking a statute limiting the overall roll to 10350. Then it could introduce regulations 'stating the class of students who are to be limited'. The Government should control the numbers entering secondary schools and secondary students should be warned that getting UE would not guarantee a place. Where a university had 'legislation on its books which limits the number of Overseas Students', entry would be on a quota system and depend on academic ability within each quota.[37]

If all the universities decided on limitation to an agreed proportion of their roll, say 8% of total New Zealand university rolls, and selected on

36 M (70) 3, 17.7.70. ibid.
37 Memorandum by Pullar, 5.8.70. ibid.

academic merit, there would be multiple applications, Massey pointed out, leading to undershooting the target one year and overshooting it the next. It argued for a '[c]entral clearing agency'. It also considered the problems in identifying superior academic performance: relating results in UE or UB and overseas HSC; accrediting; subject-blind admission ad eundem; students with UE not accepted at USP. Should an English test be applied to students from New Zealand schools? '[S]ympathetic treatment' often meant that their English was not good enough.[38]

IDC also commented before the meeting with VCC and UGC. Considering the 'sharp increase' in the numbers of private secondary and university students at the start of 1969, the Committee had raised the level of entry into secondary schools, established in 1967, and the UEB had raised the requirements for ad eundem admission to bring them into line with Australia for 1971. 'As a further means of controlling the flow of students', UEB had also made a special NZ English language test compulsory from 1971[LATOS], and it would be extended to secondary schools. The Labour Department did not exercise direct control over numbers: its role was to issue or authorise entry permits to private overseas students with entry qualifications. The Education Department determined the academic levels for private students seeking to enter secondary school. Foreign Affairs, also represented on IDC, took account of New Zealand's foreign policy aims. It was responsible for the operation of the Colombo Plan and other schemes. 'The Ministry is also concerned to see that New Zealand fulfils its international aid obligations and that the New Zealand intake of overseas students should compare with that of other countries.' The largest increase in Malaysian students in the past three years had been by direct entry – ad eundem at entry or with credits – and not as a result of obtaining UE in New Zealand. It seemed to IDC therefore that UEB and the universities were the appropriate authorities for the introduction of any further restraints, but, because of foreign policy and other considerations, any proposal should be referred to IDC for comment.[39]

Chaired by Alan Stewart, the MU VC, the proposed meeting was held at Victoria on 7 August 1970, and included the president of NZUSA, the national union of students, as well as representatives of all the universities, UGC, Labour, Foreign Affairs and Education. Sir Alan Danks, the chairman of UGC, suggested establishing 'a Central Council of Admissions' as a sub-committee of UGC. All overseas students seeking admission at

---

38   Memorandum, General Policy for Admission of Overseas Students to N.Z. Universities, 4.8.70. ibid.
39   Memorandum to VCC, 30.7.70. ibid.

entrance level would have to apply to the Council. Each university would indicate how many it could take, and the Council would assign places within those limits. The idea attracted general support. The principal criterion would be academic attainment, though some categories, such as Colombo Plan and Pacific Island students, could be given preferential treatment. In advising the number of places available, the universities would be expected to guarantee accommodation in their halls or through their agencies. Applicants would name the universities they wished to attend in preferential order. A central council, it was suggested, would be 'in a better position to ensure that available student places were spread equitably amongst applicants from under-developed regions, instead of giving weight to any one region'. It 'could help to guard against any undue influx of students from the overcrowded Australian university system'. The new arrangement could provide Government with an up-to-date statement of the amount of foreign aid the universities were providing. 'The total number of overseas students which the university system should assimilate was seen to be a matter of Government policy. The provision of additional buildings, staff and other resources needed to handle greater numbers than the universities indicated that they could take at any time, would be a matter for the U.G.C. to determine in consultation with the Government.' The 'Council' would have no policy-making powers.

'It was suggested that overseas students should be levied fees at two or three times the amount paid by New Zealand students. The revenue thus obtained could be used: – (a) to subsidise overseas students with financial problems; (b) to provide more university halls of residence; (c) as a direct source of Government revenue in recognition of the foreign aid provided by the universities. Opinions were 'sharply divided', and no action was proposed 'in the meantime'.[40]

The proposed Council was clearly not unwelcome to the universities, but it was not surprising that UGC had taken the initiative. It was UGC that negotiated government funding of the universities quinquennium by quinquennium. If foreign students were not to pay full fees – and not even Williams had gone that far – the funding for foreign students had to be included, lest domestic students were excluded. The funding so far provided had more or less allowed for that, but the increase in numbers in the late 1960s pushed at the limits. The Vice-Chancellors clearly found that provision in the quinquennial funding was inadequate and had no confidence that it would be sufficiently boosted. The new 'Council', while not determining policy, would facilitate its implementation in another

---

[40]   Report of a Meeting held ... 7.8.70, 12.8.70. ibid.

sense, too, as the reference to 'equitable' treatment of the regions perhaps suggested. It would facilitate the adoption of country quotas within the overall total.

The Holyoake government had, it seems, been rather unwilling to make a structural change. In any case External Affairs had advised in 1968 that it was unnecessary, and in October 1969 the Prime Minister, in a letter drafted there, indicated that Phillips had explained 'the background of the Council's decision' to him. 'The informal consultations held during the year with University authorities have meant that New Zealand will continue to make a contribution at an appropriate level while at the same time preserving the interests of young New Zealanders.'[41] In December External Affairs suggested that the percentage of overseas students on the roll was comparable with the percentage in Canada, the UK and Australia. Entry standards had been tightened, AU was limiting its roll, and UGC was actively considering methods of English language testing. Standards had been 'tightened' so as to contain the inflow of secondary and technical students to the present level of approximately 600. Most applicants came from Malaysia, affected by Australian restrictions, and by 'uneasiness' among the Chinese. Overall the Department thought the measures would diminish the 1971 numbers to 'a little below the 1969 level which is believed to represent a total consistent with international obligations'.[42]

The Department also noted that there were 173 overseas secretarial students in New Zealand, mostly at private business colleges. 'Concern had been expressed that two such Colleges, which advertise extensively overseas, are not providing tuition or facilities that measure up to claims in their advertising.' A 'close watch' was being kept, but 'so far it has not been thought appropriate to try to set standards for private institutions, unless their activities are such as to provoke well-founded criticism among overseas students, their parents and local authorities and in consequence to mar New Zealand's image.' One college had sought preferential treatment for the issuance of student permits 'on the grounds that it is earning overseas exchange by bringing students here. It has been made clear that policy is to regard the presence of any private student in New Zealand primarily as fulfilling aid objectives and that financial considerations are not the key factor in the issuing of permits.'[43]

In July 1970 Cabinet reached the view that further action was needed. Comments at its meeting on 20 July suggested that, certainly at AU,

---

[41] PM/Grocott, CU Stud Ass, 24.10.69. UGC Box 89.
[42] Memorandum, 12.69. PM 118/88/1. ibid.
[43] ibid.

'qualified New Zealanders' were being excluded from some courses 'because of the large numbers of places filled by foreign students'. The fees private foreign students paid 'fell a long way short of the actual costs involved', and they often pursued 'courses which would not lead to qualifications which were in greatest demand in their home countries and were often not in the category of courses which would be open to Colombo Plan and other aid programme students'. The point had been reached when, like the Australians, 'our universities would have to set their own quotas'. The UGC, it was suggested, should be asked for recommendations. Alternatively, given that the UGC was 'already fully committed with its other responsibilities', the relevant Departments should look into the matter.[44] The latter prospect no doubt prompted Danks to take the initiative and suggest what became OSAC.

Now the Cabinet agreed on legislation. The Minister of Education, Brian Talboys, emphasised that the number of overseas students which the system could accept was 'a matter of Government policy'. The proposed committee would 'provide the machinery to implement policy equitably'. Legislation was needed because, under their Acts, the universities could refuse enrolment only on the grounds of insufficiency of accommodation or teachers. 'If a university must wait until such insufficiency exists before it can restrict the entry of overseas students any restriction it may impose will be too late to serve its purpose.' The UGC believed that the right to decline to enrol overseas students had to be placed beyond legal doubt.[45] Was the reason Talboys advanced the real one? Surely 'insufficiency' could be forecast. The problem was rather that 'insufficiency of accommodation' would be a ground to limit numbers, but it would not be a ground for discriminating other than on academic merit among those who might not be admitted.

UGC convened a further meeting on 8 September and circulated a summary of the position. The Government had agreed to introduce legislation, providing Councils with authority to determine the number of overseas students who could be admitted to any university or course. Admissions at entry level would be only through the Overseas Students Admissions Committee [OSAC], though the universities individually would still handle admissions with credit. Overseas students would be defined as any person other than a New Zealand citizen, or a person who, in the opinon of the sub-committee, was ordinarily resident in New Zealand. The Committee would consist of the Chairman of the UGC and

44 Memorandum for Minister of Education, 22.7.70. UGC Box 89.
45 Memorandum for Cabinet, n.d. ibid; also Box 166.

the VCs or their nominees. It would have 'an administrative function only'. In its policy on overseas students, the Government would continue to be advised by the Departments and the UGC. OSAC would consider all overseas applicants except those admitted ad eundem with credits. It would also define those 'ordinarily resident in New Zealand' who would not have to apply through OSAC, for example 'the children of parents whose occupation has required them to take up employment in New Zealand', such as diplomats. Universities would set quotas, taking into consideration the availability of residential accommodation. Foreign Affairs would advise OSAC of places it would like reserved for Colombo Plan and other government-sponsored students, including those sponsored by the governments of 'some countries overseas'. OSAC might wish to take account of the regional origin of students and would take account of any information or views the universities might offer. Competition for places was likely to mean that admission of students from secondary schools in New Zealand would depend on UB results. A second allocation of offers would be made when overseas HSC results became available, so that students would not have to wait a year or decide to go elsewhere.[46]

Section 10 of the 1961 Universities Act was amended to provide for the appointment of a subcommittee to select overseas students to universities. In selecting students, the sub-committee might 'specify the University, faculty, school, department, course, or class in a particular subject, to which the student is selected for admission'. The Council of each university should, 'having regard to such matters as it considers relevant, determine each year the maximum number of overseas students who may be admitted in the following year in the following year to the University in any faculty, school, department, course, or class in a particular subject'. An overseas student was defined as any person other than a New Zealand citizen or a person who, in the opinion of the sub-committee, was 'ordinarily resident in New Zealand'.[47] OSAC included two representatives of each university, normally a senior academic and a relevant member of the administrative staff. In addition there were representatives of relevant government departments, Education, Labour, and Foreign Affairs, and also NZUSA.

The media response was not unfavourable. The *Auckland Star* – in an editorial headed 'Guests at our universities' – saw the legislation as 'necessary and desirable'. It argued that the first duty in taxpayer-funded universities was to domestic students, and the next to Colombo Plan and aided students. 'If there is to be any restriction, it is right that it should

---

[46] Memorandum, Establishment of Overseas Students Admissions Committee, 9.70. VCC Box 12; UGC Box 89.

[47] 1970 No. 148.

apply to those who come privately.' But the number should be 'generous initially and moved up as university accommodation increases'.[48] New Zealand universities were 'popular' because of their 'high reputation', the *Press* observed, and also because they were 'among the cheapest in the world to attend'. Earlier in the year, it noted, B.R. Philpott at LC had suggested that overseas students should be 'charged university fees which reflected the full marginal cost of their education'. That might be worth considering either as a supplement or an alternative to the legislation. The editorial went on to suggest that a similar scheme might soon have to be considered for domestic students. 'Fees, at present of the order of $40 a year for each subject, might well be doubled or even trebled without undue hardship to students', most of whom had the fees paid by bursaries or scholarships if they made satisfactory progress. 'Raising fees in New Zealand for all students would reduce numbers by discouraging those whose progress is not satisfactory; it would also discourage private overseas students from settling on New Zealand when they "shop around" for a cheap education – without laying this country open to the reproach of discriminating against outsiders.'[49]

The debate on domestic fees was not yet fully joined, but NZUSA's overseas student officer, R. Khan, had attacked Philpott's suggestion that New Zealand should use university education to earn overseas funds. 'This would mean putting the clock back 200 years by continuing a disease that plagues Asia – poverty. I am sure New Zealanders would not even give serious thought to this suggestion, as to accept it would mean that New Zealanders acknowledged for themselves a universal right they did not acknowledge for others – the right to acquire education irrespective of financial situation.'[50] Early in 1971 the NZUSA vice-president publicly opposed a government proposal to surcharge private overseas students by $100. The Prime Minister was quoted as saying that no final decision had been made; and it was just one of the proposals Government had been considering for controlling education expenditure. No one in Wellington could say how the students became aware of it, the VCC secretary commented. Either NZUSA had 'an excellent pipe-line', or the information was leaked to gauge the strength of opposition.[51]

At a seminar at VUW in May 1972 J.W. Rowe argued for 'user-pays' in higher education, where private 'appropriable' benefits were likely to be high, and a varying element of subsidy would be justified by 'spillover'.

---

[48] Star, 3.11.70.

[49] Press, 7.12.70.

[50] Press, 16.7.70.

[51] Memorandum by Hampton, 10.2.71. VCC Box 12.

Foreign students, he added, should be subsidised only as part of an aid programme.[52] A.D. Brownlie also advovcated 'user pays' at the Educational Priorities Conference later in the year.[53] The new prime minister, John Marshall, had, however, opened the conference by invoking 'open entry'. 'As one who had neither money nor influence but who was able to get as good an education as the country can provide, I am grateful for the opportunities which were mine.'[54] Despite the country's economic difficulties and the advent of 'market' theories, 'open entry' stood in the way of change. That did not, of course, apply to overseas students, but those opposed to higher domestic fees were to make the connexion that the *Press* made when higher foreign fees were introduced. Meanwhile both the attitude to education as a public good and the attitude to foreign students nurtured since at least since the Colombo Plan began meant that when numbers unexpectedly increased, New Zealand proceeded by quota and distribution, not by sale.

The notion that the admission of private students was at least informally a form of aid was sustained not only by the fact that they paid only domestic fees but also by the fact that they could come only from a limited number of countries, none of them 'developed'. Students entering on awards and scholarships – who came in on temporary permits – might come from further afield, if their scholarship so provided, Rotary for example, and so might students on various exchange schemes. But self-financing students – who entered New Zealand on study permits – could come only from the British Solomon Islands Protectorate, Fiji, Gilbert and Ellice Islands Colony, Indonesia, Malaysia, Nauru, New Caledonia, New Hebrides, French Polynesia, Thailand, Tonga, Singapore, Western Samoa, and [South] Vietnam, i.e non-Communist Southeast Asia, but not Burma, it seems, plus South Pacific countries, not India. The immigration regulations did, however, provide, in respect of US students, for what was later termed Study Abroad, a year of study in New Zealand for credit towards an already-started American degree.[55] The list was expanded as a result of a review undertaken by the new Labour government, but few other changes resulted.

That review was carried out by officials from Foreign Affairs, Treasury, Education, Trade and Industry and Labour, though it also considered submissions from the Overseas Private Students Conference – which,

---

[52] q. R. Butterworth and N. Tarling, *A Shake-Up Anyway,* Auckland UP, 1994, p. 43.
[53] ibid., pp. 42-3.
[54] q. ibid., p. 42.
[55] Secretary of Labour/Hayward, 20.9.74. AU archives.

meeting in May, had criticised the 'impersonal, slipshod and ineffficient' attitude of Governments, especially Labour[56] – from the Director of Student Welfare Services at VUW, from the Waikato Students Association, and from NZUSA, which suggested that many saw the Immigration Division as 'a monolithic ogre', 'impolite and unreasonable', 'racist', and considered IDC 'unworthy', lacking in academic expertise.[57] There were no submissions, it seems, from UGC, VCC, or the universities.

Current policy, as the 'monolithic ogre' set out, was 'geared to the admission of overseas students from developing countries, particularly those situated in the South Pacific and South East Asia, where facilities for higher education were either unavailable or inadequate'. The primary aim was 'to train students ... to a level which would allow them to return to assist in the economic, social and educational development of their own lands'. 'The most persuasive argument in support of the policy has been that the education of private students is an important form of indirect aid ... made in the main to countries New Zealand assumed obligations to under formal aid schemes.'

The escalation in numbers and the proliferation of the kinds of study undertaken had made the Department's task as permit issuing authority 'much more complex and the subject of controversy at home and sometimes abroad'. Over the past decade there was 'a growing awareness that private students ... were at a disadvantage compared to Government aided students, and it was realised that the impressions private students take away with them were just as important in creating a good image abroad as those of aided students. The fact that private students are obliged to deal with the immigration authority in matters affecting education (whereas aided students are not) does tend to create dissatisfaction in the student fraternity and among well meaning New Zealanders.' IDC had been formed 'in an effort to minimise this, and to achieve a degree of uniformity both in the fields of entry criteria and policy'. It also acted as an appeals committee in cases where students appealed, usually on academic grounds, against Labour Department decisions.

The Department suggested that New Zealand might review its educational resources, perhaps a 'somewhat imponderable' task 'in the sense that the system tends to expand according to demand'. Alternatively, 'consider adopting an arbitrary assessment based on such factors as the needs of the country of origin and emphasis on those courses in which we can offer some particular expertise'. The next step could cover 'a redefining of the aim of the policy'. That could be based on one or more of three

[56]   Press, 17.5.73.
[57]   ibid., 3.8.73.

objectives. One was to provide aid for developing countries, 'basically the existing aim[;] but we have never based our criteria on the needs or stage of development of a particular country'. Some students obtained New Zealand qualifications, and then did not return to their own country, but were granted immigration status by a third country. A second objective could be to assist in developing trade and cultural links with other countries, and that could cover countries in North America, the EEC, 'and especially Japan'. A third objective would be to make the policy 'part of a long term migration plan to provide (New Zealand trained) personnel for our own labour force'. That would extend present policy, which allowed some students to stay on to complete one or two years' practical work or 'remain on a permanent basis'.

Was New Zealand providing education of the right kind? Should it 'continue to provide places in universities rather than technical institutes or in secondary schools rather than apprenticeship or trade training schemes'? Was it providing it to the right people? There could be 'little comparison between the stages of development of Malaysia and Tonga', yet 59.6% of overseas students were Malaysian. Most of them would be 'other than indigenous Malays (i.e. Chinese). If it is considered desirable to base our policies on the needs of the country of origin, what are those needs and, more particularly, can we gain a rational picture of them, independent of the views of the Government of the country concerned? There is, of course, a recognised flaw in any policy which results in our accepting only students nominated by their own Government.' 'Is it desirable to set geographical limits which may, irrespective of political necessity exclude South East Asia, but embrace an area covered by the boundaries of the South Pacific Commission (but excluding American controlled territories)?'[58]

Immigration also raised questions about primary and secondary education. Currently children from Tonga and Western Samoa were admitted at primary level, and there were quotas for secondary school below Form 6 for South Pacific countries and for Indonesia, Malaysia, Singapore and Thailand, and students could also come from Vietnam. Should primary students be admitted from countries other than Tonga and Samoa? Would it be better to drop the quota system for secondary schooling and use the finance to offer direct aid and expertise?

The final report, presented in July 1973, confirmed that the primary aim of existing policy – 'to train students from developing countries (particularly those in the South Pacific and South East Asian regions) to a

---

[58] Immigration Division, May 1973, Appendix A to Review of Immigration Policy, Private Overseas Students, July 1973. UGC Box 89.

level which would allow them to return to assist in the development of their own lands' – was 'still a valid one'. In the eyes of the committee 'the aid function of student policy' was 'paramount', and it should 'reflect and be complementary to New Zealand's official aid policy'. It recognised, however, 'that a secondary function of student policy was to promote international understanding and culture'. To that end 'the policy could be expanded to allow the entry of small quotas of students from outside the established geographical limits to take courses in which New Zealand has special expertise not readily available in their own countries'. The limits would essentially be those of the South Pacific Commission, with the exception of the US-administered territories, and the members of the South East Asia Ministers of Education (SEAMEO), including the Philippines, the Khmer Republic and Laos, from which so far New Zealand had not accepted private students.

'In considering the labour shortages in higher vocational categories in countries from which New Zealand accepts students, the Committee felt that student policy should be "tailored" to the needs of the home countries.' It recommended 'that approaches be made to the countries concerned on a Government to Government basis, inviting them to give a broad indication of areas of education and training in which their needs are greatest.' That seems to stop short of saying that other countries would determine what New Zealand did, a course that which Immigration saw as 'flawed', while deflecting the charge that its aid could amount to interference.

The Committee endorsed the continuance of the IDC, now attended on by UGC and UEB observers, but thought its appeal function should be taken on by a separate body, the Education Advisory Committee, to be established under the Labour Department Act. There were 100 appeals in 1973, mainly, but not exclusively, concerned with student transfers and the extension or non-extension of permits. The appeal body should include student and institutional representation, but none from the Labour Department.

The Committee considered that as a general rule students should not be accepted at primary level, but endorsed the small quotas given to Tonga and Western Samoa. It did not adopt the idea that quotas at secondary level pre-Form 6 level should be replaced by direct aid, recognising 'the practical problems in assessing correctly the amount of "equivalent finance" which would be required to offset indirect aid given by way of places'.

The Committee also dealt with a number of suggestions made in the submissions it had received, rejecting many, accepting some. For example, it opposed dropping the existing regulation that proscribed taking employment other than in the long vacation: 'the cost of educating private overseas students is borne mainly by the taxpayer (it is conservatively estimated that those studying at universities alone cost over $3 million per annum) and it was, therefore, highly desirable that students should complete their studies in the minimum time'. It did not support NZUSA's suggestion that post-graduate study should be permitted if the student were accepted by the university, preferring the existing rule that required the student to have completed the first degree within one year of the minimum time. It did not support admitting private overseas students to teachers colleges, given 'the limited facilities available, and New Zealand's own need for teachers'. It supported 'the suggestion that provision be made for persons to enter New Zealand for the purpose of learning English', provided that the whole cost were met by the students. It also endorsed the view that remedial courses would improve academic performance, and that 'could represent a saving in the long term'.[59] 'All OK', the UGC thought.[60]

Government acceptance of the main recommendations was announced by the Minister of Immigration, F.M. Colman, on 2 October 1973. Those included the new appeals committee. The announcement added Laos, the Philippines and the Khmer Republic to the list of countries, also newly-independent Bangladesh. 'The primary aim is to train students from developing countries so that they can assist in the development of their homelands', the Minister declared. 'It has, therefore, been decided that there should be government to government consultations with the countries concerned to determine the areas of education and training in which New Zealand can best help them.' He promised a study of the possible provision of remedial English and of the share of the costs that students would have to bear.

'It is widely accepted', Colman continued, 'that it is in the best interest of younger children that they should be educated in their own environment. For this reason students are not normally admitted for primary or for secondary education below 6th form level. Nevertheless, Government, having regard to particular needs, has agreed to accept a limited number of students from some countries at this level.'

'The Minister observed in conclusion that the public may not be aware of the number of students from overseas studying privately in New Zealand or of the costs involved in providing their education.' Officially aided students numbered fewer than 1000. At 30 September 1972 3400 private students were in the country, two-thirds of them at universities and technical institutes. The cost – in addition to the fees they paid – he estimated at $3.5m. 'This figure does not appear in any published overseas

[59] Report, July 1973. H.O. 22/1/279. UGC Box 89.
[60] Note on Renwick/Danks, 19.7.73. ibid.

aid statistics, but represents, nevertheless, a substantial contribution to development in those neighbouring countries from where the students come.'[61]

Student permits, guidelines issued the following year made clear, were valid for one year [except in the case of Western Samoa]. Normally all students were required to return home immediately on completion or termination of their studies. A private student who had successfully completed a course of at least three years at a university or technical institute might, however, be permitted to remain in New Zealand, if he or she satisfied one of four conditions. '(i) The student possesses a qualification for which there is an urgent demand in New Zealand. or (ii) The student produces an offer of employment in New Zealand commensurate with his qualification and the appropriate New Zealand diplomatic post is of the opinion that the student is unlikely to secure a comparable positon in his own country. or (iii) The post is of the opinion that the student is likely to be subject to persecution or discrmination if he returns home. or iv. Marriage to a New Zealand citizen.'[62] The last of these provisions had been liberalised a little in the 1973 review.

The 1973 statement and the 1974 guidelines on the whole emphasise that the admission of private overseas students continued to be seen predominantly as a form of aid. Certainly there was no sense that it was a source of revenue for the institutions or of expansion for the economy. Only marginally was it seen as a source of worthwhile migrants. At the institutional level it was valued partly again because of a sense of obligation to developing countries. Overseas students were also seen as diversifying the student population and adding to the experience of domestic students.

The two Engineering faculties – the focus indeed of competition – particularly valued the work done by private students for the research components of their degrees. Many of the topics they pursued offered contributions to knowledge about New Zealand.

The regulations established no geographical limits for the admission of private foreign graduate students, 'but we prefer to accept those students who wish to undertake a course in which New Zealand has special expertise'. Applications went straight to the universities, not to OSAC. 'They should also be referred to the nearest New Zealand Post with an indication as to whether or not they are acceptable to the University.'[63]

---

[61]   Review f Immigration Policy. Policy Announcements 2 October 1973 to 7 May 1974, presented to House f Representatives. AJHR 1974, E. 21.

[62]   Labour/Hayward, 20.9.74. AU.

[63]   ibid.

Each year OSAC published an information pamphlet and also a notice in the *Education Gazette* [EG] that was directed in particular to New Zealand secondary schools which had private overseas students on their roll. Pamphlet and notice defined those who had to apply through OSAC: every person admitted on a study permit; and every person 'who has come to New Zealand from a country overseas and who is not a New Zealand citizen or ordinarily resident in New Zealand'. Citizens of the Cook Islands, Niue and Tokelau were New Zealand citizens, OSAC noted. As its statute required, it also defined the phrase 'ordinarily resident'. For example, the *Gazette* notice of February 1977, covering the admission of students for the 1978 academic year, included any person who had resided continuously in New Zealand since 1 July 1974, any person whose parents or one of them had resided continuously in New Zealand since 1 July 1976, and any person whose parent was stationed in New Zealand as a diplomatic or career consular officer.[64]

The notice also set out the academic requirements for entrance for overseas students in New Zealand secondary schools who sought admission. If their mother tongue was not English, they had to pass LATOS, unless they had already passed it with a grade of A, B or C. They had to obtain a University Entrance qualification either from the University Entrance or University Bursaries Examination. The standard at UB level acceptable to OSAC was defined as the qualification for entrance as set out in Regulation 8 of the UB Regulations 1965. 'However, for those who do not present English for the University Bursaries Examination or who fail to gain the minimum acceptable mark of 25 in English, a higher standard is required, which is: (i) A qualification for entrance as set out in regulation 9 of the Entrance Scholarships Regulations 1962 ..., or (ii) A 'B' award or better under regulation 7 of the University Bursaries Regulations. (To qualify under this provision a candidate must already hold a university entrance qualification.)'[65]

These regulations set out the framework within which New Zealand had come to deal with the flow of private international students. Largely developed ad hoc, they were based on a philosophy of aid and support developed in respect of the Colombo Plan. Though numbers had grown – particularly of Malaysians – suggestions for higher fees had not been adopted.

---

[64] EG, 1.2.77.

[65] ibid.

CHAPTER THREE

FORTY PER CENT

The first meeting of OSAC, held in July 1972, noted a reduction in first year overseas student enrolments: already down to 517 in 1971, the number was now 458, including those admitted under delegated authority to do diplomas at VUW, LC or MU. That, Danks pointed out, would 'lead in a few years to a substantial reduction in the proportion of overseas students enrolled in New Zealand universities. This may lead to charges that New Zealand is not fulfilling its obligations internationally in educational matters.' UGC would therefore include a statement on OSAC in its annual report. In 1972, it would point out, every eligible overseas student was offered a place in the course to which he sought entry, except in Eng Int, and in that case students were offered a place in Science.[1] Commerce was the other course mainly in demand: VUW took 60, AU 12, CU 20, OU 30.[2] The chairman – and perhaps the government – were somewhat defensive, perhaps for fear of domestic criticism, deriving in part from the government's own success in promoting the need to aid less fortunate countries. The chairman's remarks contrasted with those he had made in 1969 on the risk that overseas students would deprive domestic students of places. The risk was now that the measures since taken might have been too effective. The increase in domestic students, moreover, slowed down in the years 1972-4.

The 1973 OSAC meeting was told that 505 overseas students had been accepted, including those admitted under delegated authority: 832 had applied, 449 of them from Malaysia/Singapore. Substantially more

---

[1]   OSAC 1, 11.7.72. UGC Box 166.
[2]   Minutes, 11.7.72. ibid.

qualified for Eng Int than could be placed, and demand was 'again high' for Commerce.[3] The following year 613 accepted places, including 81 under delegated authority. There had been a sharp increase in the number of applicants: 1186, 838 of them from Malaysia/Singapore. Commerce was overfilled at CU and AU, and Eng Int in demand. Some doubt was expressed about offering places in Science instead, since the students had little chance of realising their hopes of entering Engineering by that route.[4] In 1975 700 accepted places, including 101 delegated. Applications had sharply increased to 1712, 1309 of them from Malaysia, 36 from Singapore. Including those from New Zealand secondary schools, and those dealt with under delegated authority, Malaysian applications totalled 1445, those from Fiji 95, and 172 came from all other countries. Commerce and Engineering dominated. The practice of offering places in Science to those denied entry to Eng Int continued, but 44 could not be found a place even there. 96 qualified candidates, 88 of them Malaysians, were not offered places at all.[5]

The kind of assurance Danks offered in 1972 could no longer be offered. But it seems likely that the change in policy that was already under consideration was not simply the result of a concern on the part of the New Zealand government about the rapid and unbalanced growth in the number of overseas students. It may be that the view of the Malaysian government was decisive. Certainly Foreign Affairs put it strongly. Informal and formal aid differed in modality. Were their objectives also in conflict? The 1973 review had hinted at such issues – Immigration recognising a 'flaw' – and advocated government-government discussions.

Sir Alan Danks had told the UGC in April 1974 that Prime Minister Kirk had on a recent visit to Malaysia discussed 'the matter of the numbers of private Malaysian students undertaking university education in New Zealand' with Prime Minister Tun Razak. 'Concern had been expressed that the increasing numbers of private students obtaining a subsidised university education in New Zealand was affecting the level of overseas aid from this country to Malaysia.' MFA had 'now suggested various ways in which the numbers might be decreased'. Danks listed the suggestions: increasing fees; requiring government sponsorship or interview at the High Commission in KL; refusing to accept the Victorian Higher Certificate as an entrance qualification; 'accepting private students only for courses which are accepted by the Malaysian Government'; increasing the level of LATOS; not accepting applications until students had actually received

---

[3]   OSAC 73/2, 31.7.73. ibid.

[4]   OSAC 74/2. ibid.

[5]   OSAC, 11.7.75, Secretary's report. ibid.

their Cambridge HSC results; or 'setting a quota for private Malaysian students'. UGC had been asked to comment to the Minister of Education.[6] It seems clear that Tun Razak sought to constrain the numbers and that New Zealand was quite ready to agree.

In the meantime it undertook to make it a New Zealand government requirement that Malaysian students should pass the MCE test in Malay as a prerequisite to study in New Zealand.[7] That, the NZUSA vice-president said, was 'another intrusion of Malaysian standards, regulations and practices into New Zealand universities',[8] and the VUW Professorial Board protested.[9] It did not necesarily put non-Malays at a disadvantage, Kirk said: the language was widely spoken by non-Malays and taught in all schools.[10]

After the riots in KL in 1969, the Malaysian government had adopted a form of nation-building more emphatically designed to favour the bumiputera, and it seems clear that Tun Razak, while unwilling to prevent Chinese from securing qualifications overseas, wanted to limit it. Certainly Malays had not been well represented in the professions pre-1969. In 1968 Malaysian medicos included 65 Malays, 808 Chinese, 771 Indians, 249 others; lawyers in West Malaysia included 92 Malays, 241 Chinese, 190 Indians, 47 others. The UM teaching staff included 51 Malays, 143 Chinese, 75 Indians, 199 others.[11] If non-Malays gained qualifications outside the country that they could not because of ethnic quotas gain within it, how would the Malays ever catch up?

Tun Razak returned the prime ministerial visit in October 1975. No action had been taken as a result of the discussions the previous year, Foreign Affairs advised, and Razak's visit was 'an excellent opportunity to provide fresh political push for a detailed consideration of the question'. About half the foreign students in New Zealand were Malaysian, and Malaysians made up 86% of the Asian students in the country. There had been 'a dramatic rise', too, in the numbers who wanted to come. The 'problem' was confined to private students. 'Very few young Malaysians enter New Zealand ... under the Colombo Plan': only three in the current year. 'In other words, the vast majority of Malaysian students in New Zealand are from wealthier Malaysian families who do not require official

6   Minutes UGC 84/1, 29-30.4.74. ibid.
7   Letter signed W.O. Broad, 18.7.74. ibid.
8   Press, 22.6.74.
9   Cotterall/Broad, 19.7.74. UGC Box 166.
10 Parliamentary Questions, *New Zealand Foreign Affairs Review* [NZFAR], 24,8 (8.74), p. 40.
11 Karl von Vorys, *Democrcay without Consensus*, Princeton UP, 1975, p. 244.

assistance and do not need to undertake the commitments it involves.'[12] The argument was at best a shaky one, but the conclusion that private students came because they were wealthy took hold.

Foreign Affairs went on to argue that it was 'a bad thing' that students from one country should be so dominant, and that it restricted New Zealand's ability to provide assistance to a wider spread of countries, Iran and the Middle East, for example. The sum involved, though difficult to calculate, probably exceeded New Zealand's regular development aid to Malaysia. New Zealand university rolls had been begun to rise and competition for university places was 'again becoming very keen'. That meant 'that a sound domestic reason is emerging for curbing the inflow of overseas students if, as a consequence of their growing numbers, young New Zealanders are to be prevented from undertaking higher studies', an argument Foreign Affairs deployed even though it would also apply if Iranis or others were found to take the place of Malaysians.

'Another important consideration', it added, 'is the high rate of "defection" among the Malaysian students.' 42% of Malaysian students completing in 1974 were granted permanent residence. 'In the political sense, the presence of Malaysian students in New Zealand has helped draw attention to Malaysia's internal affairs', focusing on 'the allegedly repressive policies of Tun Razak's Government, and on charges that the Malaysian High Commission carries out surveillance of a potentially sinister nature of all Malaysian students here'.

The activities of the High Commissioner – the 'intrusion' the NZUSA vice-president had in mind – indeed provided another context for the episode. In September 1973 he had suggested that Malaysian students in New Zealand were being subverted by Communist propaganda. 'If illegal activities are uncovered', Kirk had responded, 'they will be dealt with. But we are not aware of any evidence to suggest any illegal activities by a foreign power. New Zealand is a free society. Educational places are made available to both New Zealanders and others without enquiring into their political beliefs. We believe in the free exchange of ideas at university.' Unless the law was breached, 'there is nothing that the Government can, or would wish, to do'.[13] It could, however, limit the number of students, and Foreign Affairs clearly hoped to reduce an embarrassing problem in that way.

The question had been revived in 1974, when a former student, Khoo Ee Liam, was arrested in KL. One of the charges was that he took part in

---

12 Brief for the Visit, 10.75. UGC Box 89.
13 NZFAR, 23,9 (9.73), p. 39.

the activities of the New Zealand-China Society while a student, and NZUSA declared that the Malaysian Government was spying on its citizens in New Zealand.[14] The Associate Minister of Foreign Affairs wrote to the Malaysian High Commissioner, asking for further information about the charges against Khoo. New Zealand expected Malaysian and other students to abide by New Zealand law when they were in New Zealand, he said, but it made no differentiation between them and local students. 'Mr Walding said that many in the universities and in the community at large would feel that any attempt to penalise someone for activities which were not unlawful in New Zealand would be an attempt to extend the laws of Malaysia to this country, and would raise serious issues involving academic freedom and the civil liberties of which New Zealanders were proud.'[15]

The Malaysian government would be 'in favour of some restriction being placed on the numbers of their students going abroad', the 1975 brief continued, and the High Commissioner confirmed it was Razak's view. 'The Malaysians have been unwilling so far however, to take any initiative. The question does have implications for their internal situation, particularly its racial aspect. Almost all the Malaysians who study abroad are Chinese; to have them do so works to a degree as a social "safety valve" for the Malay-dominated Government. ... But the greater national interest undoubtedly lies in securing the return to Malaysia of the graduate skills her students acquire and of which the country is greatly in need. Tun Razak has indicated his concern over the permanent loss of so many students.'

Only two ways of imposing a limit on Malaysian students promised to have 'a major impact', raising academic standards, and imposing a quota. Attempting the former at university raised a difficulty. If it applied only to Malaysians, it would be criticised as discriminatory. If it applied 'in blanket fashion', it would penalise students from other developing countries, perhaps more than those from Malaysia. 'For these and other reasons New Zealand universities are most unenthusiastic about this possible course.' The only alternative was a quota. The Prime Minister, Foreign Affairs suggested, might obtain Razak's agreement that the two governments should consider it 'a matter of urgency', and get their officials to consider the application of a quota system.

In the communique at the end of his visit, Razak expressed appreciation for the education and training New Zealand had provided. Prime Minister Rowling assured him that it had been pleased to assist and had itself

---

[14]   Press, 5.6.74.
[15]   NZFAR, 24, 6 (6.74), p. 49.

benefited. 'In this connection however, and noting the increasing numbers of Malaysian and other foreign students seeking opportunities for higher study in New Zealand, Mr Rowling informed Tun Razak that the New Zealand Government had decided to give urgent consideration to ways of ensuring the most equitable allocation to overseas students of the places available at New Zealand educational institutions.'[16]

In KL the New Zealand High Commissioner received Lim Kit Siang and other Opposition parliamentarians. 'The number of Malaysian students who had studied in New Zealand had had a pronounced beneficial impact on "people-to-people" relations between the two countries', Lim declared. Weir said that Malaysians were taking too large a number of the places available in New Zealand, whose first obligation was to the Pacific. It was 'a kind of supplementary aid programme', but many were not returning to Malaysia, he added. That problem would not be dealt with by a quota, Lim responded. 'The reasons for ex-students staying on in New Zealand lay in the situation which existed in Malaysia itself.'[17]

The National government took up where Labour left off. On 20 January 1976 the Muldoon Cabinet sought a paper from the IDC. It concluded that it would be possible by 1978 to restrict the entry of first-year students from any one country to not more than 40% of the intake at that level in any year, and that the government could issue a directive to that effect. Malaysia was in mind, but it would not be openly stated. It could be implemented through OSAC.[18] That committee had not been established for the purpose, but its capacity to act in such a way had been recognised. Rather to the surprise of the UGC's new chairman, Alan Johns, there was no official notification till the Labour Department representative produced a letter at that year's OSAC meeting.[19]

'As you are aware there has recently been some discussion over the imbalance by nationality of overseas students studying in New Zealand', the letter ran. 'It has become increasingly obvious that at university level in particular the vast majority of places offered to overseas students were taken by Malaysian students. This is not in keeping with our aim to give priority to the educational needs of the South Pacific.' The Minister of Immigration had therefore directed that limits were to be set on the numbers of students entering New Zealand from Malaysia. Given that there were some 130 Malaysian private students in New Zealand schools who would qualify for entrance in 1977, the Minister had decided as a

---

[16]   Joint PR, 14.10.75. UGC Box 89.
[17]   Simcock/Secreary FA, 12.11.75. 125/4/1. UGC Box 89.
[18]   Draft memorandum for Cabinet, received UGC 25.2.76. UGC Box 653.
[19]   Chairman's Report, 1.8.77. UGC 103/49. VCC Box 12.

first step that no more than 70 Malaysians would be granted entry into New Zealand secondary schools in 1977, and no more than 170 Malaysians would be admitted direct from Malaysia to New Zealand universities in 1977. The intake of Malaysians into first-year studies in 1977 would thus be approximately 300.[20]

In Parliament, the question 'Why?' put on behalf of Russell Marshall (Wanganui) elicited the answer from the Minister, T.F. Gill, that the 'vast majority of places available to private overseas students were being taken up by Malaysian students', and that was 'not in keeping with New Zealand's aim to give priority to the educational needs of persons from South Pacific countries'. The restriction was intended 'to ensure that the admission of private overseas students is consistent with New Zealand's overseas aid objectives generally'. The decision was taken on the basis of a recommendation from the inter-departmental committee.[21]

The policy approved by the Cabinet and announced by the Minister in October took a somewhat different form, proceeding, as IDC had suggested, by percentage rather than by numbers. The number of private overseas students from any one country was to be limited to 40% of the total intake. That would, the Minister said, 'entail restraint on the number allowed entry to secondary schools for pre-university study'. At the same time the range of countries from which students could come – hitherto the members of the South Pacific Commission, SEATO and Bangladesh – was increased by including the Middle East. Commodore Gill invoked the aid concept, but also mentioned the contribution the students made to the universities. The changes, he said, were 'designed to achieve a better balance, more closely related to our general overseas aid objectives, in the intake of private students and in the undoubted contribution these students make in our educational institutions'.

There were other changes: though they were stepping up existing policies, they were negative in tone. 'It has also been decided, in the interests of the students concerned, that because of the recent rate of inflation, the financial undertaking students have to provide before entry to New Zealand must be raised in value. This should avoid any temptation to disregard a condition of their permits concerning employment during the academic year.' It was 'essential' that students return home 'in due course', since studying in New Zealand was intended to enable students 'to assist in the economic, social and educational development of their own countries'. Some claimed they could not find employment at home, and pressed to remain in New Zealand as permanent residents. 'In these

---

[20]   Labour/OSAC, 14.7.76. AU.
[21]   Hansard, 12.8.76.

cases, my officers are required to satisfy themselves that appropriate employment in a student's home country is not available and the only applications for permanent residence to be approved will be those which also meet the same occupational skill requirement used for all migrants.'

The government, Gill concluded, was 'anxious to discourage overseas students from entering "marriages of convenience" as a means of obtaining the right to remain permanently in New Zealand'. Private overseas students who married New Zealand residents while studying in New Zealand would be required to complete a course of study of at least three years 'and to have served a two-year probationary period following the date of their marriage before being granted permanent resident status'.[22] The last provision was not, however, implemented.

Answering a question in the House, Gill said students from the South Pacific had first preference, Southeast Asia second preference. Opportunities for students beyond those regions were to be given to those coming from countries with which New Zealand had close political and trade links. 'It has also been agreed that a secondary aim of New Zealand student policy is to provide opportunities for cultural exchanges between the people of New Zealand and people in other countries.'[23] The universities made a number of agreements for the exchange of students in the following years.

The quota on Malaysian students was deeply controversial. A motion at the 1976 OSAC meeting to defer the introduction of quotas was lost, though Danks agreed to report the discussion to the UGC.[24] NZUSA, a strong critic, wanted the matter put on the 1977 agenda. Lisa Sacksen, the President, made three points: the detrimental effects on the academic, cultural and social life of the universities and on New Zealand's aid to developing countries; the failure of the government to consult the universities; and the urgent need to review the government's policy. Johns pointed out that OSAC's function was to select and distribute students. It had no power to determine the numbers admitted to New Zealand, nor had the universities.[25] The President's motion lapsed. But the chairman did agree to inform UGC of OSAC's view that one-country quotas should be suspended until other students were available to take up the modest number of places that the universities offered.[26]

Indeed the figures put to OSAC showed that the 1976 limit on

---

[22] *North Shore Times Advertiser,* 19.10.76.
[23] Hansard, 23.11.77.
[24] Minutes, 29.7.76. UGC Box 166. Cf UGC 104/4a. VCC Box 12.
[25] OSAC 77/5. AU.
[26] Minutes, 27.7.77. UGC Box 166.

Malaysians had constrained the total number of offers and acceptances.[27] The government's objective was to get the number of Malaysians down to 40% of the 1975 quota by 1978. In that year, the maximum was to be 240. In fact only 221 took up places, and the grand total was 327. Though it had not publicly said so, the government indeed wished to reduce the total number. Its object – on which Treasury was insistent – was to reduce expenditure.

In a paper reviewing existing policy dated 29 March 1976 Treasury had recommended that the Cabinet committee on expenditure should agree that UGC should 'review the basis of the fees charged to private overseas students with a view to a substantial increase in these fees', and invite the Minister of Education, Les Gandar, to report and present a recommendation to that effect at the end of April.[28]

Unsure whether the recommendation had been adopted or not, Danks offered Gandar his comments in August, 'in case you wish to take the matter further'. First, he pointed out that fees were set by Councils. If they were to be raised, the Government would have to proceed by reducing the block grants and informing the universities that they could increase fees to compensate. 'It is certain that a discriminatory increase in the fees of overseas students will be criticised, and it is likely that at least some University Councils will decline to levy higher fees, preferring instead to accept a slightly reduced income.' Because the universities would have to administer an 'unpopular' scheme, and students would try to avoid higher fees, it would be important to have a clearer definition than suggested by the word 'private': some students were 'assisted' by other governments or organisations, some fully supported, some partially. Any scheme, it was suggested, should apply to all overseas students, except those from Niue, Tokelau and the Cooks who were New Zealand citizens.

The number of overseas students recorded by the universities in 1975 was 2747; excluding 25 from those islands, 2722. 415 were assisted by the New Zealand government, and 115 assisted by governments or organisations overseas, total 530. The Department of Labour listed 1933 overseas students at the universities. That did not include 57 from Australia, who required no permit, nor about 30 from the UK who presumably entered before permits were required in 1974. Total 2020. That left some 170 of those recorded by the universities not accounted for. Perhaps more were assisted than they recorded. Perhaps some had married and been granted permanent residence, but the universities were not aware of the change. At all events there about 2020 private students

---

[27] OSAC 77/2.
[28] Memorandum by Gandar, 17.8.76. UGC Box 653.

in a total lying between 2550 and 2720. The steps recently taken by the Minister of Immigration would reduce the number of those coming from Malaysia, but it would take time for the larger numbers admitted in recent years to work their way through the system. The grand total of overseas students might be 2970 in 1976, 2680 by 1980.

Currently overseas students paid the same fees as New Zealanders, ranging from $40 to $60 a unit in the general faculties to $200 a year in Engineering and $330 in Vet Sci. Over the whole system the average fee paid by internal students was $122 a year. For overseas students the average was slightly higher – about $135 – as more were full-time and more did Engineering. The costs for the Government could not be isolated. It would be paying $73m for 39 400 internal [as distinct from extra-mural] students in 1976, an average of $1 857, exclusive of capital costs. 'No faculty costs are available because the faculties are not self-contained and marginal cost has little meaning because up to a point another student can be accepted in a class at little or no additional cost.' At a university without costly professional faculties, such as VUW, the average cost was $1 300. The average cost for an overseas student probably lay between $1 600 and $1 900.

In the UK, Danks noted, overseas students currently paid a higher fee, but the differential was to be abolished in 1977, and all students were to pay a higher fee, averaging GBP 658 for undergraduates, 758 for postgraduates. UGC did not recommend that overseas students should be charged higher fees than New Zealanders. If the 'user-pay' principle was to be extended, 'it would prefer to see all students pay an increased fee'. If, however, Government decided that overseas students should pay higher fees, it would also have to decide how to handle the students it assisted, effectively transferring the charge from Vote Education to other votes. Should the higher fees be charged to those already on-course or only first-time students? Should there be special assistance for Pacific island students, many of whom would probably be unable to continue their studies if fees were raised?[29]

'My feeling is that this [reduction of expenditure?] is best done by reduction in numbers of overseas students rather than increasing fees', the Minister wrote.[30] It was that he recommended to Cabinet committee on expenditure on 17 August. Treasury returned to the charge in November. It estimated the cost of overseas students at around $5.6m out of the total university running cost of $73.2m, of which $947 000 was for

[29] Memorandum for Minister of Education, 10.8.76. G. 8/32. UGC Box 89, also Box 653.

[30] on the copy in Box 89.

assisted students. That left $4.65m as a 'hidden subsidy' for private overseas students. Many of them attended New Zealand universities because their own governments had 'some form of discrimination on entry to University'. Treasury suggested that a further report should be sought, along the lines of full cost recovery.[31] The Cabinet expenditure committee agreed to invite the Minister of Immigration, in consultation with the Minister of Foreign Affairs, 'to report on the administration rules regarding university students from overseas which presently apply and what further action would be necessary to reduce the number of students significantly by 1981 having regard to the requirements to provide places for assisted students under the official aid programmes and for the special needs of the South Pacific'.[32] At Cabinet itself on 20 December 'Ministers commented that officials should give attention also to a possible double approach of setting higher and (therefore differential) fees as well as reducing quotas'.[33]

In the meantime Talboys, now at Foreign Affairs, agreed that NZUSA representatives should meet the IDC. What should they be told? Student organisations had criticised the reduction in the number of overseas students and the 'deprivation' of the Malaysians. They said that they had understood that the cut in Malaysians would signal a redistribution, students from other countries replacing them. In fact only a few students were coming from the Middle East, and language difficulties, and New Zealand's lack of knowledge of the education systems, meant that rapid expansion was quite unlikely. Officials did not accept that a reduction in private student numbers 'detracted' from New Zealand's aid effort. The Government had always seen the education of private students as a 'supplement' to official aid programmes. 'For instance, while students sponsored under the aid programme are undertaking courses regarded as important to their countries' development, private students usually seek an overseas education for personal rather than national interests', and many did not return home. A substantial sum was involved, but it could not be 'seen in the context of official development'.

The cabinet committee sought a significant reduction in numbers by 1981. In fact the quotas were 'clearly working', and the recommendations Foreign Affairs had made to IDC focused on other areas, including tightening controls on postgraduate study, on admission with credits, and on admission to accountancy professional at technical institutes. Ministers had tried to blunt the edge of criticisms of the reductions already being

---

[31] Memorandum for Minister of Finance, 23.11.76. UGC Box 653.

[32] Minutes, 17.12.76.ibid., also Box 89.

[33] Minute by Secretary, 21.12.76. UGC Box 653, also 89.

achieved by suggesting that they would make room for others and would be offset by them in due course, though the Middle East would certainly not provide the numbers to do that. In fact government apparently wanted to achieve further reductions, but had not publicly declared it. Perhaps, Norrish suggested, Foreign Affairs should propose adding Africa and the Caribbean to the list of countries from which private students could be accepted. 'The numbers involved could be kept very small still – certainly not enough to offset the reductions achieved in Malaysian student numbers.'[34] Talboys agreed.

The joint memorandum from the Ministers of Immgration and Foreign Affairs reached the expenditure committee in March 1978. Though it was 'too early' to establish trends in student applications from Malaysia as a result of the quota, overall applications had fallen, while the introduction of Bahasa as the language medium in Malaysian institutions might 'reduce the number of students competent enough in English to qualify for student permits'. At this stage it was not therefore considered necessary to introduce further restrictions on the entry of private Malaysian students. Measures should, however, be taken to check a growth in applications for post-graduate study and admission with credits, for example by making LATOS compulsory for both and tightening admission to the former. A quota could be put on Malaysian entry into professional accountancy courses.

'The stated aim of private overseas student policy is to train people to assist in the economic, social and educational development of their own countries where facilities for higher education are not so readily available. It follows therefore that those chosen for study in New Zealand should be chosen on the basis of academic merit rather than on their ability to pay.' That was particularly true of the South Pacific, 'where the great majority of students would be unable to afford more than the current token fee'. IDC had considered a proposal – supported by Treasury – 'that private overseas students should meet all costs of their education by way of differential fees which would be refunded by way of a scaled subsidy administered by the Ministry of Foreign Affairs'. But the committee thought that any system of scholarships or subsidies designed to protect the poorer students would 'discriminate against the middle income students and involve an expensive and cumbersome administrative machinery which would likely negate advantages or savings to be gained from a differential fee system. Charging private students differential fees for their education is not seen as a particularly efficient system of either reducing overall student numbers or of allocating costs on a "user pays"

---

[34] Memorandum by Norrish, 20.6.77. UGC Box 653.

principle.' It was not necessary to reduce numbers, and the committee counselled against 'any action which would be seen in developing countries as a move away from the primary aim of private overseas student policy which is that it be seen as a form of indirect private aid'.[35]

Treasury did not consider that the joint memorandum answered the request Cabinet Committee and Cabinet itself made in December 1976: if they wished significantly to reduce the number of overseas students by 1981, 'then it would be necessary to examine ways for doing so *now*'. Treasury, moreover, continued to maintain that overseas students should pay fees that reflected costs, at present about $2 000 a student. 'So as not to penalise students with low incomes, a graded subsidy based on need could be paid by the Government, possibly administered by the Ministry of Foreign Affairs as part of overseas aid.' Such a proposal would not harm students from the South Pacific. Treasury recommended that the expenditure committee should reiterate its intention significantly to reduce the number of overseas students by 1981.[36]

A meeting of the committee, attended only by Hugh Templeton and David Thomson, plus officials, did not go so far. UGC and MFA wanted the quota system to continue, it was told. In 1977 170 Malaysians were admitted at first-year level direct from Malaysia, along with 70 from New Zealand secondary schools: that was a reduction of 55% on 1976. About 100 students would come from the South Pacific. None would be coming from Iran or Iraq, for which a limit of 50 had been set. Numbers from Malaysia would also be affected by the changing language requirements in Malaysia. The committee noted that the effect of existing policy was still being felt and agreed that the situation should be reviewed in 1979 with the intention of seting targets for 1981.[37]

At the same time, but apparently coincidentally, IDC suggested to the Minister of Immigration that the policy statement needed updating, so as to cover the preference for the South Pacific, and secondly for Southeast Asia, and also the concept of cultural exchange. In the following weeks the Minister questioned whether the primary aim was still valid. In 1973 – when some MPs had argued it was 'inhuman' to send students back to what had become 'foreign cultures' on completion of their studies – the review committee had agreed that students should be allowed to remain if there was an urgent demand for the qualification in New Zealand, or the student had a job offer and the New Zealand post advised that he was unlikely to get a comparable position at home, or he was likely to face

---

[35]   Memorandum, 2.3.78. UGC Box 653.

[36]   Memorandum for Minister of Finance, 28.2.78. ibid.

[37]   Minutes, 7.3.78. ibid.

persecution or discrimination. By 1975 50% of those completing were being allowed to stay. The current goverrment tightened the controls, incorporating points 1 and 2 as a condition.

Now the Minister was 'becoming increasingly concerned at the requirement that these students return home, after having spent a number of their formative years in this country, to what may be an alien environment'. He was receiving an increasing number of requests for permanent residence on humanitarian grounds: the students had been in New Zealand for so many years, their qualifications were not recognised at home, they could not find employment there. New Zealand employers who could use the skills involved argued that they should get the benefit of students' qualifications gained at the taxpayers' expense. 268 private overseas students had been in New Zealand for seven years or more.

'The Minister has asked that a complete re-appraisal of our student policy be undertaken with particular regard to determining what the future aims and objectives of private student policy should be.' Was there still a need to accept private overseas students or did New Zealand's aid programme 'adequately cover the needs and objectives of our foreign policy in regard to providing the necessary educational qualifications to developing countries'? If there were a need still to accept them, was the aim to train them to return home? The implication was that the courses they did should be only those recognised by and needed by the home country and should be 'courses which the student could not undertake in his own country'. If, on the other hand, private students were seen as potential migrants, the emphasis should be on skills of benefit to New Zealand, 'and again the courses approved would be significantly different from those which many students are currently permitted to undertake'.

If the aim was still to train students to return home, then steps might be taken to minimise their time 'away from their own country and culture'. Perhaps students should not be accepted below tertiary level, be limited to one course only at undergraduate level, not be allowed to gain experience in New Zealand, or be allowed to do postgraduate study only after spending two years at home. Maybe more places should be offered in technical institutes or apprenticeship schemes. There would also need to be consultations with other governments to ascertain their needs.

'A strong case can be made for gearing the entry of private overseas students to the needs of [the] New Zealand economy and not requiring them to return home on completion of their studies.' Some who gained qualifications at the New Zealand taxpayers' expense were sought after by 'a third country'. Students trained in New Zealand fitted more easily into the workforce than first-time migrants. Following that policy might, however, create a 'brain drain' effect that would strain relations with the other countries, 'a factor which was starting to become evident to some extent in the case of smaller South Pacific countries by 1975'.

As for the 268, many had been permitted to stay after appealing to the Education Advisory Committee [i.e the appeal committee of 1973]. If more strict controls were to be applied, its terms of reference might have to be 'tightened'. Alternatively the Labour Department might have more frequently to decline to act on its recommendations. But that would put the Department back where it was before 1974, 'when without any expertise in the field, it was required to determine academic progress'.[38]

This paper the Minister of Immigration forwarded to the Cabinet, seeking a directive to IDC 'to investigate and make recommendations on the need for continuing to accept private overseas students for study in New Zealand, and on the basis if any, on which they should be accepted'. There were a number of features in the present policy impossible to administer without causing 'considerable dispute' between the government departments on the one hand, and employers, universities, overseas students and students associations on the other. One 'example' was that 268 students had been in New Zealand for 7 years or more, 9 for 11 years, 2 for 12 years. The review should consider whether there was a need to admit private students and whether the aim was to provide assistance or seek migrants, and consider also the administrative rules necessary to implement any recommendations.[39] On 26 June 1978 Cabinet ordered the review. The universities were able to make submissions to it.

At OSAC Johns had drawn attention to the existence of the IDC. Recognising that OSAC did not have a policy role, VUW suggested that NZVCC should set up a standing committee on overseas students, in the hope of increasing consultation and influencing policy, a recommendation a committee of its Professorial Board, chaired by Stuart Johnston, had made in July 1977.[40] The OSAC secretary, Peter Morris, relayed the idea to the VCC. The VCC did not see the need for such a committee, though they wanted to be consulted by Government when policy changes were contemplated. Could the VCC have an observer at IDC meetings, as had UGC and UEB?[41] Could VCC invite IDC to its next meeting? Morris wondered.[42] There were important academic issues at stake, overseas doctoral students, ad eundem admissions, admissions with credit, the 'desirable mix'. VCC decided that a small group should meet IDC and

38   Private Overseas Student Policy, n.d. [?May 1978]. ibid.
39   Memorandum for Cabinet, n.d. ibid.
40   Report, 5.7.77. VCC Box 12.
41   Hampton/Morris, 21.10.77. ibid.
42   Morris/Hampton, 7.11.77. ibid.

report, Stuart Johnston of VUW, Tarling of AU, and Peter Hampton, the VCC secretary.[43]

That meeting took place on 10 February 1978. One question – raised in the VUW report, but also 'envisaged' by IDC – was a three-year course-length permit permit, rather than a year by year one. Another was the longstanding question of defining 'satisfactory progress', on which universities tended to be more 'lenient' than Labour wished, though its practice was to allow two years after the minimum for completion. IDC queried ad eundem admission with credit: some of those admitted by universities were below the standard of students rejected by OSAC. Tarling argued against quotas on graduates, and Johnston urged that the concept of exchange should be preserved, since New Zealand students expected to go overseas. The university spokesmen reiterated their 'distaste' for the 40% quota on undergraduates.[44]

The idea that VCC might have observers at IDC was taken up again in 1979.[45] Johns had no objection to it, and indeed Morris drafted a letter for Hampton to send to the Minister of Immigration.[46] The Minister, Jim Bolger, declined to offer the VCC permanent observer status.[47] No doubt the controversies of 1979 had not made it more likely. They did not, however, arise from the IDC review.

In August the universities were told that Cabinet had directed IDC to 'undertake a full review of Private Overseas Student Policy and make recommendations through the Minister of Immigration on: (i) the level in terms of overall numbers, and the countries and regions from which New Zealand might reasonably continue to admit private overseas students, and the types of study in New Zealand which should be open to such students; (ii) whether a certain length of stay (in New Zealand) should be a factor in granting permanent residence to overseas students; (iii) whether the aim of allowing private overseas students to study in New Zealand should be directed towards recruiting students as potential immigrants or towards providing assistance to the future development of the students' home countries, or a combination of both depending on individual circumstances; (iv) the administrative rules necessary to implement any recommendations.' Since the 1973 review, the Secretary of Labour noted, the numbers of private overseas students had increased from 3176 to 3967 in 1977. The IDC wanted to 'assess the varying views and opinions held

---

43   Memorandum, 14.12.77. ibid.
44   Notes by Hampton, 10.2.78. ibid. Tarling's notes. AU
45   Tarling, Report on OSAC, 26.7.79. VCC Box 12.
46   Morris/Hampton, 12.10.79. ibid.
47   Bolger/Secretary VCC, 5.12.79. ibid.

on this matter', and called for submissions from interested parties. It attached the statement of current policy.[48]

The NZVCC sent in a submission on 27.10.78, compiled by Johnston and Tarling, but very much relying on comments from VUW. Its reply on the first topic was prefaced by three general comments. First, the presence of overseas students was important for diversifying teaching and learning and reducing New Zealand's isolation. Second, the numbers should not be reduced, least of all at the postgraduate level. Third, restricting the entry of overseas students might rebound on New Zealand students overseas. The question itself was answered by stressing the need to consult the universities, by urging that the 40% rule be dropped, by arguing that, if it were retained, Foreign Affairs and others must encourage recruitment from other countries, and by proposing to extend the list of developing countries to include, for example, those in Africa.

On the second topic, the submission suggested that the recruitment of potential immigrants was not a necessary aim of a student admission policy. The general rule should be that students should return home. Decisions about permanent residence should be made when the student had completed a course, and take into account the employment situation both in New Zealand and in the student's home country, as well as the political climate there.

The third topic was seemingly related. The aims, the VCC submission proposed, should include contributing to the aid programme; giving individual overseas students opportunity; providing New Zealand students with opportunity for cultural experience and understanding. Overseas students should have a wide range of choice, and not be confined to a narrow concept of 'usefulness'.

Under the fourth heading, the submission referred to English language tests for graduates. It again referred to the value of continued consultation, and suggested that the Education Advisory Committee should be invited to offer advice on all the issues involved.

The submission dealt with a number of other issues. Among them was the question of language assistance for private overseas students, thought to be the more necessary as Malaysia turned to using Malay throughout, and a wider range of countries was sourced. The universities wanted permits to be granted for the minimum period of a course, and they also wanted greater flexibility over the 'work' proscription, so that students might be employed at the university during the academic year.

CU took a somewhat divergent view. The University's Academic

---

[48] Malpass/Registrar, 21.8.78. AU.

Administration Committee thought overseas students might occupy 10-12% of the roll, provided that there were adequate places for qualified New Zealanders. It referred to problems in classes with over 25%. It also suggested that there might be categories of overseas students, with domestic fees for the first 150, then nearly full cost.[49] That was not a policy the universities were likely to initiate. In any case the terms of the review did not cover the issue. But – even if the universities were unaware of the Government's unstated policy of restricting numbers and Treasury's persistence – the idea of differential fees, advocated occasionally in earlier years in New Zealand, had been gaining ground overseas.

The provincial governments of Alberta and Ontario had already decided to charge differential fees. The Canadian Bureau for International Education pointed out that the amount by which Alberta and Ontario had increased the fees did not nearly cover the actual costs. Differential fees did not therefore relieve the burden on Canadian taxpayers. '[A] small differential fee is considerably worse than a large one since it projects a negative image without saving Canadian taxpayers any meaningful amounts of money.'[50] In 1979, the year after it had sought submissions to a review the terms of reference of which did not allude to the matter at all, the New Zealand government decided on a middle-sized one.

Discussions on LATOS – which led to its abolition – had a different origin again and proceeded independently. It had been seen as a regulating device as well as an academic assessment. In 1975 UEB had raised the standard by eliminating the D provisional pass grade and by raising the cut off point for the C grade. What was in mind were failure rates at the universities and 'a vast increase in numbers'.[51] In 1976 Danks told the Board that the prospect of a quota, meaning that numbers would be 'severely pruned', made it 'prudent' to make further use of NZCER evidence on failure and raise the C cut off from the 30th decile to the 40th.[52] That was done after the quota was announced. It 'eased selection problems', though many were still left outside the quota.[53]

The test, as Morris told UEB in 1980, could 'hardly be expected to be popular among the students concerned', and there had been objections from different areas in turn, Malaysia, Singapore, Fiji, and now Western Samoa. Visiting New Zealand the prime minister, Tufuola Efi, claimed that LATOS acted as 'a discriminating barrier' to Samoan students.[54] 18

[49] Brownlie/Hampton, 21.9.78. AU.
[50] *University Affairs* [Canada], 1.78, p. 2.
[51] E38.3.2, 6.76. UGC Box 166.
[52] Memorandum, 5.76. E38.3.2. UGC Box 95.
[53] Memorandum, 6.76. E38.3.2. ibid.

students had allegedly been refused entry into New Zealand universities for failing LATOS, and his government claimed that the test had been toughened up in order to cut back on the number of foreign students.[55] In fact 8 were successful; 7 did not reach UB standard; 3 failed LATOS. Jack Caldwell, UGC secretary, pointed to the high failure rate of a trial group admitted to universities and technical institutes in 1976, 1977 and 1978 with UB passes and LATOS failures: they would have taken six years to complete a 3-year course.[56] One motive had in fact been to cope with numbers, but the debate focused on the question of ability to cope with courses and the value of LATOS as a predictor. Doing English for UB was not a substitute, UEB officials argued: it had a literary focus and was too open to the drilled answer.[57] Citizens or permanent residents of New Zealand, some perhaps of Samoan origin, sitting in secondary school classes alongside the 'foreigners' were qualifed to enter on that basis, however. No special English tests could be put on top of UE for them.

Given this somewhat but not entirely invidious situation, DOE did not support UEB/UGC,[58] and on 8 April 1980 Cabinet invited the Minister formally to request UGC to alter its position.[59] LATOS, Muldoon said on a subsequent visit to Samoa, was conceived by 'wise men with the best intentions, but who fell into a bit of foolshness'.[60] Or were they pushed?

UGC decided to set up a committee to report on the need for a test of English competence as part of the condition of entry for overseas students and the need for bridging courses for those who failed. Meanwhile LATOS would not be administered to overseas students with NZUE.[61] The committee was headed by L.V. Castle of AU. It recommended discontinuing the application of LATOS to students without NZUE [i.e. ad eundem entrants]. It did not favour bridging communication courses for those who failed any English requirement, but suggested that remedial courses open to all students who wished to take them should be considered. Dispensing with LATOS, it thought, would not lead to a substantial increase in the number of those students whose studies were impaired by language difficulties. Other factors might come into play, including the impact of

---

[54]   E46.3.2. UGC Box 166.

[55]   EP, 4.6.81.

[56]   Memorandum, 25.2.80. UGC Box 166.

[57]   ibid.

[58]   Comment by Renwick, n.d. UGC Box 166.

[59]   CM 80/12/18. ibid.

[60]   P, 4.6.81.

[61]   UGC, 28-29.5.80, reported by J.A. Ross, n.d. UGC Box 166.

the Malaysian quota and the $1500 fee.[62]

This phase was in general marked by moves to contain the growth in private overseas students. The 40% quota was largely a Malaysian initiative. The New Zealand Treasury was, however, interested in reducing numbers in order to save money. The idea of 'making' money was not yet present. Nor did it influence the decision to impose a special fee.

[62] Report, 24.11.80.

CHAPTER FOUR

$1500

Though the 1978 review had not covered the question of raising the fees that overseas students paid, such a step was being implemented in other recipient countries. Two Canadian provinces had raised the fees for foreign students, though not so that they met full costs. The desired result was to limit numbers. A fairer way, the Canadian Bureau for International Education argued, would be to impose quotas, since differential fees discriminated in favour of the wealthier inhabitants of sending countries, making a mockery of Canada's claims on equal educational opportunity.[1]

In Britain the number of overseas students had risen over the decade to 1977-8 from 31 000 to some 80 000, and the expenditure on subsidising them reached some 100m pounds. The Labour government had introduced quotas and raised fees by some 60%. The Thatcher government raised fees by a further 33% and began to remove the subsidies. To do that, the *Financial Times* estimated, would require the fees to be multiplied by two and a half. Half of the foreign contingent still came from the Commonwealth, and some ministers argued that the subsidy was a remnant of empire which the country could no longer afford. A reduction would, however, be condemned by the anti-imperialist National Union of Students. One problem was that some students came from countries no longer badly off. If full cost fees were imposed, the British government needed to provide 'generously increased funds to help youngsters who, although well qualified for British higher or further education, cannot afford to come here'. Michael Dixon, the correspondent, notes that numbers from India, Kenya, Sri Lanka and Pakistan had fallen between

---

[1]   *University Affairs*, 1.78.

1976-7 and 1977-8. The numbers from the main suppliers, Malaysia, Iran, Nigeria and Hong Kong, had increased.[2]

On 14 May 1979 Prime Minister Muldoon announced that, from 1980, private foreign students in New Zealand would have to pay a fee of NZ$1500 a year. The measure would net about NZ$800 000 in 1980, and by 1982 was expected to add $2m to government coffers. Students from the South Pacific would be exempt, as would those who had already started their courses. Most of those affected would be Malaysian. 'Mr Muldoon said most of these have wealthy parents who could afford to pay.' He did not expect the number of foreign students in New Zealand – about 4000 – to be affected.[3] What accounted for what seems to be a modest Treasury victory? The UK and Canada offered examples, and a visa fee of up to A$2000 was set in Australia. The main factor, however, was the wish to cut expenditure. Foreign Affairs had, moreover, suggested that Malaysians were wealthy enough to pay.

Brian Lythe, overseas student counsellor at AU, disagreed. 'Not all the students' families were affluent, he said. Some were already scrimping and saving to pay the students' living expenses in New Zealand. The new fee would make further education beyond the reach of many.' Malay students had preferential entry at home – by 1978 they had 64% of the 18 000 places and the Chinese 29%[4] – and Chinese opted for New Zealand 'where living and lessons were inexpensive, in comparison with some other countries'.[5] The president of NZUSA, Chris Gosling, was 'appalled'. The decision had been made without any consultation, and it was likely to be followed by other cuts and attacks on the system, including a rise in domestic fees.[6] Imposing the fee made a mockery of the call for submissions on policy, Lythe suggested.[7] A 'short-sighted' move to save money, declared Koh Chee Chung, a Malaysian student spokesman in Christchurch.[8]

A standing committee of NZUSA, the National Overseas Students Action Committee, prepared a background paper, countering the Prime Minister's assertions. The students, NOSAC claimed, did not come, as Muldoon asserted, from wealthy families. They were not given bursaries. They mostly returned home at the end of their courses. They could be

---

[2] *Financial Times* [FT], 10.8.79.
[3] NZH, 15.5.79; Press, ibid.
[4] FT, 28.4.79.
[5] NZH, 15.5.79.
[6] ibid.
[7] NZH, 2.6.79.
[8] Press, 15.5.79.

taught at marginal cost. The change, made without consultation, would make the intake more elitist, and reduce the aid involved. A pamphlet NOSAC issued made the same points, adding the suggestion that New Zealand had a moral duty to help the students, having shared the benefits of the colonial exploitation of their country. The move was an attempt, it alleged, to cut numbers still further.[9] It organised a National Action Day on 15 June 1979. A petition, signed by nearly 12 000 students, was presented to Parliament in July, and NZUSA made submissions to the Select Committee on Education.

The Deputy Prime Minister, Talboys, argued that the step was 'reasonable'. He was 'surprised that the Government should be the butt of criticism. ... Other developed countries, many of which have greater resources than New Zealand, require overseas students to pay their way and the fees they charge are far higher than ours; for instance, in Great Britain, the average charge is $2160; in Canada, charges are upward of $2500, depending on the province; and in the United States, fees charged at private universities range between $3000-$4000. It is entirely logical and reasonable that if private students wish to come to this country they should pay. This in no way means that I do not recognise the value of overseas students to the universities: the contribution they make to cultural environment, mutual understanding and research work. But none of these need be affected by the charge of a fee. The fee is not designed to reduce the entry of overseas students or to penalise them; it is purely a fiscal measure. And I repeat, it is perfectly logical and reasonable that these students should make some contribution for the facilities that this country is providing them.' $1500 was 'the Government's assessment of what is a fair level', arrived at only after careful examination.[10]

In earlier argument against such a measure, Danks had pointed out that Councils set fees, and that it would be implemented by cutting quinquennial grants, then leaving it to Councils to decide. That was now attempted – in September UGC sent each university the draft of a possible Council resolution – but met opposition. VUW decided to seek a legal opinion. 'Is it a proper exercise on [sic] its power under Section 48 [of the VUW University Act] for the University to impose this fee at the direction or request of the Government?' Did the Council need to be satisfied as to the reasons for doing so? 'Is it sufficient reason for the Council to pass the appropriate resolution that funding from the Government for the University will diminish according to the fees the University would be

[9]   Background Paper, Pamphlet. AU.
[10]   Talboys/Tarling, 24.7.79. AU.

collecting if it imposed the requested charge?' Could the Council discriminate among students from certain countries as the Government directed or did that breach the Human Rights Act? It was possible that a student group would take legal action if it felt that the courts might overrule the measure, and that in itself was sufficient reason for VUW to be sure that it acted properly.[11]

The opinion of J.T. Eichelbaum QC dealt first with the implications of the Human Rights Act 1977. Section 26 provided that it was unlawful for an educational establishment to admit a student 'on less favourable terms and conditions than would otherwise be made available ... by reason of the colour, race, ethnic or national origins, sex, marital status, or religious or ethical beliefs of that person'. The proposal would exempt some students and thus discriminate by national origin and so infringe Section 26. Under s. 93, nothing in the Act was to affect any enactment or administrative practice that distinguished between New Zealand citizens and other persons or between British subjects or Commonwealth citizens or aliens. That did not apply, for the proposal would distinguish between New Zealand citizens and *some* aliens.

Eichelbaum then dealt with the Council's power to prescribe fees. That involved the exercise of a discretionary power, and if the Council merely rubber-stamped the recommendation of UGC or another body, the validity of its decision could be challenged. S. 48 required the University to have the concurrence of UGC for its scale of fees. That did not, however, give UGC the right to direct, though its view might prevail. The Council, he concluded, must reach its own opinion 'on reasonable consideration', and then submit its scale to UGC. The answer to the Council's first and third questions was no and the second yes. It should have regard to the current legal position, though it was 'idle to suppose that Government could not force the issue, by legislation if necessary'.[12]

Johns told VCC on 11 October that the Crown Law Office agreed that the legality of the matter was in question, and that it could be settled only in the courts. 'The Vice-Chancellors agreed that an overseas student challenging one of the universities in court was not a desirable course of action', and that the chairman of the UGC should discuss the issue with the Minister.[13] No more was heard before a bill to amend the Education Act of 1964 was introduced into Parliament.

The amendment was referred to the Select Committee on Education, and that provided an opportunity for submissions. The VCC objected to

---

[11]   McGrath/Chapman Tripp, 27.9.79. VCC Box 7.

[12]   Opinion, 3.10.79. ibid.

[13]   Statement, n.d. ibid.

clause 2, which gave the Director-General the right to issue regulations to prescribe fees for university students, set out how they were to be assessed, and provided for reductions or exemptions. That would over-ride the universities' right to set the fees, 'a basic tenet of the autonomy of the universities', embodied in each Act. If the Government thought that it was necessary to provide for the payment of fees by private foreign students in certain cases, it could be done by other means: they could, for example, be collected by the appropriate government department when permits were issued or renewed.

'The discriminatory imposition of fees on overseas students is now practised in several Commonwealth countries to the detriment not only of the universities, whose staff and students are inevitably deprived of the considerable cultural and intellectual benefits of direct association with representatives of other cultures, but also in the long term to the detriment of a better understanding and more cordial international relationship with other nations both within and outside the Commonwealth.' The VCC quoted a resolution from the AGM of the Association of Commonwealth Universities, just held in London. That urged the need to avoid or mitigate 'the potentially harmful effects of such financial deterrents'.[14]

'Financial gain – or avoidance of loss – differs from economic advantage', added AU's submission, 'and even if the problem is measured in such material terms it seems to us that insufficient thought has been given to the proposition that foreign students who train in New Zealand often become opinion leaders and power wielders in their own countries. As such they are in a position to influence trading patterns, and pre-disposed to favour the country that nurtured them and furnished their technical skills.' AU also argued in terms of aid. 'We have heard it argued that some foreign students are better able to meet the full cost of their tuition than are many domestic entrants. True or not, that seems to us to be beside the point. The benefit derived by their countries of origin is an undeniable and universally approved form of aid to the under-developed world.' It was easier to provide, and more effective, than direct 'giving'. Like many other countries, New Zealand aid did not reach the 1% of GNP advocated by the UN, but if it was necessary to fall still further short, 'let us not chip away at the most efficient aid given'. The University also argued that, while New Zealand might gain a few million dollars, it would lose its mana in the South Pacific and Southeast Asia 'as a friend and mentor', and its 'repute in both pure and applied learning and research'. Had the long-term consequences of the proposal been thought through? The government had made no attempt to pursue a cost-benefit

---

[14] Submission, 20.11.79. ibid.

analysis and had admitted $1500 was an arbitrary figure. If a deferment were allowed, AU would be prepared to undertake such an analysis.[15]

VUW's submission ranged less widely. Its task under the Act was 'the advancement of knowledge and the dissemination and maintenance thereof by teaching and research'. It regarded 'non-academic restraints on its ability to receive and transfer knowledge, either through entry restrictions or other means as highly undesirable'. The selection of overseas students, it argued, should depend on their academic ability, not on 'their being in favourable financial circumstances'. In its submission to the 1978 review, it had called for an overall policy. The current proposal was brought forward without consultation and out of context. It breached the Council's powers to control entry and, in conflict with the Human Rights Act, was also at odds with 'the University's strongly-held opposition to discriminatory action which affects its corporate wellbeing and that of its students'.[16]

The submission of the Association of University Teachers [AUTNZ] drew attention to the impact on graduate students. 'New Zealand has benefited greatly from the opportunities for post-graduate studies made available to young New Zealanders in North American and European, mainly British, universities. Should New Zealand encourage the dismantling of this valuable system of international exchange?' New Zealand, too, had benefited from the work done by overseas graduate students at Masters and PhD level in engineering and science. 13.1% of the total postgraduate students in the universities were from overseas, nearly 20% of those who were full-time. The 617 students formed 21.5% of the total overseas students in New Zealand. If the proposal could not be dropped altogether, it should not apply to graduates. Alternatively scholarships should be greatly increased.[17]

The Education Committee made some changes to the Bill. It added further categories of exemption, and provided more fully for grandparenting. It did not change the power given to the Director-General to notify universities when the fee was to be levied.[18] It was passed on 14 December 1979.[19] Under it the Director-General was to notify secondary schools and tertiary institutions that a person was a 'private foreign student', when that person was not a citizen or permanent resident of a South Pacific country, was not the holder of a scholarship provided by the New Zealand government or by any intergovernmental organisation, was not under a reciprocal exchange scheme approved by the Minister, or

---

[15]   Submission, 21.11.79. ibid.
[16]   Submission, 11.79. ibid.
[17]   Submission, 23.11.79. ibid.
[18]   VC (79) SA 8, 14.12.79. ibid.

under the Commonwealth Postgraduate scheme, or sustained by Government funds, was not enrolled before I January 1980, and had been granted a temporary permit to enter New Zealand for study or training. Such a person had to pay the fee prescribed for the course being taken.

The fee was set by an Order-in-Council made on 22 January 1980. Its first schedule listed the South Pacific countries: Federated States of Micronesia, Fiji, Kiribati, Nauru, New Hebrides, PNG, Solomon Islands, Tonga, Tuvalu, Western Samoa. The second schedule prescribed the fee for private overseas students at tertiary institutions, viz, $1500 for a full-time course; $2 for every hour of tuition in a part-time course at a technical institute or community college; and for a part time course of study at a university, '[a] fee that is the same proportion of the product of $1500 and the minimum number of years required for the completion of the course of study of which that part-time course forms part as, in the opinion of the Director-General, that part-time course is of that course of study'. A third schedule set out additional fees for study at technical institutes and community colleges.

A UGC memorandum – noting that Australians were also exempt – set out the mechanism. 'Private overseas students entering New Zealand to take up courses are required to pay the fee in their home country before an entry permit is granted. These payments are being credited to the Education Vote and they will be gathered in a trust account for subsequent payment to the universities. Students in New Zealand who are liable for the fee will pay it direct to the universities and present the receipt to the Department of Labour for their entry permit. Appropriate adjustments will be made subsequently to [quinquennial] grant payments.'[20]

Applications by Malaysian students fell by some 300. The decision to charge $1500 was, the *New Zealand Herald* reported, believed to be the reason for the drop. The Prime Minister had argued that most Asian students had wealthy parents, but it seemed that 'many families cannot now afford to support their children at New Zealand universities'. There would, however, be no problem in filling the places available, it was suggested, since only 240 places were open to Malaysians.[21]

An editorial next day suggested that Muldoon had been proved wrong. Diplomats in Southeast Asia, it claimed, had disagreed with him. 'They said "New Zealand old boys" were a useful pool of influence in the professional and administrative positions for which their New Zealand qualifications had qualified them.' They had also argued that Malaysian

[19] No. 148.
[20] Memorandum, 11.1.80. AU.
[21] NZH, 23.1.80.

Chinese sent their children to the UK or the US if they were wealthy, but to New Zealand if they had to 'scrimp'. The Prime Minister had looked for an income of $800 000, but numbers were down, 'so it would appear the Government's decision will do little, if anything, to help our balance of payments. All New Zealand may stand to gain is resentment.'[22]

NZUSA returned to the charge in 1981, an election year, making a submission to the Minister of Education prepared by Ian Powell, NZUSA's research officer.[23] Again it argued that the typical Malaysian student in New Zealand was not wealthy: students came to New Zealand because education was less costly than elsewhere, and it was possible to work in the Long Vac. The case was supported by comments from Lythe and his colleagues at other universities. The government, the submission suggested, was 'creating the situation which [it] inaccurately claims already existed'. Moreover, the government referred to Malaysians: it did not assert that students from other developing countries were wealthy, though they would also have to pay the $1500. In 1976 it claimed indeed that it wanted to attract students from such countries, including countries in the Middle East. Had that policy been abandoned? A fall in numbers suggested that the revenue the Prime Minister anticipated would not in fact be generated, while, on the other hand, foreign exchange earnings would fall.

The emphasis on revenue, the submission also suggested, was 'in direct contradiction of the underlying principle behind any aid programme'. The Governor-General's speech on the opening of Parliament on 17 May 1979 coupled Southeast Asia with the South Pacific as areas in which New Zealand especially sought to contribute to peace and stability and develop friendly relations and cooperation. Yet now it was implied Southeast Asia did not need aid. Hitherto ministers – Colman in 1973, Talboys in 1976 – had seen the provision of places for private overseas students as a form of assistance to their countries. That the Minister, Merv Wellington, now denied: 'Private overseas students have never been seen as part of New Zealand's foreign aid policy', he had told NZUSA in 1979. The chairman of the Select Committee, J.G. Elliott, said the same. In fact there had been a policy change.

While NZUSA believed 'that it would be desirable if there was a more even distribution of overseas students from their countries of origin', there were, its submission argued, 'special reasons' for the high demand from Malaysia. Colonialism had distorted the priorities of government in such countries, and education had suffered. Malaysia had 12m people, but its tertiary student population was 30 000, compared with New Zealand's

---

22 NZH, 24.1.80.
23 Submission, May 1981. AU.

40 000. The Malaysian Minister of Education, Datuk Musa Hitam, had told the Wellington *Evening Post* that his country could not keep up with the demand for tertiary places.[24] In an interview on Radio New Zealand, he had said he did not want to interfere with the New Zealand government's right to set conditions, but did want 'to try to persuade as gently as possible the New Zealand Government to say that the increase in fees might have some negative effect in terms of the capacity or the ability of young Malaysians to come to this country and to take advantage of the excellent facilities in education that you have got.'[25] The majority were, as the submission said, were Chinese Malaysians, affected by the quota at home. The Malaysian government spoke up for them, no doubt partly because their access provided a safety valve, and nothing was lost by so doing. In addition, of course, it was bitterly opposing the steps the Thatcher government had taken.

The NZUSA submission argued that the presence of overseas students helped to counter the insularity of New Zealand universities, a point Talboys had made in 1976, and Elliott had made on introducing the Bill. A reduction in numbers would be unfortunate not only for the overseas students concerned, the Student Counsellor at Massey, Bill Zika, argued, but 'possibly even more so for New Zealanders who will be denied the enhancement of their own culture through the input and sharing which people of differing cultures have to offer'. The submission drew attention to the difficulties faced by students who had completed a first degree, but now found a fee standing in the way of their going on to a masters. It also drew attention to the fall in the number of applications OSAC had reported, and also to a dramatic rise in the non-acceptance of offers. The total number of overseas students would fall.

That indeed it did. It was not, however, at odds with the Government's wish to economise, then the prime objective. And while numbers fell, they did not altogether collapse: indeed they recovered a little in subsequent years. In the short term, therefore, the Government's move was not, from its own point of view, entirely unsuccessful. Like the 40% quota, however, it tended to destroy the advantages the unplanned policy had brought, without calling it to a halt: a practice that evoked goodwill was coupled with negativity. The episode also revealed, however, the kind of opposition within New Zealand that bigger and more long-term changes could be expected to face. Indeed it arguably increased that risk. It was to be overcome only in the context of the overall changes in Government ideology, in education as in other fields, in the later 1980s. The main feature of the

[24] EP, 21.11.79.
[25] Radio New Zealand, 19.11.79.

change was the idea that university places would be sold to overseas students on a full cost basis. That idea was not, however, entirely new, and it had been traversed in the course of the review which Cabinet had instituted in 1978, but which had not reported at the time it decided to introduce the $1500 fee.

The review had begun in the context of the Government's publicly unstated wish further to reduce the overall number of overseas students beyond the reduction achieved by the quota set on the largest supplier. The Treasury's desire to impose a realistic fee also reappeared in that context. But some ministers began to realise that it could be put in a different context. If students were prepared to pay a fee – and the practice was becoming widespread overseas – then places could be sold, and viewed as a source of revenue. The restrictions on the number of subsidised students could be turned to account, even intensified, not with a view to economising, but with a view to earning. The fact that universities – anxious to argue against the restrictions – seemed to have places available – suggested indeed that there was spare capacity, which could be increased by further restrictions and turned to profitable account. That shift was still some way from a policy of expansion based on the provision of places paid for by charging full fees, a policy finally approved only in the fourth Labour government's second term, and effectively implemented only in the 1990s. But it was a significant shift, and it had, albeit somewhat covertly, begun in the second Muldoon government.

For the preparation of the report on overseas student policy, a Treasury official joined the IDC. That committee, Johns told UGC in May, had been deliberating in terms of aid. In early meetings, a Treasury official had made a 'tentative remark' about full cost payment, 'but nothing definite emerged until very recently when he announced that the Cabinet Committee on Expenditure had recommended a $3000 charge to cover fees, social services etc. He went on to advocate removal of any quotas or prohibitions on particular countries, on the argument that if New Zealand could make a profit out of taking students, it should. The development meant a radical re-shaping of the Committee's paper.' UGC took up the question of the $3000 with the Minister and the Cabinet Committee, indicating that it was 'out of line' with Britain and Canada, while Australia was not charging. Then came the 'unexpected' announcement of a fee of $1500.[26]

The Labour Department had offered its views to the IDC in January. The aim of admitting private students had been stated as 'permitting persons from other countries to study in New Zealand to train them to a stage where they will be of value in the development programmes of their

---

[26]   Memorandum, 5.79. UGC 114/7. UGC Box 166.

own countries'. First preference was given to the South Pacific, second to Southeast Asia. Opportunities beyond that were made available to students from countries with which New Zealand had 'close political or trade links'. A secondary aim was 'to provide opportunities for cultural exchange between the people of New Zealand and people of other countries of the world'. The Department did not consider that current policy was achieving those objectives. Some South Pacific countries had indeed complained of a 'brain drain', since so many students stayed in New Zealand. Many students sought a 'back-door' means of entering New Zealand permanently. The policy was hard to administer equitably.

It was the Department's view 'that the aim of allowing private overseas students to study in New Zealand should continue to be integrally linked with the needs of the developing countries', particularly those of the South Pacific and Southeast Asia. 'In the past, the acceptance of students, particularly from Malaysia and Singapore, from ethnic minorities and others who have been permitted to enter simply because they have been unable to obtain places in similar courses in their own country, has led to a situation where many students have been unable or unwilling to return to employment in their own countries'. At school level, the Department thought that the admission of primary and lower secondary students should be dropped: it was not in their interests to 'leave their home environment at such an early age'. At above Form 6 level, there was no need for students from Malaysia and Singapore to undertake secondary schooling in New Zealand. Above the school level, the Department considered, students should in future be admitted only if the type of course were not available in their own country – a criterion so far 'interpreted very loosely' – and only in order to undertake 'courses which will lead to a qualification which is recognised officially in the home country and which is expected to continue to be in demand in that country'. They would have to be 'sponsored' by their own government, by which the Department meant that it would have to agree that the criteria were met. 'On this basis it could well be argued that New Zealand should no longer accept students from Malaysia and Singapore.'

For some time the Department had been concerned about postgraduate study. It considered that proceeding to that should be allowed only if the undergraduate course had been completed in minimum time. Students who wished to proceed to PhD study should be allowed to do so only if they had completed their Masters degree with first class honours, 'and if they can produce evidence that the further course of study will enhance their employment opportunities on return home'. A number of students who had secured PhDs had found that they were 'far too highly qualified for the employment market in their own country'.

The Cabinet had also asked whether a certain length of time in New Zealand should be a factor in granting permanent residence. The Department considered that, if its suggestions were adopted, all students should return home on completion. If they wished then to apply, they could be considered under normal immigration policy.

Exception would be made only where students married New Zealand citizens or permanent residents while in New Zealand. Some argued that students who spent a long time in New Zealand became alienated from their home environment, while New Zealand employers argued that they should be able to use skills the acquisition of which had been subsidised by the taxpayer. The Department favoured limiting the total length of time a student might spend in New Zealand to five years.

It argued that the policy, which involved assessing qualifications and examination results, should be primarily administered by the Education Department, not by the Immigration Division. Many of the 268 students who had been in New Zealand for over seven years had been allowed to do so after appealing to the Education Advisory Committee on academic grounds. Its terms of reference should be tightened.[27]

Not all this proposals were included in the final report, offered to Cabinet by the Minister in October.[28] The overall policy was redefined. It retained the emphases on development, but dropped the reference to Southeast Asia. Preference was given to the South Pacific, and opportunities were made available 'in the light of New Zealand's national political and economic objectives'. The secondary aim was 'to provide opportunities for promoting international understanding through cultural and similar educational exchanges between the people of New Zealand and people of other countries of the world'. Requests from governments not on the approved list to sponsor their own students – it currently included Iran and Iraq and China had recently been added, following the charge's approach to Corner[29] – would be considered by ministers on the recommendation of IDC, and provision would be made for the inclusion of 'some developed and richer developing countries'.

The decision to charge $1500, made during the course of the review, was 'reflected' in its recommendations, IDC observed. The primary aim of overseas student policy had been to offer relevant training and provide for exchange, assistance to private students being seen as 'an adjunct to the official aid programme'.[30] The committee had explored an alternative approach: opening

27 Submission on Review of Private Overseas Student Policy, 1.79. H.O. 22/1/279-2. UGC Box 653.
28 Report. UGC Box 97. Memorandum for Cabinet, 3.10.79. Box 653.
29 3.8.78. MFAT Box 3497.
30 Report, pp. 8-9.

the system to any person ready to pay tuition costs and some of the hidden costs, including building maintenance. That would mean a fee of about $3000 above present tuition fees. The decision to charge $1500 in total was 'seen by the Committee (in the absence of other specific guidance) as an indication that a move to such an "open entry" system is not contemplated by the Government at present'.[31] IDC thus turned what might have been conceived as a step towards full-cost fees into an argument for not introducing them and for retaining the traditional emphasis.

The 40% limit would be retained, but the committee did not favour setting global or country-specific quotas. Given that the effects of the new fees, and of the changes it recommended, would take several years to show themselves, it thought that numbers would tend to decline, then stabilise.[32]

No primary students should be admitted, the report proposed, and generally secondary students would be admitted only from the South Pacific and only at Forms 6 and 7. Provision, it emphasised, was 'a function of residual capacity', not a license to establish new courses or justify the expansion of facilities.[33]

At tertiary level the committee said it had considered two approaches to approved courses of study: no restrictions; or preference to students from developing countries doing courses unavailable at home and of value in development programmes, and to students wishing to undertake courses in which New Zealand had special expertise. Given the imposition of the $1500 fee, which would not cover full cost, the committee did not think it practical to proceed on the basis of no restrictions, and so chose the second approach.[34]

The committee was opposed to admission to undergraduate courses with credit except in special circumstances, such cases to be recommended by the IDC. Such students, it argued, had already had the opportunity to gain a tertiary education; consistency could not be ensured across the universities; 'some students with failing records at home gain entry on the basis of a minimal grant of credit'.[35] Admission to a second undergraduate course would be allowed 'only for compelling reasons'.

Current arrangements for postgraduate work should continue, but extensions of permits should be approved only if the undergraduate course were completed in minimum time, and, for PhD studies, only if students had gained first-class honours.[36]

[31] p. 6.
[32] pp. 16-17.
[33] p. 37.
[34] p. 38.
[35] p. 43.
[36] p. 49.

Students would be admitted on temporary permits to do short English language courses at technical institutes approved by IDC.[37] Temporary permits would also be available for students attending Bible colleges, the NZ Administrative Staff College, and similar 'private places of education'. Such courses, normally not exceeding two years' duration, would also be subject to IDC approval.[38]

The length of time spent in New Zealand was a factor in granting permanent residence which Immigration had found difficult to handle, and sometimes the arguments used were unfair to those who completed in minimum time. The committee suggested that, when the policy was publicly announced, its basic aim should be stressed: contributing to the development of the home countries. Length of stay should not 'in itself' be a ground for granting permanent residence. New Zealand would not as a general rule recruit students as settlers. They would return home on completion of their courses, unless they had married, and any subsequent application would be considered under normal immigration policy. Applications from students in New Zealand would, however, be 'favourably' considered if they could satisfy Immigration that, while their course was in demand at home on commencement, there were no opportunities at the time of completion, and that they possessed skills in demand in New Zealand and had 'an offer of employment for which no suitable labour is available'.

On 8 October Cabinet referred the report to its Committee on Family and Social Welfare. Chaired by George Gair, it included Templeton, Bolger, Allan Highet, and Wellington, with Talboys and Aussie Malcolm, then Under-Secretary for Labour and Immigration, also present, and officials from Social Welfare, Treasury, Labour [Cross], Foreign Affairs [Jermyn], Education, the PM's Department and UGC in attendance. The first part of its discussion on 19 March 1980 indicated general support for 'a flexible overseas student policy'. It needed to recognise 'that there was a link between our trading relations with a particular country and the desire on the part of that country to send some students abroad for training. We had to give positive recognition to the fact that our future lay with the countries of Asia and it would be to our advantage to forge sympathetic links by providing nationals of friendly Asian countries with a New Zealand education'. The report seemed 'too rigid' and gave insufficient emphasis to 'the changing international situation'. If secondary and tertiary rolls fell as demographic forecasts suggested, it was remarked, 'there would be sufficient spare capacity in all parts of our educational

---

[37]   pp. 51-2.
[38]   pp. 53-5.

system to accommodate additional numbers of overseas students'.

Officials responded that the report did not dictate firm quotas, and that there was scope for an annual review. They also pointed to the problem of the 'long stay' student and the difficulty of administering the current provisions. Perhaps the report could be regarded at least as an interim policy. The Committee directed them to submit a summary of the key principles of private overseas student policy, any differences among departments, 'and the room for manoeuvre in the future'. They should first address the immediate problem of immigration, 'and keep in mind the long term fact that there would be surplus educational capacity by the end of the decade and the advantages that a common educational background would provide when we have to deal with friendly Asian countries'.[39]

Draft memoranda circulated in the IDC suggested that its report had been influenced by the decision to impose the $1500 fee – which still involved a substantial subsidy – and had not therefore looked for major changes. Since the report was prepared, however, spare capacity had been reported. That required investigation, but it might mean that the government could announce, as a second stage in the review, an opportunity to take able-to-pay students, which would help to maintain teaching opportunities and avoid the deletion of courses. In the meantime the officials' proposals could be implemented in respect of the $1500 fee students.[40]

The $1500 fee, and some of the other recommendations in the report, might 'convey the unfortunate (albeit unintended) impression that the New Zealand Government is appearing to be unduly disadvantaging Asian students and trainees wishing to come to New Zealand while looking to New Zealand's responsibilities in the Pacific', and ministers, another draft suggested, might want to take account of 'these longer-term considerations' before finalising their recommendations'.[41]

Briefing the Prime Minister the previous November for a visit by the Malaysian Minister of Education, Foreign Affairs had suggested that the Malaysian government did not see the fee as itself the problem – it was introducing a loan scheme – but was more concerned that it betokened a wish to limit access. That, the Minister could – less than candidly – be told, was not the intention. Foreign Affairs had also noted the Malaysian government's wish to introduce its own scholarship scheme for sending students overseas, to which Talboys had responded positively when in

---

[39]   Minutes, 19.3.80. FS (80) M 1 Part 1. UGC Box 653.

[40]   Draft memorandum, 27.3.80. ibid.

[41]   Draft memorandum, 28.3.80. ibid.

Malaysia.[42] Both the governments of Malaysia and Singapore wanted to support more students, officials noted, and were ready to pay $1500 or in some cases full costs. Other countries were making similar enquiries. There might be 'a unique opportunity for New Zealand to put some substance on otherwise insubstantial and distant relationships at little real cost to ourselves'.[43]

The notion that there was 'spare capacity' and the apparent readiness of the governments of successfully developing Malaysia and Singapore to pay substantial or full fees suggested to officials that there was some 'room to manoeuvre', such as the Cabinet committee sought. But again it was not so much a sale of places as a government-government package that was in mind. In the Malaysia case the effect would no doubt be that Malays would take up places normally going to Chinese, but Foreign Affairs did not make that point.

Going down such a track might, however, be less unfriendly than the policy the 1979 report advocated. MFA also reported concern at its Asian posts over the idea of limiting secondary school entry to Pacific students, which it had vainly contested during the preparation of the report. The existing links with ASEAN should continue, though the focus was on the Pacific. 'The point would be to strengthen the network of informal associations between New Zealand and the politically and socially influential groups in these societies. The issue is again essentially one of *not* appearing to present an unnecessarily restrictive attitude.'[44]

By July IDC had reached agreement on a summary submission. Officials recommended four principles as the basis of private overseas student policy: '(a) to provide education and training that will be of value to developing countries with which New Zealand has an aid relationship, especially those in the South Pacific region; (b) to make available opportunities for other students from other countries in the light of New Zealand's national political and economic objectives; (c) to promote international understanding through educational exchanges between New Zealand and other countries; and (d) to ensure that access to New Zealand education is not abused as a means to obtain permanent residence.' Insofar as subsidy continued, the education covered under principle (a) could be seen 'as an indirect but valuable adjunct to New Zealand's official aid programme'.

So far as immigration was concerned, officials more or less repeated

---

[42] Brief by Ag Minister for PM, Call by Malaysian Minister of Education, 19.11.79. UGC Box 90.

[43] ibid.

[44] Draft memorandum, 28.3.80, as above.

the recommendations of the 1979 report. They also reiterated the recommendation that no private students should be accepted at primary level. Students from Southeast Asia as well as the South Pacific would be admitted to Forms 6 and 7. Access to undergraduate study was to be at entrance level only, not with credit. Doing a second undergraduate degree would not normally be allowed, but postgraduates would continue to be admitted without restriction by country of origin to courses in which New Zealand had 'some special expertise'. In 1981 entrance to tertiary institutions should be on the basis of existing policy, undergraduates from the South Pacific and Southeast Asia being admitted to courses relevant to the needs of their country and offering the prospect of gainful employment there. Before policy was decided for 1982 officials should be directed to report on the present and future capacity of New Zealand tertiary facilities to accept overseas students, course by course, and the cost of so doing. They did not favour deciding at the present time whether New Zealand should 'embark on a conscious policy of "selling" educational opportunities to private overseas students'. Nor did they advocate setting a target.

The $1500 fee charged to university students, they noted, did not meet the full cost, perhaps at least $3000. The taxpayer was still contributing, although each student, they also noted, was probably bringing in foreign exchange of around $4000 for living expenses. Ministers would have to decide whether to charge more – New Zealand charged less than Australia and much less than the UK – or whether other factors, such as 'maintaining educational opportunities for South Pacific and ASEAN countries', weighed against it. If there were surplus capacity, Ministers would have to decide whether to use it to cater for overseas students, or to eliminate it. If, as officials believed, there were 'positive advantages to be gained from providing for overseas students', it would be necessary to decide whether existing policy should be maintained or whether undergraduate study should be opened to a wider range of countries. 'The government would need to decide whether our educational capacity should be regarded as a potential earner of overseas exchange (as well as of goodwill) like other service industries and thus whether access to certain specialist courses (e.g. medicine, veterinary science) should be open to anyone prepared to pay the full economic cost.' Some government would like to sponsor students, 'and we need to decide whether this should be specifically catered for'. [45]

The Cabinet Committee discussed the IDC report, but did not at once

---

[45] Draft for Chairman Cabinet Committee on Family and Social Affairs, 22.7.80. UGC Box 653.

reach 'firm conclusions', as Bolger told the cabinet: 'they are still considering in particular, the question of whether people who do not qualify in terms of the policy recommended by the IDC should be allowed to enter if they are able to pay fees to cover the full costs of their education and training in New Zealand'. The Minister thought there was 'some urgency in reaching a decision on this matter in view of the forthcoming absences of the Prime Minister and Deputy Prime Minister'. He proposed that Cabinet should in general endorse the policy aims defined by the IDC and its recommendations on access. Access to secondary education would be limited to countries without sufficient capacity of their own, but the access of Southeast Asian students would continue, their future access perhaps on a full-fee basis being considered in the studies the Minister also advocated. Access to undergraduate study would be at first-year level only and to courses relevant to the needs of the students' countries and offering the prospect of employment there. As a general rule under-graduates would come from the South Pacific and Southeast Asia, but there would be no country limits on postgraduates.

The studies Bolger envisaged would also include the examination of spare capacity. If that proved to exist, it would be necessary to determine whether it should be used for private overseas students, and to consider both the possibilty of making it available at primary, secondary and tertiary level 'on a full cost recovery basis', and the desire of some govern-ments to sponsor their own students. Such a proposal would strengthen links with friendly governments, bring some commercial advantage and generate some foreign exchange. There were also disadvantages. Students might use access as a back door to permanent residence. 'There might also be some criticism from people who claim that our educational system is being opened up to those who can afford to pay rather that those who have the most ability'. Some of those who could pay might come from countries with which New Zealand did not currently wish to have contacts. Bolger was not prepared to support the extension of the policy until the extent of spare capacity had been ascertained, and it was clear that the disadvantages could be overcome. He thus asked the Cabinet to accept the initial recommendations and have the further proposals investigated.[46]

Cabinet accepted his suggestions on 4 August. The proposals were referred to Immigration, Foreign Affairs and Education for joint consideration and implementation as appropriate. The IDC was directed, as it had requested, 'to undertake a study on the feasibility and desirability

---

[46]   Memorandum for Cabinet, 30.7.80. UGC Box 90.

of further extending the access of private overseas students' and report to the Cabinet Committee on Family and Social Affairs.[47]

IDC took the initiative on carrying what Cabinet had approved. It invited the ministers to implement the decision not to admit primary students from 1982. In effect that meant students from Tonga, and the High Commissioner had pointed out that it might be opposed by the elite, who saw a New Zealand education 'as an important part of the making of a Tongan aristocrat'.[48] The recommendation that entry to secondary school should generally be confined to Forms 6 and 7 would mainly affect students from Western Samoa, and so far as they were concerned the new policy should apply only from 1983.[49] Outside the state sector current policy provided for training mainly at a number of Bible colleges and secretarial colleges. '[P]rivate institutions have been frustrated in their attempts to bring overseas students to New Zealand because their courses have not been recognised under our private overseas student policy.' IDC was the appropriate body to consider and make recommendations to ministers on the suitability of private institutions to accept students, who would receive non-working temporary permits.[50] Students would also be able to enter New Zealand for attendance at short-term English language courses of not more than six months' duration, approved by the IDC, at tertiary or other appropriate institutions.[51]

The final draft on access to tertiary institutions emerged only in December 1980. It argued that Cabinet's decision that undergraduate entry should be at entry level only would generally rule out entry with credits, and also transfer to a university on the part of a student who had successfully completed a technical institute qualification. The decision that students not be admitted to a second undergraduate degree should 'for consistency' apply to students already in New Zealand. IDC reiterated its view that only first-class honours or A students should be allowed to stay on for postgraduate studies. No particular quotas, target or ceilings should be established, though the size and composition of the overseas student body should be kept under review. 'The Committee notes that in courses where entry is restricted, qualified New Zealand students should not be

---

[47] Memorandum for Minister of Immigration from Secretary to Cabinet, n.d. CN 80/31/32. Appendix A to Report by Cross, 10.80. UGC Box 90. Wendy Cook, 'The "export" of education: the development of overseas student policy', MA thesis, AU, 1995, p. 9.

[48] Memorandum by Cross, 10.80. H.O. 22/1/279-2. UGC Box 90.

[49] Another memorandum by Cross, 10.80. ibid.

[50] Further memorandum by Cross, 10.80. ibid.

[51] Fourth memorandum, 10.80. ibid.

excluded to make a place available to an overseas student.' A paper on the availability of excess capacity and the question of providing places on a full cost basis was under preparation. 'Any recommendations arising from this paper will have an effect on any proposal for an extension of source countries in the light of New Zealand's national political and economic objectives.'[52]

The notion of 'spare capacity' was somewhat inconsistent with the concept of EFTS funding, but perhaps not entirely so, given that buildings were then funded outside the EFTS system, and academic staff were still considered to enjoy 'permanent' tenure. The belief that it existed, or might exist, was partly based on the government's decision to reduce the medical intake, and partly on demographic projections. It was also supported by the size of the quotas that the universities continued to offer OSAC, even though, thanks to the 40% quota and the $1500 fee, they were no longer taken up, or were in courses never popular with overseas students. That was itself done partly because the universities were largely opposed to those measures and preferred the aid-oriented emphasis of earlier years: they still wanted to welcome overseas students, who added to the diversity of classes, and many of whom had performed very well.

It was, however, a risky line for them to take. Caldwell pointed that out in May 1980. The universities were setting quotas unrealistically high compared with the uptake. That provided interested groups, inside and outside the universities, 'with a strong propaganda argument; they are able to claim that the universities have the room to take more overseas students, are anxious to do so, and could do so at little cost'; and they could attack government policy on limitation of entry and special fees. That was not, however, the UGC's current concern. It was concerned rather with the implication that more students could be absorbed because the increase in costs was marginal and could be ignored. That made it difficult to argue for improvements in Government funding. 'The plain fact is that the university system bases its claims for funds on the size of the student rolls; to turn later to Government and say that more students of any variety can be taught at no extra cost is naive and likely to be harmful.' Caldwell suggested that the quotas offered should be more closely related to the likely take-up.[53] He did not point out that the concept of excess capacity had another aspect: it encouraged the idea of selling places. The discussion of that issue was still confidential.

Early in 1981 the UGC advised the universities that IDC had asked for 'information about the extent of excess capacity in the universities which

---

[52]   Final draft, 12.80. UGC Box 653.
[53]   Memorandum to VCs, 12.5.80. UGC Box 90.

could be made available to overseas students. The information is being sought because the Government might wish to respond to the increasing number of requests being received from foreign governments for opportunities for training in New Zealand. When making these requests, the governments concerned have indicated that they are willing to pay realistic tuition costs for the students they sponsor. In short, the arrangements would be different from those for the private overseas students currently admitted where an aid component is involved, even though the $1500 is paid.'

Determining 'excess capacity' was no simple matter, and UGC sought the universities' help in drawing up a series of questions which it could then send to them. The Secretary stressed that there should be 'no reduction in the intake of qualified New Zealanders in order to make places available for overseas students'. It was, he added, 'not intended that present quotas for overseas students should be reduced to accommodate this new category'. There was 'no commitment about the proportion of "realistic" fees that the universities will receive. The matter has not been discussed.' Estimates had to be made 'on the basis of currently available accommodation, i.e. no new buildings or extensions to present buildings are envisaged'. Additional students would 'obviously increase the total roll and, therefore, under the block grant review agreement, ultimately affect total staffing', but 'the object of this enquiry is to find out the extent to which additional students can be adequately taught within the present staffing of the faculty concerned'. There were, however, 'situations where the provision of only one extra staff member can greatly increase the capacity to take in more students to a particular course. In such circumstances, especially where a course is very popular or has a restricted intake, a case for extra staffing could be worth making.'[54]

The University of Auckland replied that, because of insufficiency of accommodation and/or teachers, it imposed entry restrictions at undergraduate level in all professional faculties and in some departments in Arts and Science. 'Whilst such restrictions are in force it would not be desirable to refuse admission to New Zealand students and then on the other hand admit overseas students, beyond present quotas, even though they may be paying the full cost of their tuition.' The University looked rather to the postgraduate area, in particular to cooperative graduate research, using university facilities, and funding from the overseas foreign government.[55] Waikato was prepared to restore its quota of 100, cut as a result of Caldwell's earlier letter. It also responded to his request on a

54   Caldwell/Maiden, 14.1.81. AU.
55   Maiden/Caldwell, 23.2.81. UGC Box 90.

questionnaire.[56] Other universities did not reply, but VCC discussed the question on 20 February 1981, and, pressed by Aussie Malcolm, Caldwell wrote again on 17 March.[57]

That produced two further suggestions from Waikato: the admission of overseas graduates who wished to gain a teaching qualification, particularly students from Malaysia who had difficulty in gaining access to teachers colleges; and the admission of graduates who wished to obtain honours or masters degrees.[58] CU could not go beyond the OSAC quotas at undergraduate level, but was 'sympathetic with the suggestion about a selective increase in the intake of post-graduate students'.[59] Lincoln indicated that it could take a limited number of students, provided the fees covered the additional staffing and/or operating costs involved.[60] At Massey the Deans mostly felt that not much could be done without extra resources or staffing.[61]

VUW was always ready to consider special requests such as that which had led to the creation of its English Language Institute twenty years earlier. Most faculties had room for a small number of overseas students, but would need extra funding 'if such additional numbers were to regularly and substantially exceed the normal intake'. There was a shortfall in the take-up of places in Arts and Science. That could not be identified as 'spare capacity as the general increase in enrolments in these Faculties substantially exceed the number of places involved'. The OSAC quotas did, however, 'represent a willingness ... to reserve the stated number of places', and the University would be ready for the places to be taken up to those limits.[62] Additional staffing and resourcing would provide places in a considerable number of Otago departments, but not many could be provided without it, and none would be available in Computer Science.[63]

'The most popular undergraduate courses sought by overseas students are engineering, commerce and computer science', Caldwell told IDC. The returns he summarised showed that for undergraduate places other than in languages and arts – 'not much sought after by overseas students' – additional resources would be needed, particularly staffing. 'The best opportunities appear to be in the postgraduate and research areas', but

[56] Llewellyn/Secretary UGC, 16.2.81. ibid.
[57] Caldwell/VCs, 17.3.81. ibid.
[58] Gordon/Caldwell, 1.4.81. ibid.
[59] Brownlie/Caldwell, 27.3.81. ibid.
[60] Stewart/Caldwell, 15.4.81. ibid.
[61] Comments by Deans, n.d. ibid.
[62] Wilf Malcolm/Caldwell, 15.4.81. ibid.
[63] Irvine/Caldwell, 13.4.81. ibid.

there, too, funding for materials and staff was a pre-requisite. 'The possibilities for a broad-based scheme for marketing university education have not been planned for and, not surprisingly, do not exist in a form which could be presented as a package deal. The picture that emerges is one of bits and pieces here and there – probably significant in total, but not readily marketable in a commercial profit-making sense.' Faculties 'closed' to overseas students could offer nothing.[64]

The Malaysian Government's decision to divert Malaysian students, private and government-sponsored, from the UK – where fees had again been raised – had perhaps attracted Aussie Malcolm's attention. The previous year's increase, the High Commission noted, had led students to go to Canada, Australia and the US, not New Zealand. Canada had mounted a recruitment campaign, and Australia and the US had been positive. New Zealand, by contrast, 'gave the appearance of having very restricted study opportunities'. That, coupled with 'our current cumbersome application procedures and the quotas', persuaded students not even to apply.[65]

The application procedures were disputed between OSAC and Foreign Affairs and its High Commission. The main issue was the offering of places conditional on the achievement of results available in February, so that students might start in March. Both the UK and Australia waited for the results, and students were not admitted till the following academic year, delaying the students several months. Offering a chance to avoid that delay advantaged New Zealand, OSAC argued. Waiting for the following year would force it to compete with Australia, and distance might give that country the advantage. The pool of Malaysian students from which New Zealand drew, already reduced by the $1500 fee, would be further reduced.[66]

Norrish discussed the matter with Johns. Foreign Affairs shared Education's view that it was in New Zealand's interest 'to continue to educate a fair number of Southeast Asians ... since among them will be many future leaders'. Yet the number of Malaysians was declining. He did not think that resulted from the fee, which was lower than in the UK and Canada. 'It seems to me', the Secretary for Foreign Affairs wrote, '... that the lengthy application procedures together with the limited number of places that are available anyway, and the uncertainty of success until very shortly before the time the student will have to leave Malaysia, are

[64] Memorandum for IDC, Possible Capacity for Additional Overseas Students, 5.5.81. ibid.
[65] W.S. Sharpley for HC/Secretary FA, 10.4.81. ibid.
[66] Caldwell Memorandum for MFA (Smithyman), 17.2.81. ibid.

leading many students either not to bother applying to New Zealand in the first place or, if they do, to apply to other countries at the same time – countries which offer a much greater chance of being accepted and which have a much speedier notification system.' Norrish suggested that OSAC should drop the present procedures and require students to apply to the High Commission in May on the basis of completed qualifications.[67] The reply suggested that other issues – quota, fee, restrictions on desired courses, the low secondary quota – were more relevant. Johns did, however, suggest a meeting.[68]

That, including the Director-General of Education as well, took place on 4 June 1981, and there was 'broad agreement' that applications should be accepted only on the basis of results and that the secondary quota should be increased.[69] One difficulty appeared after the meeting. Only well-qualified Southeast Asia applicants and those in Arts and Sciences could be placed by, say, 31 August. The reason was that OSAC also had to place students from New Zealand and the Pacific, whose results would be available in January.[70] OSAC was presented with the decision.[71] Some universities agreed with it, others not. The High Commissioner in Singapore protested.[72]

Norrish had also indicated that the capacity study was of some urgency. That, too, was discussed on 4 June. All agreed that it needed 'to provide sufficient material to enable officials to deal with Ministers' interest in making full use of our education facilities in pursuit of our overseas interests and even in a purely commercial way'. To do that, 'the study needs to indicate, course by course for universities and technical institutes and more broadly for secondary schools, approximately how many places could be made available for overseas students'. It should indicate what constraints existed, staffing, equipment, etc. 'The cost of providing places for overseas students should also be indicated although we agreed that it would be premature to undertake a major exercise to establish the costs in detail.' Could it be done by mid-July? In August it would be a year since the Cabinet asked.[73] UGC thought it could be done. 'It would cover two broad categories such as Arts and Science and would not include closed departments. There is no hope of our doing anything on the

---

[67] Norrish/Johns, 7.4.81. ibid.
[68] Johns/Norrish, 15.5.81. ibid.
[69] Norrish/Renwick, Johns, 12.6.81. 118/88/1/3A. ibid.
[70] Johns/Woods, 11.6.81. ibid.
[71] OSAC 81/5. ibid.
[72] 28.10.81. ibid.
[73] Norrish/Johns, Renwick, 12.6. 81, as above.

restricted entry faculties.[74] Foreign Affairs thought it necessary to proceed course by course and to include the closed courses. 'We need to indicate to Ministers, for each course, whether there is likely to be any capacity to take overseas students in the future even if the courses are closed at present.'[75]

A meeting at the UGC – Richard Woods and Chris Smithyman from MFA, and Peter Morris and Caldwell from UGC – followed this up on 26 June. 'After some discussion, MFA accepted that it was not possible to produce a year by year survey.' The data could, however, be presented course-by-course in more detail and with more commentary. The meeting also discussed costs. 'Where there is space available and students could be accepted, there must be an addition to the block grant for recurrent costs. $4000 per student at February 1981 prices.' What would it cost to open up closed schools? to increase capacity in Engineering and Commerce? 'It might be possible', Caldwell suggested, 'to offer those universities with a shrinking roll, e.g. Otago a deal they would respond to. "Otago filled to capacity within existing resources .... if it had more resources it could take....."' Ministers 'saw saw a situation of falling rolls and thought foreigners could take up the slack'. In fact, Caldwell said, it was not so: he showed a graph of actual and forecast rolls, 1980-84.[76]

The point was elaborated in the memorandum subsequently sent to IDC. 'The general assumption behind the belief that spare capacity will occur in the university system is that its rolls, like those in primary and secondary schools, will fall sharply over the next few years. It has been assumed that such a fall will create spare physical capacity which (with the addition of the necessary teaching resources) provided the capability for taking overseas students additional to those already given places.' A June forecast of university rolls extending to 1984 showed, however, that rolls were expected to rise, and were in fact rising 'at a much greater rate than might have been predicted from the demographic considerations'. General physical capacity might be found only in such subjects as the languages, chemistry and physics, and some arts disciplines. In the 'highly popular' faculties, there was some physical capacity in civil engineering, since students had shifted to electrical, chemical and mechanical. In computer science, management, commerce and accounting, teaching resources were taxed to the limit. If more were available, New Zealand students would fill the extra places. Applicants for staff appointments were 'scarce'. In the 'closed' faculties, UGC reiterated that was nothing

[74] Johns/Woods, 11.6.81, as above.
[75] Norrish/Johns, 22.6.81. UGC Box 91.
[76] Jottings from meeting at UGC, 26.6.81. UGC Box 90.

spare. Medical school intakes had been reduced, 'but the lack of capacity for clinical training' ruled out any increase in that area, except for a few Pacific Island students at AU. The memorandum added that the universities were interested in adding to their research base, and there was some physical capacity for taking postgraduates.[77] Ministerial intervention followed.

In this phase some ministers, if not the Cabinet as a whole, were shifting towards the sale of places, rather than cutting back numbers, even looking for revenue. But the focus was still on existing places, which might be 'spare'. That tended to obscure the issue rather than promote the cause.

---

[77] Memorandum by Caldwell, 2.7.81. UGC Box 653. Graph in Box 90.

CHAPTER FIVE

AUSSIE AND AFTER

Becoming Minister of Immigration, Aussie Malcolm endeavoured to press forward with the policies that, on the recommendation of his predecessor, Cabinet had deferred and sent to IDC for further study. The most intractable was the question of full-cost fees, which challenged the concept of aid on which New Zealand had based its policy towards overseas students, and which affected its treatment of private overseas students who had begun to arrive unplanned at the same time as the fully-aided. The aid had itself been seen in the context of the Cold War and its projection into Asia. That had changed, with the recognition of the PRC, the conclusion of the Vietnam war, and the rapid economic growth of Malaysia and Singapore. The conclusion that New Zealand should widen the geographical scope of its overseas student policy was quite readily accepted. It was more difficult to decide whether it should continue to be aid-focused. New Zealand's own economic situation – once an argument for focusing on technical cooperation rather than capital projects – had become an argument against the extensive reception of students that had become the dominant form of that cooperation. Government had sought – though not very openly – to limit numbers and had imposed a mid-level fee. It had also taken up – though without publicity – the question of a full fee. That – though not without international example – raised more issues.

In order, perhaps, to make it more palatable, if not more feasible, 'cost-recovery' had been conceived and presented generally in terms of selling spare capacity, rather than funding expanded capacity. It became important to ascertain, not only if there were spare capacity, but to insist, more firmly than hitherto, that no New Zealander would be deprived of a place. If the notion of selling spare capacity was intended to ease the way towards selling tout court, it may have been counter-productive. Like the $1500 fee, it stirred up criticism without much practical reward. The Muldoon government, perhaps divided itself, and well aware of its falling public support, was unwilling to offer a reasoned and persuasive new policy that would reshape the bundle of arrangements that had grown up in ways that would take account of larger changes in the political and economic contexts. Even the case the fourth Labour government was finally to make was more ideological than reasoned.

Aside from the availability of places – which in a more market-oriented system was to assume the form of 'supply-side' difficulties in the provision of adequate staffing and in ensuring 'quality' – there were other problems in integrating a sale of places policy with current policies, not only in respect of New Zealand students, but with respect to aided students. New Zealand could not abandon aid altogether. To which countries should it go and on what basis? The tendency to re-emphasise the South Pacific was one response. That still raised questions. At what level should the aid be given and in what form? But if that region were not to be the sole focus, how should the aid delivered elsewhere be combined with the sale of places? Southeast Asia had remained the other main focus, despite the rationales of 1976. Would New Zealand drop aid to Malaysia and Singapore? If not, who would be aided and how?

Aussie Malcolm addressed IDC at its meeting on 8 July 1981. He wished, he said, to make a political input into the discussion of overseas student policy, adding that the priorities he outlined had been decided on after consultation with the Ministers of Education and Foreign Affairs. He envisaged a three-tier structure: (1) moving towards an intake from any geographical area at any level, provided all costs, including capital costs, could be recovered from the student, and subject to the proviso that no New Zealander would be disadvantaged by the scheme, such a proposal providing for the expansion or maintenance of existing facilities and courses; (2) current student policy with emphasis on the South Pacific and Southeast Asia and limitations on the availability of some courses; and (3) scholarships for academically able but impoverished South Pacific secondary students. Richard Woods of Foreign Affairs said his department 'broadly supported' such an approach: it would have political benefits; promote Pacific development; earn foreign exchange. IDC was asked to prepare a paper on full cost recovery and Pacific Island scholarships.[1]

In the following weeks officials tried to hammer out a paper, starting with a draft by Woods. 'The prime responsibility of [the education] system is to train New Zealanders, and overseas students and trainees cannot be

---

[1] IDC meeting, 8.7.81, minute 9. MFAT Box 3497.

taken if this means depriving New Zealanders of educational opportunities.' If there were capacity, it should be used because New Zealand had, and was increasingly seen by other countries to have, 'a particular responsibility for the political stability and economic and social development of South Pacific nations', and because it had 'close links with South East Asia and a direct interest in the region's economic and political progress'. It could also be used to strengthen traditional links with Europe, America, South Asia and Japan, and new contacts, such as China and the Middle East. It was in New Zealand's interest 'to have future political, business and professional leaders in other countries who have been educated in New Zealand and who retain feelings of goodwill towards New Zealand'. The education system was 'a resource which could be used to small but tangible economic advantage in the earning of overseas exchange at little or no cost to the taxpayer'.

The draft then went on to consider spare capacity. That existed in most primary schools, and the Education Department thought the secondary system could take 1000 a year, 5000 in total. It also thought there was a limited capacity in technical institutes, and that up to 300 students might be taken by teachers colleges. The draft mentioned the need for remedial English mainly in relation to secondary students. It summarised the returns UGC had made and made estimates of fees based on 'full cost recovery'.

It then turned to proposals for the future. After mainland New Zealanders, the first priority went to other New Zealand nationals, those from the Cooks, Niue and Tokelau, who should retain their unrestricted access. The second priority was 'the rest of the South Pacific', students from which were, and should continue to be, charged domestic fees. Places on a full-cost recovery basis might, however, be offered to primary and secondary students and to some others whose courses fell outside the criteria, for example, those whose courses did not meet the 'development' criterion. Southeast Asian students would have unrestricted access to primary schools, state or private, on a full cost basis, and to secondary schools, though with no guarantee of being able to go on to tertiary study, where they would have to compete with direct applicants, for whom a proportion of the available places would be reserved. Each Southeast Asian government would be able to sponsor 50 entrants at Form 6 level paying New Zealand fees. They would have access to tertiary courses recognised as relevant to their country's development, their priority directly after South Pacific students, the fees being $1500. The same would apply to other Southeast Asian students, provided there were places available, and their courses were relevant to and provided job opportunities in their home countries. Students from other countries would generally be admitted on a full cost basis.

Where fees were payable, they would be collected and retained by the institution. The new system would start in 1983 and run 1983-7, with a review in 1985 to iron out problems.[2]

Treasury was 'broadly ... in favour of ... employing surplus capacity ... to expand overseas student intakes and, at the same time, to earn additional foreign exchange'. In view of the difficulty in 'accurately forecasting future surplus capacities', it felt that 'a relatively cautious approach should be taken. We would prefer to see the water tested, as it were, with a limited programme, rather than any move to take up all the assessed surplus capacity in the short run. A gradual approach would also tend to promote a greater degree of stability in student intake numbers from one year to the next.' The expanded intake should be on the basis of full cost recovery, including capital costs. The general taxpayer should benefit rather than the institution. 'In the case of Universities it could be most practicable for administrative reasons for the Universities to collect the full fees and to deduct the sums collected from the levels of Government funding that would otherwise be provided. Under this procedure it is accepted that it would be reasonable for the Universities to request additional Government funding for additional costs actually incurred as a result of the taking of the additional students.'[3]

From UGC Peter Morris offered three general points. First, he could not see the universities giving priority on the basis of area or payment. Academic merit was their criterion, though, through OSAC, there was a minor departure from this in the case of New Zealand-government sponsored students and South Pacific students. Second, no overseas student could be guaranteed a place in a restricted faculty, and that might make full-cost study at secondary level or for Intermediates unattractive. Morris' third point related to the references to the relevance of courses to a country's needs and to employment opportunities. They were not issues in current policy, and the attempt to apply such formulae in relation to students who wished to extend their course or stay in New Zealand led to 'humbug and deceit'.

Morris was also concerned that in its summary the draft failed to account for the places currently made available on the 'concessionary' [$1500] basis. He offered a redraft, indicating that the universities reserved 521 places for them in 1981, plus 15 for sponsored students, leaving some 222 as 'spare'. Adding 'spare' and 'concessionary' together, he felt, 'threatens the "subsidised" places as Ministers may well take the view that the number of such places could be reduced in order to boost that of

---

[2]   Draft, 27.781. UGC Box 653.
[3]   Westrate for Secy/Woods for Sy, 3.8.81. ibid.

"full-cost" places. I should imagine a sharp reaction from the universities and the "Malaysian constituency".' He questioned – rightly in view of Treasury's comment – whether the institutions would retain the fees collected, though universities and UGC saw it as 'essential'.[4]

The Department of Labour opposed the admission of primary students even on a full-cost basis. They might become eligible for 'a wide range of Social Welfare benefits after a period of residence here', resulting in 'a new economic loss to the New Zealand taxpayer'; and the length of time such students would spend in New Zealand if they went on to secondary and tertiary education might make them unwilling to go home. Generally, 'young children are best educated in their home envronment'. Labour had similar doubts about access to the lower secondary forms. At tertiary level, the Department thought, giving priority to the South Pacific and Southeast Asia would mean that few or no students from non-traditional sources would be able to secure places. Quotas would be needed. It did not see that introducing cost recovery would have 'any significant effect on the number of students entering New Zealand under current policy'. Most would continue to apply under the current scheme. 'Exceptions to this might be those students wishing to take courses of study which are not open to them under current policy. ... We believe[,] however, that the large cost differentials involved would result in only a few students following such a course of action.'[5]

After a further IDC meeting on 17 August, Woods prepared a draft for the Minister of Immigration. It responded to the Cabinet directive and took account of the Minister's proposal 'to open the New Zealand education sysem to all-comers on a full cost recovery basis'. Overseas student policy should be 'positive and outward-looking' because New Zealand would benefit by contributing to the development of the South Pacific and Southeast Asian regions, strengthening its relations with 'countries of traditional and new interest to us by providing educational links with present or future business, professional and political leaders', and 'earning foreign exchange through using our education system as a commercial asset'. At the same time, IDC recalled that the first priority was the education of New Zealanders.

Against that background it recommended 'access to any educational course in New Zealand, where capacity exists, for any overseas student on a full cost recovery basis, a new policy'; continued access without fees to Forms 6 and 7 for South Pacific and Southeast Asian students with an

---

[4]   Morris/Woods, 5.8.81, ibid. Memorandum, Future N.Z. Overseas Student Policy, n.d. ibid.

[5]   DOL/MFA, 7.8.81. ibid.

increased annual limit of 150 on the annual intake from any one country, and to Forms 3-5 for Kiribati, Vanuatu, Tuvalu, Solomons, with no limit; maintenance of concessionary access to tertiary institutions – free for South Pacific, $1500 for ASEAN – without the 'unenforceable' requirement that the course taken be relevant to the needs of the home country and offer the prospect of gainful employment; restriction of the concession to ASEAN rather than Southeast Asia as a whole; and provision for reducing or waiving fees under government-government schemes.

IDC recommended that the Minister should consider the proposals with his colleagues in Education and Foreign Affairs. If they were acceptable, 'and bearing in mind your wish to finalise this matter before the election', he might feel able to submit them direct to Cabinet, rather than take them to the Committee on Family and Social Affairs.[6]

Perhaps fearing that they would lose rather than votes, he did not apparently do so. IDC now amended the longer draft Woods had prepared in July. It would permit access to primary schools on a full cost basis; allow access up to Form 5 on a New Zealand basis for students from Kiribati, Solomons, Tuvalu and Vanuatu, and on a full-cost basis to others; allow access on a New Zealand basis to Forms 6 and 7 for 375 students in total. It would allow South Pacific students access on a New Zealand basis for any university course without reference to needs or employment prospects.

The concessions on access to secondary and tertiary institutions granted to Southeast Asian students would now be limited to ASEAN, which was 'consonant' with the government's foreign and aid policy. The concessionary fee should be 'reviewed in due course, particularly in the light of economic development in those countries', and an attempt should be made, both within current and future policy, to encourage a flow of students from ASEAN countries other than Malaysia, which currently provided most of them. ASEAN students would have access to primary schools, state or private, on a full cost basis. They would also have access to secondary schools, state and private, below Form 6 on a full-cost basis, moving to a New Zealand basis in Form 6, but with no guarantee of tertiary access. At the tertiary level, ASEAN students, whether or not sponsored by their own governments, would have access to courses where capacity was available without restriction on numbers except for the current limit on undergraduates of not more than 240 from any one country. They would generally pay $1500. 'Should the limit of 240 be reached, consideration would be given to identifying courses to which access would then be permitted, only on a full cost recovery basis.'

---

[6]   Draft, 15.9.81. ibid.

In respect of other countries, the proposal was to allow unrestricted access to any course where capacity was available on a full cost basis, consideration being given to waiving or reducing the fees on a country-to-country basis, for example where governments sponsored their own students or the students were under a recognised exchange scheme. The proposal did not say what would happen to the current system, which, for example, had non-aided postgraduate study open to all comers paying $1500.

The paper covered procedures, adopting the Treasury's proposal so far as university fees and funding were concerned. The usual immigration provisions would apply to full fee students: they would normally be expected to return home on completion or termination. The new policies would be implemented for 1983. The draft now envisaged only reviewing the fees in subsequent years.[7]

Early in November IDC sent the paper to the Minister, prefaced by a revised version of the summary memorandum drafted in September. That now included a fuller justification for rejecting the attempt to define available courses according to a country's needs and the employment opportunities it offered. It was 'politically (as well as practically) very difficult to identify certain courses as not relevant to countries' needs'. In theory that opened the doors wider to concessionary students; but in fact it continued the present practice 'under which the universities do not discriminate according to course except in terms of available capacity'. It was unlikely to lead to any great increase in numbers. Even if it did, it would be consonant with the first and second objectives. 'The potential of the third objective [earning foreign exchange] is in any case limited by the relatively small capacity available to take additional students. This capacity should, however, have more chance of being utilised by opening the doors to people from outside the concessionary areas.'[8]

The Department of Education circulated the proposals in January 1982 – after the cliff-hanging election – to 'the whole range of educational institutions and interest groups'. They were, it was said, confidential, but the Director-General was prepared to discuss them. They reached the universities – not included in the 'whole range' – only in early March 1982.[9] Their comments were affected by the implementing of other measures that IDC had recommended, removing entry with credit, and raising the standard of pass required to enter postgraduate study. Originally conceived as reducing numbers, those could now be seen as increasing 'spare capacity'.

---

[7] Draft, 10.81. ibid.
[8] Bond/Minister, 11.11.81. UGC Box 90.
[9] Memorandum, 11.1.82. AU. Johns/VCs, 1.3.82. UGC Box 90.

Over them, moreover, the universities were not consulted at all. At VUW the acting Pro-Vice-Chancellor, Wilf Malcolm, pointed out that the VCC submission of 1978 had stressed the need for consultation.[10] The Deputy Vice-Chancellor at CU, Miles Kennedy, observed that abandoning entry with credit had not been discussed at OSAC, but had been announced in the guide to overseas students.[11] Morris replied that OSAC's function was to administer the entry of first-year students. The policy change had been based on recommendations of the IDC, where UGC and OSAC officers had observer status, and a university view did not 'necessarily prevail'. Concern had been expressed over the performance of students given credit, in contrast with those admitted at entrance level, and 'there seemed to be no strong case for continuing this avenue of admission especially as it was not subject to any Government control on numbers'. Immigration would not now issue permits in this case.[12] It seems that one university abused the system by offering entry with credit, describing the credit allowed as nil. That did not, however, justify bypassing consultation with the universities, and then implementing the change by using the study permit system more rigorously.

A press release from Immigration of 18 February 1982 announced that permit extensions for postgraduate study would be granted only to students who had achieved A-level results in their first degree – defined by those that would be needed to retain an A Bursary – and permits for doctoral study only to those with first-class honours.[13]

Jim Stewart, the LC principal, offered his personal view on the officials' paper, influenced, as he put it, by his involvement in the aid programme. 'If New Zealand accepts that a large part of its future is in the near north, then we are going to need a lot of influential friends. I am convinced through observation and experience that there is no better way of ensuring this than by educating them here.' He argued from this for marginal rather than average costing, and accepted $1500 as a reasonable estimate of it. 'We need to recognise that we are not a preferred country for tertiary education': charging full costs 'will largely result in very few private students'. He also supported 'a relatively open policy on post-graduate students'. At Lincoln they greatly contributed to the applied research programme. New Zealand would be 'the loser unless we use any spare capacity we have in post-graduate places to actively encourage them'.[14]

---

[10]   Memorandum, 11.2.82. VCC Box 13.
[11]   Kennedy/Johns, 3.3.82. VCC Box 90.
[12]   Morris/Kennedy, 8.3.82. ibid.
[13]   ibid.
[14]   Stewart/Johns, 12.3.82. ibid.

The document, Robin Irvine at Otago pointed out, spoke of the desirability of 'further' expanding access, though Government policy since the inception of the quota system had been to limit it, and the recommendations did not match the 'protestations of the desirability of an overseas student policy which is "positive and outward-looking"'. It was difficult to welcome 'a document which purports to be encouraging the admission of overseas students, but whose whole tenor is to discourage'. The feeling was 'enhanced when it is learned by accident that, without reference to Universities, policy has been established to deny access to private overseas students who wish to be admitted ad eundem statum to our Universities with credit for work successfully completed at overseas universities'.[15]

Despite his earlier remarks on cost recovery, Brownlie expressed CU's regret at the 'very high fees' contemplated. He also expressed concern over the statement on access. Did it mean that no overseas student could be accepted if a qualified New Zealander had been declined entry? If so, that would be 'a major policy change'. It would be contrary to present practice and CU would oppose it.[16]

Also commenting on the officials' paper, AU condemned the third principle, not only novel, but 'both impractical and undesirable' from the universities' point of view and from that of New Zealand in general. The implications of regarding the universities as a 'commercial asset', as distinct from 'the national asset we believe them to be', needed to be more fully considered before the new policy was sanctioned.

The University suggested 'that the presence of undergraduate students in classes who will have paid such widely varied sums for their tuition [would] add to tension among the students, and put the relationship between student and teacher under considerable strain'. Possibly universities whose rolls might be likely to diminish would be ready to accept these risks. But at Auckland a wide range of restrictions was already in force, and the courses most likely to appeal – computing and data processing, commerce and engineering – were those under pressure in all the universities. Given that entry could be allowed only 'where capacity exists after satisfying New Zealand demand', it might be that there was 'nothing to sell at undergraduate level'.

Possibly, the University suggested, the officials thought places could be 'obtained'. Not all the OSAC places had been taken up in recent years. Apparently, too, it had been decided, through denying visas, to cancel the policy under which universities had discretion to admit students with

---

[15] Irvine/Johns, 16.3.82. ibid.
[16] Brownlie/Johns, 29.3.82. ibid.

credit. At Auckland that had been done on a scale limited through internal quotas. Over the period 1976-81 384 had been admitted ad eundem with credits. Discounting those from the US, the UK, Australia, Canada and Europe, as likely to be mostly returning New Zealanders, some 124 overseas students were left in the category, not all private.

'We question whether either the elimination of this category or the non-fulfilment of the OSAC quotas guarantees the availability of places that are incontrovertibly not required to satisy New Zealand demand. Where restricted entry and selection exist it has been the practice to set aside limited quotas for overseas students. That has been acceptable, possibly even to the New Zealand students who do not obtain places, because of the element of aid involved in making places available to overseas students. But if the places are to be sold at full rates, the attitude of those not selected will be quite different, and members of the public would surely find the policy quite unacceptable.'

There could be places for some graduate students in certain areas, and filling them would enhance the research capacity of the graduate schools, which had been damaged by the $1500 fee. It was not going to be achieved, however, by charging full-cost fees to students from outside ASEAN. Currently at AU there were 65 Masters and PhD students from outside ASEAN and the South Pacific, many of them private. 'This source may dry up', and it was not clear what would replace it. Would students come from developed countries or from non-ASEAN countries at full cost? Would they meet the criteria recently invented, without consultation, by Immigration? It seemed to have been forgotten, moreover, 'that almost all of the research done here is likely to be New Zealand-oriented, and it seems questionable policy and of doubtful equity to charge private overseas students full cost for doing it'.

'No one could be more aware than we are that other countries have entered the business of "full-cost" fees. But we question the relevance of the U.K. model to the New Zealand situation. The U.K. is a traditional venue for overseas study for students from the Commonwealth and elsewhere. Many of its institutions have all the same been hit by the policy. Numbers have fallen – overseas undergraduate applications in U.K. were down in November 1981 by about 60% on November 1979, when "full-cost" fees were introduced (*Times*, 19.11.81) – and quality may also have declined. New Zealand is not a traditional objective for overseas students, and the consequences for numbers and quality seem obvious.'

The high fees imposed by the UK and other countries had had adverse effects on the numbers and prospects of New Zealand Postgraduate Scholars, those funded by UGC: the funding would not now go so far. 'Maybe the policy now proposed would seem more acceptable if there was a way of channelling overseas funds back into our UGC PGS scheme so that it could help our students meet the charges elsewhere. But it would still involve robbing Peter – e.g. say a South African student – to pay Paul – a Thatcherised university.' Some New Zealand students might wish to do graduate work in countries not charging the high fees, e.g. non-ASEAN parts of Asia. 'The whole scheme – which works so much against world-wide academic exchange – would be particularly invidious here.' Perhaps, too, it was relevant to remark that New Zealand owed a great debt to other countries, like the US and the UK, that had in the past offered minimal-cost high-level research training to New Zealand graduates or to others who had come to New Zealand after receiving it. 'It seems lamentable that, now that we in turn are in a better position to assist other countries, we should try to turn our universities into revenue-raising enterprises.'

The University thought that the third objective would work against the other two. 'The education of private overseas students has in the past brought and could still bring long-tem good will and other benefits to New Zealand, as well as contributing to our research programmes and giving our students a novel range of contacts.' But those advantages were diminished by the $1500 fee and would be 'virtually eliminated' by full-cost fees. 'The policy as a whole seems self-defeating.' The deterioration in Anglo-Malaysian relations had been brought about partly by the UK fees. Nor would the policy earn much exchange. Numbers might fall, and there would be fewer spenders.[17]

VUW was also 'concerned to stress the importance of providing opportunities for students to pursue personal objectives in higher study because it expects such opportunities to be made accessible to New Zealand students at overseas universities'. It drew attention, too, to the non-economic benefits derived from the presence of overseas students, though they were less tangible than foreign exchange earnings. 'A diversity of overseas students taking part in the academic, social and cultural life of the university is a great asset in the task of educating New Zealand students to the richness and complexity of human thought and behaviour.'

Charging some overseas students full fees required 'careful considera-tion'. Most universities did not charge such fees. 'Moreover the number of overseas students who come to New Zealand from countries other than those in the South Pacific and ASEAN regions is very small. The effect of charging such students full cost fees may well be to propagate a negative image of New Zealand for the sake of extracting a very small amount of foreign exchange from a very few students who have the praiseworthy

[17]   Asst VC/Chairman UGC, 16.3.82. AU.

aim of pursuing personal goals of scholarship.' VUW also stressed its statutory obligation to nurture research. Postgraduates from the US, Canada and the UK ought to be encouraged, not charged full fees. Commonwealth countries were discussing ways of increasing the mobility of postgraduate students following the introduction of full fees in the UK. It would be 'most regrettable' if New Zealand undercut their efforts by itself introducing full fees.

VUW also discussed the steps taken in respect of the admission of overseas students with credit. The numbers admitted to Victoria were small (21) – though there were many enquiries – and the rationale was difficult to understand. The universities had not been consulted on this, nor on the new requirements for going on to postgraduate study. B passes were a sound prerequisite for an honours course, it agreed, but each case needed to be examined carefully. Some overseas students without this prerequisite had succeeded in the past. The university also pointed out that its honours degree differed from those at CU and OU: it was entered only in the fourth year, not at the start. Again it could not see any validity in requiring first class honours as a prerequisite for doctoral study. 'Experience at this university has shown that many students who gain good second class honours degrees proceed to do excellent Ph.D work and subsequently follow careers as high quality research workers.' And the numbers, again, were small.[18]

The VCC chairman also wrote to Dr Johns. He listed categories of student who would be hit by cutting out admissions with credit, students with Law Int from USP, students with credits from Atenisi, Malaysian students entering Architecture in the 3rd professional year, Fijian students who had done part of a degree in India. The purpose of the policy was unclear, 'although it has been suggested that it is linked to the proposed plan for introducing "full cost fees"'. It would affect students who had in fact demonstrated that they could undertake university study. Stewart also considered that the requirement that overseas students would have to reach a higher level before undertaking doctoral study 'unacceptable'. 'Some highly successful Ph.D work – often of importance to New Zealand – has been done by students with less than first class honours.' The judgement of the universities should be respected. 'The fact that the U.G.C. can no longer give Post Graduate Scholarships to other than A and A+ students, does not mean that Ph.D studies require such a high standard.'

The VCC chairman thought the officials' first two objectives were 'entirely realistic and commendable', but the third, 'unrealistic and impractical', was 'incompatible'. Even if it were practical, 'its success would

---

[18]   VUW Paper, 3.82. AU.

depend on the assumption that New Zealand was a preferred country for tertiary education for students from developed countries, who will be the only ones who can afford the suggested fees. There is of course no such evidence. New Zealand policies unfortunately have discouraged graduates from developed countries from undertaking graduate studies here in the past.' Full fees had had a drastic effect on overseas enrolments in the UK. 'The price-elasticity of demand, if it is so high in the U.K. [,] will be much higher in New Zealand.' The policy would be 'self defeating, in that the main benefits of our universities to the fostering of good will in countries of inestimable importance to New Zealand in the future will be dissipated'.[19]

The policy changes, Johns replied, were made by Government on the recommendation of IDC, on which UGC and UEB had observer status, and discussions had to be confidential till announced by Cabinet. Examples would, however, show the kind of advice UGC had been asked for and the use to which it had been put. 'The basic aim of Government policy towards overseas students is to give them the opportunity to achieve an appropriate first-degree qualification and then to have them return home as soon as possible to apply their knowledge for the benefit of their country. As a concession, and recognising the laudable desire of the universities to have the best students proceed to higher level study, the Government is prepared to allow those students with outstanding records to remain here to undertake postgraduate work. To determine which ones, the UGC was asked about its criteria for selecting postgraduate scholars and for comparable standards for honours or masters.' The advice had been 'translated' into the criteria about which Stewart had written. 'The IDC has, of course, hanging over it the overall desire, expressed forcibly by some Ministers, to be able to sell places in our education system.'

UGC had not been on firm ground in countering the Immigration Division's concern over the poor performance of students admitted with credit. Many cases had gone to the Appeal Authority. UGC did not have records of them, but it had the impression that 'some universities at least have been very lax indeed in setting standards for entry with credits'. Johns thought the IDC 'not receptive to changes in their present thinking until it is realised that few, if any, students are likely to be attracted to "full cost" courses'. But he would make a submission to the Minister of Education if the universities could supply evidence of the achievements of students admitted with credit and of the success of Masters students with honours in the first division of the second class.[20]

---

[19] Stewart/Johns, 30.3.82. AU.
[20] Johns/Stewart, 6.4.82. AU.

News of the 'confidential' officials' paper had, not surprisingly, 'leaked'. The *New Zealand Times* of 7 March 1982 contained quite an accurate summary. 'And education authorities are touchy about it.' The Minister's Press Secretary asked for the *New Zealand Times* source. 'When told this was confidential and we were seeking comment to balance the story, he said: "As long as you understand that the shutters will go down from here." He hung up the telephone.' Sources in primary education said the proposals were 'farcical'. 'They said the concept of making money out of education was "appalling", and they would not support administration of the proposals if they went ahead.' At the UGC, Caldwell said that 'overseas students able to afford the costs would not be attracted to New Zealand. "The areas where we have space have limited attraction to students who are prepared to pay", he said.' Brian Small, president of NZUSA, called the proposals 'horrendous'.[21]

The Minister of Education, Merv Wellington, told the *Herald* he would not discuss the document. 'It is only comment from officials.' Asked his views, he replied: 'I am only a member of the Government and speak as that. It is for the Government to decide and it has not even been to a cabinet committee yet, so I am not prepared to make any comment.' Education leaders said that 'study in this country would be beyond the means of all but the wealthy if the new fees were adopted'. The president of NZEI, David Stewart, described the proposed charges as 'niggardly'. The Opposition spokesman on education, Russell Marshall, said that the government would be 'cutting off its nose to spite its face' if it introduced the scheme. 'Investment in overseas students is the best overseas aid New Zealand can make', he said. 'It is most unfortunate to have any fee at all and this is clearly going to mean a reduction in overseas private students.'[22] In the *New Zealand Times* for the following weekend, Paul Hemsley was reported as saying that Merv Wellington had not seen the officials' paper, though he would see it 'in due course'. Brian Small said that the Minister could not 'hide in the beehive any longer', that he had had time to read the paper, and that he had 'a responsibility to inform the public of his reactions.[23]

Immigration's new policies were also coming under fire. E.T. Chock, president of the Union of Malaysian Students in New Zealand, hit out at a 'tightening of the screw' on overseas students, saying that the new restrictions on postgraduate study were 'as draconian as the $1500 annuual tuition fee imposed in 1980'. He knew of 'several Malaysian students who had recently abandoned plans for postgraduate study and

---

21   NZT, 7.3.82.
22   NZH, 8.3.82.
23   NZT, 14.3.82.

were preparing to go home after receiving a letter from the Immigration division of the Labour Department', indicating the new requirements for entry into Masters and PhD studies. The letter also said that postgraduate students were expected to complete their course in minimum time. That, Mr Chock said, meant that overseas students were 'discriminated against, not only on financial grounds, but also on academic grounds'.[24]

The counsellor at the University of Auckland, Brian Lythe, described the new regulations as 'unnecessary bureaucratic intervention'. Hitherto, it had been the universities' decision whether a student was qualified to proceed to higher studies. 'Some departments very rarely granted first-class honours in masters' degrees, and PhD studies were very rarely completed on time because of delays in obtaining specialist equipment or tutoring.'[25] At Massey the Deputy Academic Registrar felt 'a little silly' when a student approached him on the matter. 'We had accepted the student for post-graduate work and he then received a letter from the Immigration Department saying he would have to leave the country under the new policy.' The policy came as a surprise, Stewart declared. The approach was 'unduly restrictive', harsh on students working in a second language. New Zealand gained from research done in postgraduate studies. The Association of University Teachers shared these views. 'It seems to be a policy of get it done and get out.'[26]

The Minister of Immigration, Aussie Malcolm, defended the change. 'Previously private overseas students could be considered even if they had achieved the bare marks and had taken an extra year to graduate', he said. 'This meant that post-graduate facilities were frequently made available to students who had found even the basic degree difficult.'[27] '[A]sked if he thought it was the proper role of his division to lay down qualifications for postgraduate study', Malcolm replied: 'Absolutely. The department has the role of setting policies governing people who are migrants. Private overseas students are allowed to come here under certain conditions. All that has happened is that some of these guidelines have been tightened', he said. 'If they come here and make use of expensive and scarce resources and follow extended qualifications, we expect them to be students of the top level.' The move was one of a number of 'small changes', made following a review, and designed 'to restate policies always intended'.[28] The criticism seems, however, to have been sufficient for the

24 NZH, 8.3.82.
25 ibid.
26 NZT, 14.3.82.
27 ibid.
28 NZH, 8.3.82.

restrictions on postgraduate admission to be postponed. 'But an immigration spokesman in Wellington said yesterday that it was intended to implement the tighter controls from next year.'[29]

Responding to Dr Johns' invitation the universities had collected information on the achievements of overseas postgraduate students. The Dean of Engineering at Auckland, R.F. Meyer, told the *Herald* 'that the previous year Asian students undertook one-third of the postgraduate research in his faculty. 'New Zealand graduates tended to go straight into the work force because of the high salaries offering. "The overseas students want to get the highest qualification possible before returning home and make a very important contribution to post-graduate research", he said. 'Almost without exception this research is on problems very important to New Zealand." Some of the projects were sponsored by Government departments.' Meyer feared further restrictions on private overseas students 'as the Govenment's cost-cutting drive continued'.[30] The report does not say – as the facts show it could have done – that students had done well even though without a first class record.[31]

Collecting information, the Assistant Vice-Chancellor also urged that the policy towards overseas students ought to be fully considered and take better account of New Zealand's interests and obligations. The interests were partly educational. New Zealand's current policies had 'secured the access of some very bright students particularly in competitive fields like engineering'. The research output of overseas students – not all with first-class records – had been considerable and often of direct relevance to New Zealand. Overseas students had 'helped to diversify and enrich the cultural experience of an isolated country, though to a lesser extent than if students from a wider range of countries had been admitted'. A fourth interest was 'reciprocal access' for New Zealand scholars to overseas institutions. Access had been constrained by the high fees levied by the UK and other countries. 'But it is arguable that New Zealand's relatively restricted policies towards Malaysians contributed to the problem that prompted the U.K. to act, and N.Z. has not itself permitted free admission of students from developed countries. To adopt a "full-cost" policy in N.Z. towards all non-ASEAN and non-Pacific students seems hardly justifiable or politic.'

There were also economic interests. Spending on goods and services and contributing to the balance of payments might be more significant considerations for New Zealand than for the UK, but the fees might drive

[29]   NZH, 5.6.82.
[30]   NZH, 25.5.82.
[31]   List attached to Memorandum by Asst VC, 21.5.82. AU.

off the students from developed countries at present in the universities. The wealthy in the oil-rich Middle East might be a market, but to admit them might not be in accordance with the high standards Immigration was setting. 'Moreover the greatest pressure is likely to be in areas already under pressure from local and ASEAN students. To admit "full-cost" students would require the exclusion of either or both of these groups', or the provision of extra facilities. Encouraging future export orders for NZ goods and services was another factor in providing education for overseas students: 'most British firms were in no doubt that it was helpful to their cause.'

That issue had to be seen in the broader context of promoting goodwill towards New Zealand. The policy-makers were aware of that, but the policies, operated and proposed, perhaps tended to diminish the goodwill that the principles behind them deserved to win. Some Malaysians had apparently acquired the notion that New Zealand's policies were 'discouraging, if not hostile', even though that did not seem to be their intention. 'The manner in which policies are formulated, announced and implemented has much to do with this.' The policy towards the South Pacific failed 'to win as much goodwill as it might'. The proposal not to charge full-cost fees had been coupled with the decision to abolish admission with credit, though that fell quite heavily on some categories of Pacific and ASEAN students. An examination of the records of the 22 students admitted with credit at AU in 1977 and 1978 showed that no more than 5 were unsatisfactory. The decision to abolish the category had 'lost goodwill with no compensatory benefit'.

'The benefits of an overseas student policy to N.Z. should, finally, be considered in a yet larger context. It is to N.Z.'s interest to promote values like adherence to constitutionality, respect for minorities, tolerance, and the rule of law. Subsidy to overseas students is to be seen as a particular form of international co-operation supportive of liberal and democratic values, and thus ultimately a source of security.' That led the Assistant Vice-Chancellor to discuss obligations as distinct from interests. Some of them were formal, obligations under the Commonwealth Scholarship agreements, for example, or under government-government or university-university exchange agreements. 'There are also more informal responsibilities, the need to assist developing countries, more especially those in our neighbourhood or, like those in ASEAN, with which we now have historical links. The proposed policies preserve these responsibilities, and indeed envisage a desirable expansion to other countries, though in detail somewhat limiting their impact and damaging the goodwill they might evoke.'

The memorandum concluded by recommending that the admission and retention of graduate students should be left to the academic judgment of the universities. Admission with credit should be retained, 'perhaps on the basis of guidelines agreed after discussion involving the universities'. The proposal not to charge fees to Pacific students should be retained. The $1500 charge to ASEAN students might be extended to Commonwealth countries in Africa and the Caribbean. Full-cost fees should be charged only to students from countries that themselves charged them, and should be used to boost the fund for overseas awards to New Zealand postgraduate students.[32]

In December UGC considered a paper on entry to the universities, covering both the proposals that had been implemented, and those suspended. It canvassed the reasons for the immigration restrictions. One was the length of stay in New Zealand: the maximum reached was 14 years, but many stayed for as long as ten years, and wanted to remain in a country where they had spent their adolescent years. 'For this reason, and also for the reason of meeting the "aid to undeveloped country" criterion as well as the cost to the taxpayer, the government became quite hard-nosed about looking at the optimum or even the minimum period in which the objectives of the overseas student training scheme could be met.' Countering arguments opposed 'discriminatory' treatment. 'It is further asserted that a major criterion is the ability to benefit from an additional degree. Obviously the educational and immigration objectives can and do conflict with one another, and on occasion one must prevail over the other.'

It was proposed that UGC support 'easing' the requirement for first-class honours as a prerequisite for PhD studies: a II.1 student could become 'a good researcher'. The requirement for an A bursary standard in the final year before entry to an honours degree was, however, justified. Nor should the decision against entry with credit be abandoned. The practice had varied from university to university and the results, recently surveyed by VCC,[33] while themselves varied, did not compare with the results of overseas students in general. The longstanding practice of not accepting an overseas graduate for a second first degree might, however, be changed. That would fill part of the void, and, for example, enable graduates from the South Pacific to do law and engineering.[34] The UGC meeting on 10 December adopted these proposals.[35] IDC accepted them at a meeting on 20 December.[36]

---

[32]   Memorandum, 21.5.82. ibid.
[33]   Cf Hampton/Caldwell, 4.10.82. UGC Box 90.
[34]   UGC 134/10. ibid.
[35]   Minutes, 10.12.82. ibid.
[36]   Changes in Entry Policy, reported to OSAC, 21.7.83. VCC Box 12.

That meeting also considered the proposals in the officials' paper. Aussie Malcolm had declared in July that it was necessary to 'bring to a head the final stages of the outstanding issues' and get a paper to the Cabinet Committee. Among the issues was one that 'keeps confronting me headlong', but IDC was 'running away from'. If a course were not relevant, and led to no employment opportunities, 'then the private overseas student policy simply becomes a ludicrous and expensive method of back door entry to New Zealand on humanitarian grounds. If we refuse, it becomes a back door entry to Australia or Canada on occupational grounds at New Zealand's expense.' Assurances could surely be obtained from the student or the government. The course should be not only be useful: it should be recognised. 'At present we have the silly situation of Malaysian private overseas students studying for the NZCE which the Malaysian Government does not itself recognise.'[37] IDC questioned this. But it suggested that its belief that students took responsibility for the choice of course coincided with the minister's notion of obtaining assurances from them.[38] MFA supported this view.[39] The mode of levying fees at school level was also in question. The minister now seemed to lose patience.

In August 1980, he reminded the chairman of the Cabinet Committee, the Cabinet had asked IDC to examine 'the feasibility and desirability of further extending the access of private overseas students'. He had received a report in November 1981, asked for clarification, and had received two further responses. 'It is my view, and the view of the Ministers of Education and Foreign Affairs, that progress in this area has been slow and it would now be timely to refer the entire matter back to the Cabinet Committee to review why it is taking so long to finalise and what role Ministers or Government might play in bringing the issue to a conclusion.' He suggested it should 'instruct a course of action in the areas in dispute' and set guidelines for formulating a policy for consideration by Cabinet.[40]

The three issues still unsettled, Treasury told the Associate Minister of Finance, John Falloon, related to the way fees should be collected, to the proposed scholarship scheme for secondary PI students, and to the possibility of identifying the relevance of courses. 'Our principal concern is that if the New Zealand education system is to be opened up to foreign students, it should be on the basis of correct economic pricing.' Full cost recovery, Treasury recommended, should 'include an economic return on the capital employed'. Even though there was surplus capacity, 'the

---

[37]   Memorandum for Bond, 13.7.82. UGC Box 653.

[38]   Reply a.i. from DOL, 3.9.82. ibid.

[39]   Bond/Minister, 22.10.82. ibid.

[40]   Malcolm/Chair, n.d. ibid.

resources employed have alternative uses', and should therefore be valued at opportunity cost. 'This is necessary to indicate the economic cost of retaining resources in the education system for the benefit of overseas students at the expense of their alternative uses.' Figures so far given should be updated and amended so that 'the capital recovery item is adequate to amortise the capital employed over a reasonable period, say 50 years'. That would range from $600-1000 p.a. for high schools to about $5000 p. a. for universities. 'Provided educational services for overseas students were correctly charged for, there would be no need for administrative control on the number of students admitted. The price mechanism would indicate the extent to which it was economic to commit resources in New Zealand to the education of overseas students.' If the Government wished to retain free and concessionary entry for South Pacific and Southeast Asian students, 'the differences between full economic costs and the concessionary fees actually charged should in our view be regarded as a foreign aid expenditure, and deducted from the aid budget. This would enable the recipient countries to weigh the benefit of educational services against other forms of aid.'[41]

The Cabinet Committee met on 27 October. It was told by officials 'that there was both a demand among S E Asian countries for education in this country, and a willingness to pay for it'. MFA did not expect an adverse reaction in Southeast Asia to full-cost fees, provided more students were admitted. 'The reaction in Malaysia several years ago when New Zealand had raised fees had stemmed from lack of consultation coupled with the steep nature of the increase.' It was hard to predict numbers, 'although it was confimed that there would be a modest but constant demand from students in the S E Asian area'. The likely sources were Singapore, Malaysia, Hong Kong, Thailand and Sri Lanka. Opening up the field more to entrants to Southeast Asia would not harm relations with South Pacific nations, 'so long as care was taken to maintain our interests in that area'.

Practical difficulties related to the need to legislate for full-cost recovery and to the mechanics of fee-collection: DOL did not wish to mix immigration with fee collection, nor did teachers' organisations wish to be involved. 'Other foreseeable problems were related to the education system itself. There was a possibility that private schools might look to the development of a "total education" package for overseas students, and also that private hostels might be established to accommodate overseas students attending public schools. Such developments would defeat the purpose of any new policy, i.e. to make available to overseas

---

[41]   Westrate for Scy/Falloon, 26.10.82. ibid.

students the educational infrastructure existing in New Zealand.'[42] Clearly it was not pursuing growth in the private sector.

Supporting full-cost recovery, the Committee called for further reports on the matters discussed, to cover the range of options, and also an outline of the changes in policy since 1980. Treasury elaborated its argument. 'The question of whether it is in New Zealand's national economic interest to devote resources to the education of private overseas students is determined by the willingness of potential students to meet prices which reflect the cost of resources which would be committed to their education. For this reason, correct pricing on a full cost recovery basis would indicate whether resources would be productively employed in providing educational services to overseas students, or whether these resources (for example labour and capital) would be better employed elsewhere in the economy. If educational services were correctly priced, it would be economic to accept all the students wishing to come to New Zealand at that price. The number of students coming would be automatically regulated by the number willing and able to pay the full economic price. From New Zealand's point of view, it would be economic to expand the system to adjust to that number. Administrative control on the number of students admitted would therefore not be necessary.'

Only in the teachers colleges was there surplus capacity. There prices might be set on a short run basis. Elsewhere in the system capital expenditure was still being incurred. Adding overseas students would require more capital, and the price they were charged should reflect the long-run costs. Treasury prepared estimates of fees based on this distinction, also distinguishing three categories at the technical institutes and universities. It might be desirable to introduce 'a finer breakdown, in order to isolate the different costs of providing different courses. It could also be desirable to introduce differential charging between institutions, to reflect differences in real costs of providing capacity. Charges should be reviewed annually, and in Treasury's view this should include a review of the concessional fees charged to ASEAN students, many of whom are from upper-income families who would be able to pay full economic costs.' If charges were lowered for foreign policy reasons, the difference should be treated as aid, and quotas would be required for those given the concession. 'There would be no economic objection to accepting over-quota students who were prepared to pay full cost recovery.'

Private schools could set and retain the fees, but would have to exclude the students from the calculation of government grants. State institutions could include them in their calculations of per capita grants, with the fees

---

[42]   Minutes, 27.10.82. ibid.

being paid into the Consolidated Account, either through immigration procedures, or through teaching institutions.[43]

An IDC draft of 14 December set out current policy, then summarised the new proposals. The aim was to provide access to any educational course on a full cost basis, while maintaining the current fee concessions for South Pacific and Southeast Asian students. There would be an overall quota at Form 6 and 7, intended to limit pressure from subsidised students seeking university study. There would be unrestricted access at all levels for full cost students, including those not within the quota and those from other parts of the world. The subsidised students would be receiving a form of aid, and the conditions and amount should be considered each year in the context of the development assistance programme and reported as such. The draft then presented the Treasury's argument on the pricing of full-cost students. University rolls were expanding, owing to a rising participation rate, and nationally only the teachers colleges had spare capacity. In all cases there would be additional staffing costs. At the very least cost recovery should include full operating costs. Aside from the teachers colleges, the fees should include capital costs as well. Officials were now agreed that the fees should be collected initially at the overseas post and then by the Immigration division on the annual renewal of permits. Private schools should be free to set their fees and take the numbers they saw fit, but would receive no government grants in respect of them. Legislation would be required to allow the charging of fees at schools and teachers colleges and to cover a number of other matters.[44]

A further draft, dating fom February 1983, included a table of costs, based generally on amortising capital cost over fifty years. Foreign Affairs appears to have taken fright. The fees, it suggested, should be introduced gradually if New Zealand, entering the market late, were to be attractive. It recommended a top limit of $5 500 or operating costs only, whichever was the lesser. Treasury thought that lowering the price might indicate that New Zealand had no comparative advantage. If the Foreign Affairs view was accepted, there would be a subsidy and there should be a quota on the subsidised.[45]

Yet another draft was sent to UGC on 16 May 1983. It reiterated the proposal that above-quota students could be admitted on a cost recovery basis, but pointed out that it would 'create contrasting categories of students from the same country', and make it difficult for OSAC, which admitted two sets of students at different times, to decide which students

---

[43] Draft memorandum, 17.11.82. T 62/21/6/1. ibid.

[44] Draft, 14.12.82. ibid.

[45] Draft, 4.2.83. ibid.

merited inclusion in the secondary quota. On the question of fees, however, officials had been unable to reach agreement. Foreign Affairs contested the Treasury's pricing argument. One aim was 'to try to build up, over the longer term, constituencies in important countries such as, say, Japan, Mexico and Iran through having some of their future decision-makers live and study in New Zealand'. That was a long-term operation, and to start it up, fees would have to be set at market prices. A literal interpretation of the concept of full-cost fees would price New Zealand out of the market. Australia's fees were nowhere near that level, and the UK had found that 'the political cost of a full recovery system (literally interpreted)' had 'proved to be excessive given the comparatively low earnings involved'. Students had to bear travel and living costs. Adding either the total or the operating costs identified by the Treasury 'would discourage any active interest from those countries with which we seek to develop our relations'. Foreign Affairs thought the fees should be set on the basis of operating costs plus 10% for overheads.[46] Education agreed.

In the report finally sent to the Cabinet Committee, the difference had been removed or rather, perhaps, glossed over. It added to the statement that extended access of overseas students was consistent with New Zealand's economic interests the proviso 'that the additional students entering on a cost recovery basis are not counted in justification for capital works and other operating cost proposals'. Previous discussions had been based on spare capacity, the report noted. That existed mainly in the school and teacher training areas. 'Because of the number of additional places which could be available in the universities and technical institutions [sic] are so few, it is reasonable to exclude capital cost in computing a fee. To do this, it would be necessary to ensure that the students concerned were not included in the student numbers used for capital works proposals. It would be quite practicable to do this.' The basis of fees was to be cost recovery plus 10%. Collection of the fees, it was now agreed, should initially be by overseas posts, and then by the tertiary institutions, or, in the case of schools, by Immigration. Legislation would have to be added to the 1983 programme.[47]

The Cabinet Committee, meeting on 24 August 1983, accepted the proposals. 'Treasury expressed concern that prospective students should be warned that there were few places available at tertiary level', and also about the need to distribute secondary students across the country 'so that there was not an imbalance'. The necessary legislation should if possible be introduced in 1983. The scheme would operate from 1985,

---

[46] Report, 16.5.83. ibid.
[47] Memorandum for Cabinet Committee, n.d. UGC Box 91.

the Committee proposed, although private schools would be able to proceed earlier.[48]

On 29 August 1983 Cabinet approved the recommendations of the Committee. The announcement was made by the Minister of Foreign Affairs, Warren Cooper, on 4 September 1983. His press statement included the principles behind the policy, but 'using surplus capacity to earn foreign exchange' was altered – by hand – to 'using surplus capacity on a user pays principle'. The Minister explained that 'it would be mainly in the schools and the teachers colleges where surplus capacity exists and additional students could be accepted. The universities and the technical institutes had very limited capacity for additional students', particularly in areas that were 'the first choice of foreign students'. There would be no limits on access to private (non-integrated) schools, but 'arrangements would need to be made for the recovery of per capita grants in respect of foreign students on a cost recovery basis'. The legislative changes would be introduced in 1983 and the policy implemented in 1985, though overseas students could apply to enter private schools in 1984. Fees would be collected where possible by High Commissions and by institutions and, in the case of schools, by the Department of Labour via visa renewals. The statement did not explicitly refer to 'Kiwi first' – perhaps from political caution – but it is implicit in the emphasis on surplus capacity.

Circulating the statement, UGC indeed told the universities that it was 'based on Government policy that overseas students will not be admitted to courses unless capacity exists after New Zealand has been satisfied. Universities will not therefore be permitted to offer places to overseas students in any course from which qualified New Zealand students have been excluded.'[49]

Before the announcement, Tarling had offered Johns some comments, coincidentally not entirely unlike those Foreign Affairs had advanced. 'Dedicated to scholarship and its international values, the universities could only welcome the concept of drawing on a wider range of countries that the new policies have in mind. But they would stress that this is an area where goodwill is likely to be built up only over the long-term, though it can be damaged by the pursuit of other possibly short-term objectives. The long-standing links with the UK and the older Commonwealth countries and with the U.S. have rested not only on common language, similar objectives and government support, but also on the network of personal and institutional relationships built up over a long period.' The

---

[48]   Minutes, 24.8.83. ibid.
[49]   Memorandum from Johns, 5.9.83. AU.

Thatcher government's initial steps were criticised for 'drastically interfering with this structure'.

'In New Zealand's case something like such a connexion has been built up with some Southeast Asian countries, though again at times N.Z. has damaged some of the goodwill it should have earned by abrupt and, if not ill-considered, ill-explained measures towards Malaysian students. The proposals for full-cost fees are not likely to build up a net-work of new relationships, though they may damage some of those that exist. The device is too crude. The countries with which it is concerned are too various in their resources, in their education systems, in the opportunity they have offered or might offer our students. India, for example, is a more likely source of suitable students than Saudi Arabia, but the latter might be more able to produce a full-cost fee.' Japan was a suitable destination for New Zealand students and offered scholarships. Was a policy of full-cost fees for Japanese students an appropriate response?

'A coherent policy could take account of these diversities by working out a number of objectives and establishing a range of devices for meeting them.' The objectives might include (a) 'A contribution to international goodwill and the values of a free society, including aid where N.Z. can appropriately make it available'; and (b) 'A commitment to the international values of scholarship, which would take account not only of N.Z.'s attitude to overseas students but also of the overseas needs of N.Z. students.' Using the education system as a 'commercial asset' could not be regarded as 'an appropriate objective at university level', though the objectives would not 'exclude a more wide-ranging consideration of the benefits to N.Z. as well as the costs of the overall policy'.

The devices to be used for realising these objectives 'would include many of those now in existence[,] but they might be applied in new ways or in new contexts appropriate to the particular countries or groups of countries or institutions concerned'. They included exchange agreements, provisions for waiving fees, provision for scholarships as part of aid programmes or by academic or other institutions. The objectives and the means of attaining them would need to be reviewed from time to time.[50]

Such arguments for a more differentiated and niche-based approach did not affect the outcome, but influenced AU's official response to the Government decisions. New Zealand, it agreed, stood to benefit by stengthening relations with countries of traditional and new interest by building educational links with their leaders. 'But New Zealand also stands to gain by stressing the international aspect of education. All possible means of transferring knowledge need to be kept available to a relatively small

---

[50] Memorandum in Tarling/Johns, 6.7.83. AU.

country that must live by its wits. Even apart from the benefit to individual students, the New Zealand community as a whole stands to benefit from a relatively free traffic in university education, particularly at the research level.' The University favoured access from a wider range of countries. 'But it is opposed to the higher fees with which such a widening is associated, and feels that coupled with the need to make sure that qualified New Zealanders are accommodated, and the academic standards which the Universities, if not Government itself, will require, these will tend to negate the change of policy.'

Indeed it might inflict some damage on 'current and developing relations'. The University was pleased that students from the Pacific and from ASEAN countries were not being charged 'cost recovery' fees, but considered that other countries that had supplied worthwhile graduate students in the past, such as India and Pakistan, ought to be placed in the same category. Though speaking of new and traditional interests, the policy took too little account of the way interests were developed in the university world, the University added. It had longstanding contacts with the UK, Europe, the US, Canada. Gradually it was establishing contacts with China and Japan. 'But that requires not only formal agreements but a range of personal contacts that only time and experience can foster. Abrupt changes in policy and the levying of high cost fees only inhibit such developments, to the possible disadvantage of our students and indeed of New Zealand.'

If the policy were carried out, UGC should endeavour to ensure some flexibility, so that it might be possible to seek exemptions, 'for example for post-graduate students (particularly perhaps if their work is likely to be of direct benefit to New Zealand), for students from needy non-ASEAN countries, or for students from countries that offer substantial support to New Zealand students, and so that exchange agreements can be made that provide mutual waivers of fees'. The University pointed once more to the UK example. High fees had damaged its relations with Commonwealth partners, especially Malaysia, and it had introduced 'a countervailing scholarship scheme'. If New Zealand had to enter the cost-recovery business, it, too, should sustain a larger scholarship scheme for its own and overseas students.[51]

Such 'views and attitudes' had been presented, 'most several times', during the discussions prior to the announcement, Dr Johns wearily replied. 'While the UGC was able to attend the meetings at which the policy changes were considered UGC was not able to consult with Universities on the proposed changes prior to their announcement', and it

---

[51]   DVC AU/Chairman UGC, 20.10.83. AU. For UK, see THES, 11.2.83.

was therefore happy to receive from VCC, the universities, and other interested groups 'suggestions on how the new policy can be modified and/or clarified to ensure that New Zealand's best interests are served'. Government strongly supported the policy changes, 'so any attempts to revoke the policy cannot succeed at this time. There are however, several areas which need closer study so that the implications of the new policy can be studied and appropriate interpretations arrived at.'[52]

Another letter from the UGC indicated the significance of the broad hint that the Chairman was giving. IDC, it said, was considering the implementation of the new policy. 'In brief, all *private* students from countries other than Pacific Island countries, ASEAN countries and Australia will be liable for full fees.' Currently no undergraduate students from other areas were admitted 'except under special schemes', and that would continue to be the case. 'However, postgraduate private overseas students from such countries as USA, Canada and Britain have in the past been admitted on the same basis as students from ASEAN countries.' Under the new policy, those students would be required to pay full fees, with the exception, of course, of those funded by the New Zealand government or on exchange or 'other recognised schemes'. Johns suggested that the universities might wish to comment: he had arranged that their views could be presented to IDC. 'Evidence of the numbers and countries of origin and of the value in research of such students, with a few brief specific case studies, would be the best way to have this move modified. Ministers are more likely to be influenced by actual examples rather than by general statements and it is they who will ultimately decide this issue.'[53]

The University of Auckland, like the others, prepared a list, excluding DSIR, UN, Colombo and BAP students, also excluding a few unsatisfactory students and others who would have been ruled out by the 1982/3 rules on student visas. The list included students from India, Taiwan, Hong Kong, Pakistan, Bangladesh, Japan, the USA, Canada, Great Britain and France, and covered Masters and doctoral studies in quite a wide range of disciplines, including Botany, Zoology, Cell Biology, Physics, Geology, Engineering, Anthropology, Psychology and Education. Much of their work was on topics of direct value to New Zealand. A substantial number came from non-ASEAN Asian countries, such as India and Pakistan, which had low per capita income. Others came from wealthy countries which had 'done a great deal for New Zealand students in the past, in particular by providing low-cost education, scholarships, and/or tutoring opportunities. Even now, the British are making up for some of their high fees

---

[52] Johns/Tarling, 26.10.83. AU.
[53] Johns/Maiden, 18.10.83. AU; also UGC Box 90.

by scholarships, Government or University-funded, while Monbusho scholarships are one of the main means by which New Zealand students get to Japan.'

'[A] case could be argued – on the benefits to New Zealand and its students, if not on the basis of the values of international scholarship – for allowing admission to postgraduate students at the concessionary rate of $1500: (a) if coming from non-ASEAN countries in South and Southeast Asia; (b) if coming from countries which are deemed on the advice of the UGC to afford satisfactory supportive facilities and finance for New Zealand students. These would presumably include U.S., Canada, Japan, U.K. and some EEC countries. It would also induce others to afford similar support.'[54]

UGC made the case, both direct to the Minister of Education, and to IDC. Johns argued that, while some of the countries to which New Zealand postgraduate students went theoretically had high fees, in many cases they were remitted for able students. New Zealand should not be out of line 'when our own students are generously treated overseas. Because of our small size we need access to overseas research experience to a greater extent than most of the countries which currently accept our postgraduate students.'[55] A paper for IDC argued for the status quo, again deploying the reciprocity argument. Using the returns from the universities, it emphasised that most of the research done related to the development of New Zealand's resources, and its benefit outweighed any fees paid. Postgraduate students reached senior positions at home more quickly than undergraduate and that also brought benefits.[56]

No legislation had been passed by the time Muldoon dissolved Parliament in June 1984. In the meantime the agitation against the $1500 fee had continued and the issue was put on the election agenda. AUTNZ had pursued a correspondence with Warren Cooper, published in its Bulletin.[57] In September 1983 NZUSA announced that it was taking a case to UNESCO. 'We have exhausted all available channels for change in New Zealand', said the acting president, Roger Tobin. 'The Human Rights Commission reported that it found merit in our view that the current $1500 fee imposed is discriminatory and contravenes international agreements the Government has signed.'[58] The complaint was presented

---

[54]   DVC/Chairman, 7.11.83. AU.
[55]   Johns/Minister, 30.3.84. UGC Box 90.
[56]   Wills/Bond, 28.3.84, and enclosures. ibid.
[57]   Nos. 78, 8.82; 84, 3.83.
[58]   NZH, 7.9.83. Cf Report to the PM ... Pat Downey, 3.83. VCC Box 46.

to UNESCO in December as 'a last resort'.[59] The last resort was, however, the electoral process itself.

The Labour Party had committed itself to abolishing the $1500 fee, though its leader, David Lange, confessed some second – and rather Muldoon-laden – thoughts in March 1984. He was reported as saying that New Zealand should charge at least some overseas students the full cost of their education plus a percentage. 'I have been around the East and met those people who were part of the Colombo Plan, and I went to their near-palaces', he said. 'They could have paid time and time again. And I have met others who should never have been charged a cent. Indeed, we should have paid them to come because they come from developing countries and poor households.'[60]

Equivocation indeed marked the policies of the new Labour government, as it had those of the government it replaced. In its second term, however, it came out openly for the policies that Treasury had with increasing forcefulness been advocating.

59   NZH, 20.12.83.
60   NZH, 29.3.84.

CHAPTER SIX

MARSHALL PLANS

The Labour government came to power with a number of unequivocal commitments, but also – initially less noticed – an equivocal attitude to change: was it to be along traditional Labour lines or to follow the kind of path advocated in Treasury's briefing paper *Economic Management?* The new minister, Russell Marshall, pursued the commitments, but, despite his endeavours, was unable to obtain a compromise between the directly-opposed viewpoints suggested by the attitude to change. He secured the abolition of the $1500 fee. But the Treasury's paper went beyond the views it had so far been expressing in the overseas student debate, and, as NZUSA apprehended, applied its rationales to tertiary education in general.

Tertiary education was 'more a private than a public good', and the government was involved in order to 'offset able to pay constraints on tertiary participation'. Problems with tertiary education, as in other areas of public provision, were 'associated with relative insulation of suppliers from consumers, low incentives to minimise costs, and sluggish ability to change resource distribution for optimal return. In addition, the gradually increasing use of relatively inefficient quota methods of rationing course demand is becoming apparent, with clear labour market consequences.' A case could be made for 'greater use of market processes in the provision of tertiary education'. Initially 'services' could be more fully charged for, and financial support differentiated. In the longer term, private providers could be encouraged to participate. 'This would improve the responsive-ness of tertiary sector supply to consumer monitoring in terms of teaching performance and the range and nature of services.'[1]

---

[1]   *Economic Management*, Wellington, 1984, pp. 268-9.

Essentially tertiary education was a 'service' or a commodity that the individual chose to buy. If that attitude came to prevail, there were no obstacles – other, perhaps, than practical ones – to the creation and selling of places by private or public institutions. It did prevail, though only after a somewhat contradictory phase of fee reduction. It prevailed more readily and completely in respect of overseas students than domestic. The latter had a political constituency that could be deployed with some effect against market-oriented rationales. The former had none. The arguments about neighbourliness and goodwill lost purchase, their advocates were weakened, and some aid continued, offsetting the 'able to pay constraints' in the South Pacific. But it took some time for the 'market' to validate the policy, so far as it ever did. Only in the later 1990s did really large numbers of overseas students come to New Zealand, and then one country came to predominate, rather as one country, a different one, had predominated in the 1970s. Again, push factors prevailed over pull.

The new minister indicated, the UGC informed the universities on 9 October 1984, that the Government's legislative programme did not include the introduction of the 'cost recovery' fees policy for overseas students announced by its predecessor. He was aware that universities had been holding enquiries from postgraduate overseas students while the question of their fees was resolved. 'He has therefore agreed that overseas students may be advised that they may enrol in postgraduate courses during 1985 on the same basis as in 1984.' That meant that those from specified South Pacific countries would pay the basic tuition fee [ie the flat domestic rate, now $208], while others would pay the concessionary fee [ie the $1500].[2]

The following month Marshall announced that the government had reduced the tuition fee payable by overseas students from countries other than specified South Pacific countries from $1500 to $1000 from the beginning of 1985. The specified South Pacific students continued to pay the basic fee $208 for a full-time course. 'The Government has also indicated that it will review the level of the fee again before the commencement of the 1986 academic year with a view to the abolition of the fee.'[3] Marshall said it was 'still committed to scrapping the fee altogether'. The president of the Union of the Malaysian Students in Auckland, Robert Ling, said that at $1000 it was still a deterrent, particularly for those from poorer families. Overseas students had no bursary, and were not eligible for government-subsidised student summer jobs. NZUSA also supported scrapping the fee.[4]

[2] Wills/Registrars, 9.10.84. AU.
[3] Wills/Registrars, Sy VCC, 19.11.84. AU.
[4] NZH, 12.11.84.

The full-cost proposal had raised another issue, and it did not disappear with the full-cost proposal. That had insisted that it was government policy that no overseas student should occupy a place for which there was a qualified New Zealand student. Hitherto, no places, it was accepted, were available in Medicine, where there quotas on the number of domestic students. But in Engineering some places had been kept for able foreign students, even though there were qualified Kiwis who could have filled them, and such 'quotas' had been adopted in other courses as demand grew.. The plan to sell spare places raised an issue over which the universities had exercised their discretion. Though the legislation had not been passed, the policy it had prompted remained, and presented universities and politicians with a dilemma.

In 1984 the AU Engineering School had been closed to private overseas students. It looked as if Law and Commerce would follow suit in 1985. 'New Zealand has had a long-standing policy that private overseas students can occupy only places in the university which were not taken up by New Zealanders', the *Fiji Times* reported. Overseas students, it added, had formed a group to fight the closures. It sought 'the allocation of quotas for private students for all professional courses in Auckland'.[5]

The status of this 'long-standing' policy was somewhat in question. When Dr Maiden and Professor Brownlie saw the Minister about the quinquennial grant, they also discussed access by overseas students. 'You will remember', Marshall wrote to Maiden, 'that I was advised that a handwritten note had been sent by my predecessor to Dr Johns as Chairman of the University Grants Committee indicating his and his Government's wish that New Zealand students should have priority. I understood from this conversation that the message through the University Grants Committee had been taken in some universities to the point where places for overseas students in professional schools were being reduced if not cut out completely.' The Minister said he was 'particularly aware' of the 'pressure' on the University of Auckland and of the decision 'under that policy' to close off several more courses in 1985.

He had 'on several occasions lately received nervous messages from various quarters, particularly from would-be students, believing that the change of Government will not effectively mean a change in university policy for 1985. I am aware of the fact that there is very little room to move and that in a sense the ball is in the Government's court. The question of access for overseas students is a matter which will have to be carefully considered by the Government when funding arrangements for the quinquennium are made and when further reviews are undertaken.'

---

[5] *Fiji Times*, 5.7.84.

It would, however, be 'helpful' if he could be 'sure that overseas students were not to be excluded from consideration from the range of professional courses at the University of Auckland next year', particularly those available to them in 1984. He was concerned 'that the direction by the previous Minister of Education should not be felt in any way to put any obligation on the universities for enrollments [sic] next year'.[6]

AU wanted in fact to ensure that it could take some private overseas students. It wanted, if possible, to take more postgraduates, especially research-oriented. It wanted to take some undergraduates, and not only the New Zealand government-aided, at present accommodated even in closed courses. 'What it would be interested in doing, if, as must be expected, resources remain constrained, is setting a quota for private overseas undergraduate students within each of the faculties, including those currently "closed" to them. Such a quota would necessarily prejudice the chances of qualified New Zealand students at the lower end of the academic scale, though if it were not taken up, New Zealanders could fill the vacant places.'

That involved, the Deans Committee believed, a change in government policy, 'in turn involving an essentially political decision'. Inasmuch as the issue had national implications, it deserved an overall review. 'Indeed we have long wanted to see a coherent overseas student policy, formulated in consultation with the universities.' That would take time, however. For Auckland the matter was urgent, and it was receiving unfavourable publicity. The matter should be taken up with UGC.[7]

That process was in train when the Minister's letter arrived. The memorandum formed the basis of Dr Maiden's reply, which indicated that the University could provide limited quotas for Law Int, Commerce and Engineering Int, as it had in 1984. 'Though sensible of the advantages of having overseas students in our classes, the Deans felt that you and your Government colleagues should be clear that this will almost certainly result in the exclusion of some qualified New Zealanders from such Faculties' as Engineering, Law and Commerce. 'They conclude that this in now acceptable to Government.' In the longer term, the matter needed fuller consideration. The University would welcome the opportunity to make an input, through UGC, into the review of policy to which the Minister alluded.[8]

The New Zealand student organisations of the day supported the overseas students in this case as they had over quotas and fee differentials.

---

[6]   Marshall/Maiden, 6.11.84. AU.
[7]   Memorandum, approved 8.10.84. AU.
[8]   Maiden/Marshall, 16.11.84. AU.

AUSA argued for reserving a minimum number of places for private overseas students, and collected 2500 signatures, mainly from students, for a petition. That, presented to Helen Clark MP in August, argued for the presence of overseas students: it generated goodwill, it was a valuable form of aid, it contributed to 'the development and understanding of multi-culturalism in New Zealand', the students contributed to the academic side of the university 'through high grades and research work'. The petition opposed the present policy. The answer was 'not to exclude private overseas students followed by other students such as mature age and poor students but to create more places through more adequate funding of universities'.[9]

Helen Clark was the convener of a Caucus committee Marshall had set up in August[10] with a view to 'a complete review of OSP', its other members being Richard Northey, Eden, son of the Professor of Public Law at AU, and Clive Matthewson, Dunedin West.[11] The sentiments of the committee were not very different from those of its petitioners. New Zealand, it reported in early October, should allocate places to BAP students and overseas students paying domestic fees 'in such numbers as we can afford, bearing in mind our responsibility as a member of the club of developed nations to other developing coutries'. It spoke of minimum quotas for overseas students.

Marshall's response to the AUSA was also to endorse its sentiments. 'Frankly, my dilemma is that there is very considerable constraint on Government expenditure across the board and education is not exempt from that. If I have a small amount of money extra it is, to be honest, not likely to go into the university area.' He subsequently announced a review of tertiary education, in tandem with a more specialised review of university education.[12] It may appear in retrospect that he was attempting to pre-empt devotees among his colleagues who looked for more drastic change – though at the time the universities were apprehensive lest they were reviewed by the Department of Education – just as on the overseas student issue he set off against them the young but-old fashioned idealists in the caucus committee.

In December, when the quinquennial grants for 1985-9 were approved, Cabinet directed the UGC, the Department of Education, and Treasury to report on a number of matters by 31 August 1985, when the funding for

---

[9]   Petition in Lythe/Deans, 8.10.84. AU.
[10] Cook, p. 30.
[11] Marshall/Mullins, 24.9.84. AU.
[12] NZH, 10.11.84.

the remaining years of the quinquennium would be further reviewed. The matters included fees, student assistance, open entry, staffing, and procedures by which UGC would be able to report at the end of the quinquennium the extent to which the universities had achieved 'the policy objectives set for them'. The trio were also to report on the implications for open entry, university funding and university accommodation of government policy on overseas students, when determined.[13]

The review of overseas student policy Marshall had begun by asking IDC to report to the Cabinet Committee on External Relations on its current state. The paper it offered on 31 August also sought the Committee's guidance on the future course of the policy. It drew attention to a number of problems with the 1983 decisions. It would be difficult to report subsidy as aid, and in any case OECD was re-examining the question, on which it would be difficult for it to secure consensus. At secondary level it would be difficult to allocate places fairly among countries, between direct entry and progressing students, and between the free and cost recovery students. Most, moreover, would expect to go on to university, but the expansion of rolls since 1980 ruled out the idea that spare capacity would continue to exist, and admitting secondary students, and then not to have openings for them, was 'a prescription for disappointment'. IDC saw four options for relieving the capacity problem: 1. allow qualified New Zealanders to be displaced; ii. increase university funding through Vote: Education; iii. provide funding from the aid vote for the next ten years to create facilities for students from developing countries in development-oriented fields; iv. introduce cost recovery. That Treasury had favoured in 1983, but other IDC members had seen as pricing New Zealand out of the market.

The $1500 fee, IDC noted, met only a small proportion of the actual cost, and, with the falling dollar, its real cost to the student had diminished. Labour had committed itself to abolition, but had made no reference to the new cost recovery system. Abolishing the $1500 could be seen as 'a gesture of goodwill' in ASEAN countries. But it should be considered against the loss of revenue involved, and 'the possible inconsistency of abolishing a concessionary fee, while maintaining a higher cost-recovery fee for students from developing countries outside the Pacific and ASEAN regions'. Treasury favoured retaining the cost recovery structure. Any concessions were a subsidy from New Zealand taxpayers which should be identified and justified. That view it would apply to postgraduates as well as undergraduates.

IDC recommended that the Cabinet committee should consider a

---

13   Butterworth and Tarling, p. 79.

submission covering temporary facilities at VUW for 60 ASEAN Commerce students p. a. for five years and decide whether to direct officials to prepare costings that would maintain at 1983 levels a constant number of places for private overseas students through to 1995. It should advise whether the $1500 fee should be abolished, whether the cost recovery fee should be introduced for developing countries or others, whether some kind of concessionary fee should be maintained for graduates because of the value of their research to New Zealand, and whether unrestricted access to private schools should continue. It should decide whether, given the restraints on university places, it should direct officials to put forward recommendations on the means of restricting entry to secondary schools.[14] The Minister of Immigration forwarded the recommendations to the Committee.[15]

The committee met on 17 October with Lange in the chair. The previous government's policy of open access to private schools had raised expectations that could not be fulfilled, it was observed, introducing 'further complications ... into an already tangled subject'. If the cost recovery scheme was to be 'in place for the next school year', legislation would be needed in 1984: that was 'impracticable', since the policy had 'yet to be developed to the point where drafting instructions could be produced'. The committee did not favour 'at the present time ... including any assistance to students from developing countries as official development assistance'. It was 'a volatile issue', and the policy to be adopted had to be examined 'very carefully. It was observed that if New Zealand had pressed ahead with the proposal, then this country would suffer most decidedly in comparison with other members of the OECD.' The committee directed officials to prepare a further submission 'establishing an overall framework for overseas student entry', agreed to receive a submission on Commerce students at VUW, directed officials to cost maintaining 1983 places to 1995, deferred the introduction of the legislation for cost recovery, declined to agree to the policy of unrestricted entry to private schools, and directed officials to make recommendations on restricting entry to secondary schools.[16] For Marshall, the decisions were a victory only in the sense of a delaying action. Would that work or would it be counter-productive?

Since no legislation was required, the previous government had allowed full-fee paying foreign students into private secondary schools from the start of 1984. In addition, though the required legislative changes had not

---

14 Memorandum to Chairman, 31.3.82. UGC Box 92.
15 ER (84) 7, 15.10.84. ibid.
16 ER (84) M 5. ibid.

been made, overseas posts had been working on the assumption that they would be admitted into state schools.[17] The result was, as Johns had written to Norrish even before the election, that 246 Malaysians in New Zealand secondary schools would be eyeing 240 places in New Zealand universities, and that would rule out the traditional direct-entry Malaysian Chinese.[18] Foreign Affairs agreed that there was 'a risk of prejudicing our longstanding educational connections with the leadership of ASEAN countries'. Extra Engineering places could not be provided in the short-term, but Commerce ones could. The cost of 60 extra students at VUW would be provided by the UGC and Vote; Foreign Affairs, Item: Bilateral Aid.[19] That was the proposal on which the Cabinet Committee agreed that a submission should be made.

Treasury preferred to 'defer expanding university facilities to cope with overseas student demand until an overall framework for overseas policy' had been developed. 'The Government should then be in a position to more accurately gauge the demand for university places from those it wishes to assist together with those who are prepared to meet the full costs of their education.' Current policy did not target countries or students most in need. Deferring the proposal could strain relations with ASEAN, however. If the government wished to proceed, it should approve funding from Foreign Affairs only for 1985/6 and only by reallocation within budget, while giving VUW assurance of funding for the future either out of Foreign Affairs or student fees.[20] Cabinet adopted this approach.[21] UGC advised VUW.

Marshall also announced that the government could not endorse its predecessor's open-ended commitment to the entry of overseas students into secondary schools 'because of the pressure this would place on university places in 1986'. New Zealand 'could not admit unlimited numbers of foreign students to … secondary schools without their being assured of a place at university once they qualified'. The government had therefore deferred a decision on cost-recovery entry to state schools, and the topic would be part of a review of overseas student policy. It had also decided to withdraw the 'unrestricted entry' policy in respect to private schools. 'However, he said, 69 places would be provided for Malaysian seventh form students in private schools in 1985, as part of the quota for Malaysian student entry.' That would provide for all those who had been

[17] Cook, p. 18.
[18] Johns/Norrish, 10.4.84. ibid.
[19] Memorandum for Cabinet by F. O'Flynn, 21.9.84. ibid.
[20] Memorandum for Minister of Finance, 25.10.84. ibid.
[21] 29.10.84. CM 84/42/17. ibid.

accepted. The government would also permit entry by all other students who had been offered places and who had applied for entry permits by 30 October. 'The essential point to be made is that the problem has arisen because of the messy and inconsistent policy operated by the previous Government. They were shutting doors for tertiary students while opening the floodgates to secondary students.'[22]

Before the officials could start on the 'framework', the Prime Minister wrote, 'they need an indication from Ministers on their thinking', and he arranged a meeting of the ministers involved.[23] He outlined the main issues. Did the government wish to continue taking in 'a reasonable number of overseas students', knowing that, unless more places were made available, that could have 'adverse consequences' for qualified New Zealand students? If it did so wish, should it offer places primarily in the form of assistance, or on a user pays basis, or both? Would it wish to make provision by fixing a percentage? Would it be prepared to accept more students at secondary level than could subsequently be accommodated at tertiary level?[24]

The ministers concluded at their meeting that open entry at secondary level 'would build up expectations that could not reasonably be satisfied in respect of admission to New Zealand universities'. At the tertiary level, they talked in terms of a quota and saw the need for quotas that would protect New Zealand students from competition in faculties that had restricted entry. They wanted to consider a policy 'which was a mixture of New Zealand government assistance to overseas students and some form of user pays'.[25]

A further meeting of ministers took place on 16 May. Its decisions made for greater 'transparency', one of Treasury's objectives. In effect there would be three categories of overseas students: full fee students on a cost recovery basis; full scholarship students, i.e. awards including subsistence; and students who would receive fees scholarships awarded by the New Zealand government and would not therefore be disadvantaged by selection policies adopted by their own government.[26]

Ministers subsequently prepared guidelines for officials: 'i. Suitably qualified New Zealand students should not be deprived of the opportunity for tertiary study; ii. The number of overseas students (except graduate

---

[22]   NZH, 16.11.84.

[23]   Memorandum for Ministers of Immigration, Education, Finance, 19.3.85. UGC Box 97.

[24]   Enclosure in ibid.

[25]   Notes by Renwick, 27.3.85. UGC Box 92.

[26]   Cook, pp. 38-9.

students and those meeting the full costs of their education) to be admitted to tertiary institutions and secondary schools should be controlled by quotas; iii. Overseas students should be admitted in three categories in the following order of priority: a. students funded under approved bilateral assistance programmes and other approved international programmes; b. students from South Pacific and ASEAN countries, including those sponsored by their home government and private students, assisted by the New Zealand Government to the same extent as New Zealand students (except for the Tertiary Assistance Grant); c. tertiary students from all countries who would meet the cost of their education. iv. There should be provision in 7th forms for overseas students who wish to proceed to further study in a New Zealand tertiary institution.'[27]

Officials considered the guidelines and reported to the Cabinet External Relations and Security Committee. First, it was necessary to indicate the quota levels that might be discussed with interested organisations. Given present levels of funding, it was estimated that 490 places would be available for first-year overseas undergraduates by 1990. 'Officials for the most part consider this number too low.' MFA expected a growth in ODA students, and there was a demand from own-government sponsored students. To ensure that the number of private students was retained at current levels, 175 additional places should be made available by 1990, and that would involve capital and operating expenditure. 100 extra places at technical institutes could use existing physical facilities. An additional 200 places would be required for an intake of 850 in schools.

Financial provision – reaching $11m in 1990-1 – would be transferred from Education to Foreign Affairs as ODA. Students meeting full costs would have to meet capital as well as operating costs. The $1000 fee would be abolished. These two changes would involve legislation, though the fee could be abolished without it. Decisions would need to be made and legislation passed by the end of 1985 if the changes were to be implemented in 1987. Given the intention to consult interested organisations, some changes might be delayed, particularly those relating to full cost students.[28]

The Committee met on 16 October with Frank O'Flynn in the chair and Marshall in attendance. The discussion stressed that the courses taken by assisted students should reflect the needs of their countries. Students sought university rather technical institute courses. Degree courses were often more relevant to New Zealand conditions, and many graduates

---

[27] q. Memorandum for Cabinet ER and S Committee, 2.10.85, attached to ER (85) 16, 7.10.85. UGC Box 92.

[28] ibid.

sought permanent residence. 'Attention was also drawn to the advantages which could accrue from actively selling places in New Zealand courses to private overseas students. It would increase the numbers of potentially influential people overseas who were educated in and had some ties with New Zealand. There was also the possibility of economic profit and of the institutions involved receiving indirect benefits from economies of scale. For example, larger faculties often support more extensive research facilities.' Priority had always to be given to New Zealand students, and overseas students could be placed only where vacancies existed, 'or could be created without disadvantaging New Zealanders'. Australia's charges were 'much higher'. New Zealand had 'a comparative advantage', reflected in 'a sharp increase' in applications. The Committee agreed to the officials' proposals, but included the notion that 'advanced educational institutions' might actively sell places overseas in the matters for consultation with interested organisations.[29]

The comments recalled old arguments on the types of course suitable to overseas students and on the tendency not to go home. They also covered speculation about the same of places. An increase in applications did not prove that New Zealand had an opportunity, since the applications were for places charged at $1000. Nor was it certain that purchasers at any unsubsidised rate would sustain the same ties with New Zealand that aided students fell.

UGC circulated the proposed guidelines for comment. The government sought submissions on the admission of ODA, home government sponsored and private students within intake quotas rising to 665 in 1990 for undergraduates, 230 for technical institute students, and 850 for 7th formers, and 'the opportunity for admission of students who will meet the total costs of providing their education'.[30] Quotas provided the answer to the problems the government had seen in the proposals of its predecessor, though it was not clear how the favoured quota – those paying domestic fees – would be selected. It set limits to the tertiary places which it intended to fund which would it guessed preserve the opportunities for qualified New Zealanders. It also set limits to secondary school enrolments, which had been recognised as having flow-on effects.

At Otago the Senate welcomed the proposed increase in the number of overseas students in New Zealand. It also appoved the idea of admitting full-cost students, 'provided that priority always is given to New Zealand students and that overseas students should only be placed in courses where vacancies exist or could be created without disadvantaging New Zealand

---

[29]   Minutes, 16.10.85. ER (85) M 11. ibid.
[30]   Hall/Maiden, 18.10.85 AU.

students'. Graduate students – not mentioned in the guidelines – should, Otago thought, be 'exempt [from] any requirement to pay full costs because of their value in Departments in providing stimulation, but should be required to pay no more than the appropriate fee payable by New Zealand students'.[31] AU also noted the apparent exclusion of graduate students from the guidelines. That was welcome. 'The ability of New Zealand universities to attract research students from overseas should not be limited by quotas or high fees. The Universities, and indeed New Zealand itself, directly benefit from research done by them.'

The University continued, however, to be critical of the proposal for charging students full-cost fees. 'On the policy front, ... it removes any element of "aid" in respect of those students. On the University front the attendance in the same class of students who have paid enormously different sums for their education may produce tension. More generally, it is imitating, and thus encouraging a practice adopted in other Commonwealth and foreign countries, which is in breach of the international traditions of scholarship.' That said, the policy might have 'limited impact' on AU. 'Constraints of space and pressures on entry will make it difficult for us to offer places of this nature at the under-graduate level.'

The proposal was coupled with quotas on students from ASEAN and the Pacific. 'While the coupling may not be entirely logical on general grounds, again we feel that it is acceptable in Auckland.' Some faculties could not take overseas students without excluding qualified New Zealanders, and the provision of a quota, and the resources required, would be an advantage.

The University concluded by raising some other matters. One was the provision for exchange agreements, which many universities were seeking. Would fees still be waived? Another was the question of admission with credit. Reversing the decision to disallow it 'might be seen as providing more economic use of aid resources. The question of attempting a professional degree in New Zealand on top of a general one elsewhere should also be revived.'[32]

The quota was still below the 1976 peak intake, NZUSA pointed out. It objected to the above-quota proposal: 'any scheme which is based on cost-recovery fees is in direct contradiction to the Government's stated policy of education for overseas students being a form of aid to developing countries.' It would 'only benefit those who are wealthy', and would 'create a dangerous precedent for other consumers of education in this country'. NZUSA disliked the reiteration of the 'New Zealanders First'

[31]   Girvan/Hall, 14.11.85. AU.
[32]   Tarling/Hall, 12.11.85. AU.

policy: it put overseas student policy in the negative context of "depriving New Zealand students" of education. The real problem was cutbacks in university funding which created a crisis in high demand courses like Engineering and Commerce. NZUSA proposed that a minimum of places, say 5%, should be reserved for overseas students in all courses.[33]

AUTNZ, somewhat contrastingly, reaffirmed 'that the top priority of the New Zealand university system must be to provide the opportunity for all New Zealand students to have the education of their choice', but also stressed the responsibility to provide foreign aid. It was 'especially important' not to restrict postgraduate admissions, and it urged the drop the restrictive criteria imposed in 1982. The Association had 'considerable doubts regarding the concept of selling New Zealand overseas. It is especially inappropriate to be considering a proposal to sell off places in our university system at a time when universities are already suffering from worsening staff:student rations and as a result are being forced to further restrict entry to New Zealand students.'[34]

On 6 December Marshall reported that the proposals had generally been accepted, but a number of issues were raised. At school level the proposals limited access to Form 7, except for students from a few South Pacific countries. The Thai government wanted access to Form 6 and below – it sought opportunity for upgrading English skills – and so did independent schools. Officials from Labour, Foreign Affairs, Education and UGC opposed unlimited access, since it would build up pressures for access to tertiary courses that would difficult to resist. Treasury and Trade and Industry argued the other way. First, it could be made clear that there was no obligation to make tertiary places available. Second, if tertiary institutions could recover their full costs with a margin for profit, 'the present capacity for private overseas students would increase so that a greater number of those who study at secondary school in New Zealand and wish to continue through to the tertiary level would be able to do so.'

The proposals limited the access of private assisted students to those from Southeast Asia and the South Pacific. The Government Caucus Committee on External Affairs and Security wanted a specific quota for African students and suggested that 'the proposed focus ... be spread somewhat to provide for students from other parts of the world'. A recent aid mission had suggested a number of new awards for African and Indian Ocean countries, and they could be accommodated within the number of ODA-BAP awards available.

The policy provided for students who would meet the cost of their

---

[33] Submission, 11.85. AU.
[34] *Bulletin*, 109 (November-December 1985).

education. Treasury and Trade and Industry recommended 'that this policy not only apply to the *surplus-capacity* available in the less market-related post-compulsory education alternatives available but also that the institutions involved should have the liberty to charge such fees [as] they consider appropriate (full cost-recovery and a margin for profit) to enable them to *create a capacity* to meet excess demand'. The institutions would 'operate in a manner not dissimilar to a business. They would market their product, work in a competitive environment, seek to improve their management, lower costs etc and retain profits for their own use. Caution would need to be taken that no cross-subsidisation occured and the courses are suitably costed and charged. The two departments believe there may be beneficial flow-down effects on the management of the non-commercial side of the educational institute.'

The Government Caucus Committee on External Relations opposed marketing education as an export commodity. It considered that any surplus places should be included in an increased quota for overseas students and that no discriminatory fee should be charged. Other organisations also opposed cost-recovery, including AUTNZ, AU and NZUSA. 'It was seen as inappropriate at a time when entry to under-graduate courses was being restricted for New Zealand students. A marginal-cost basis was argued where there was "genuine" spare capacity. There was a widely held view that cost-recovery would benefit the wealthy.' The presence of assisted and cost-recovery students in the same class might produce 'tension'. '[T]here was a fear that cost-recovery for overseas students could lead to the same for New Zealand students.'

Marshall proposed to announce the policy, and recommended that the Cabinet Committee decide on the way in which capital costs should be calculated, confirm the abolition of the $1000 fee, and decide whether there should be unlimited access to private schools on a cost-recovery basis.[35] The Committee referred the recommendations to Cabinet, but on 18 December Cabinet referred them back to the Committee for considera-tion at a meeting early in 1986.[36]

In January, when he attended the Southeast Asian Education Ministers Conference in Brunei, Marshall briefed Southeast Asian officials on the government's proposals. They included, he told the *Herald* by phone, the abolition of the $1500 [$1000] fee and an increase in the quota of 30-35% over a four-year period. 'And the possibility of providing further places over and above the quotas for foreign students able to pay the estimated full capital costs of their courses was also discussed.' Because of

[35] Memorandum, 6.12.85, attached to ER (85) 20, 9.12.85. UGC Box 92.
[36] Memorandum for Minister of Education, ?3.2.86. ibid.

the 'difficult political implications', however, more work was needed on the cost-recovery proposals. The cost was around $12 545 for each student, he said. The problem was, however, that the demand from foreign students was likely to come in areas such as medicine that were now closed. 'If you start to allow foreign students to come in because they are able to pay for the full cost of [sic] recovery of the course, then New Zealand students are likely to ask why they cannot get in if they are prepared to pay the full cost. We still have to work this through.' There were 'differing views' in Caucus. 'Some members were against full recovery of costs on the ground that, if New Zealand were to take any students, it should do so without charging them at all, while others favoured the policy in principle, he said.'[37]

Before the Committee met in April, Treasury put in its comments. It emphasised that the cost-recovery element of the policy was a critical part of it. 'Given that the legislative log jam precludes the institution of cost-recovery until 1988', it was ready to agree with the idea that officials should 'use the time available to study and evaluate recent Australian experience where a liberalised private overseas policy was instituted in 1985'. That need not, however, delay the confirmation of the proposals: it would provide a basis for considering implementation. Treasury agreed that the $1000 fee should be abolished, but it should occur at the same time as full cost recovery was instituted, not before. If it were abolished in 1987, there should be compensatory savings, a lower quota, for example.[38] The Committee did not accept Treasury's view on abolishing the fee, which was to be dropped for 1987. It did, however, confirm guidelines on cost-recovery for non-quota overseas students, the details of which would be reviewed after study by officials who would should take Australian experience into account, and report to the Committee by 1 October.[39]

The Government's decisions were announced on 1 May 1986. The $1000 fee was abolished: postgraduate students from all countries and undergraduates from ASEAN would now pay the same as domestic students. The government recognised that additional funding would be required to ensure that the capacity to take overseas students, particularly in vocational degree courses, would not 'decline to unacceptable levels', and it planned to increase the number of university places available to a total of 665. It had also considered 'admitting a non-quota category of students who would meet the total costs of their education', but it was not prepared to take a decision on that until 'a close study' had been

---

37 NZH, 27.1.86.
38 Memorandum, 8.4.86. T 62/9/17. UGC Box 93.
39 Minutes, 9.4.86. ER (86) M 2 Part i. ibid.

made of the Australian attempts to implement such a policy.[40] The press release thus avoided the 'confirmation' Treasury wanted.

The changes in immigration policy provided another context.[41] The most significant change dislodged the 'traditional source' criterion. It was 'not factually and historically correct', since migrants from China, Hong Kong, Greece, India and Yugoslavia had all all established communities in New Zealand. 'Selection according to national origin is inherently discriminatory in that important decisions affecting individuals have been made on the basis of the applicant's nationality. Difficulties have been experienced by employers wishing to recruit good quality migrants whose occupational skills are at least equal to those available from previously preferred sources. More generally, the traditional source approach has restricted the entry to New Zealand of people from countries and regions of present and future economic and political importance to New Zealand. If non-traditional markets for New Zealand exports are to be developed and expanded it is important to build up personal as well as commercial relationships and the inflow of capital is more likely to proceed in an environment which welcomes human as well as financial investment.' The Government therefore decided with effect from the beginning of 1986 'to abolish national origin as a factor in immigrant selection and to assess applicants solely on criteria which evaluate personal qualities, skills, qualifications, potential contribution to the New Zealand economy and society and capacity to settle well in this country'.[42]

'[F]or the sake of completeness' the Govenment's review alluded to the examination of New Zealand's policy on overseas students that was being carried out alongside, and referred to the guidelines. It did, however, add that the abolition of the 'traditional source' preference had implications for some overseas students. 'Hitherto students from developing countries, even though appropriately qualified, have not been eligible to acquire permanent resident status in New Zealand on occupational grounds and have been required to leave this country on completion of their studies. With the removal of national origin as a criterion in migrant selection this rule is no longer appropriate and it will be open to private overseas students with the requisite skills or qualifications who also meet other standard immigration requirements to be granted permanent residence.' Home government-sponsored students, or those in New Zealand under bilateral or international assistance programmes, would, however, have to discharge their obligations.[43]

[40] PR, 1.5.86.
[41] PR, 14.8.86. Immigration Bill, Review. AU.
[42] ibid., pp. 15-16.
[43] iid., p. 34.

The change in immigration policy were closely associated with the 'free-market' policies the Government was pursuing in other spheres. So far as overseas students were concerned, the report disposed of a whole policy and attitude, that aid was being given – even, more or less, to private students, now about to pay only domestic fees again – and that they should or must go home to help their countries. Moreover, the basis of the argument was mistaken. National origin had nothing to do with this policy, and so removing it as a criterion was really no argument for reversing it. Dropping the 'traditional source' criterion was, however, presented as a means of promoting good relations, which had been an argument for aid to Southeast Asia. The trend of the argument also worked towards the sale of education, as NZUSA saw. Would that win friends and influence people?

In September 1986 NZUSA offered the Minister of Education a submission on the proposal to admit overseas students to surplus places in New Zealand universities on a cost-recovery basis, drawing on the experience in Australia and Britain. The proposal, it argued, 'completely negates the reason why New Zealand admits overseas students in the first place'. The overseas student programme was 'established and continues to be, an effective and inexpensive form of aid to developing countries. Marketing full cost education is in direct contradiction to this concept of aid. Instead of targetting [sic] those who will benefit most from the programme, New Zealand would be selling education to the wealthy who already have a privileged position in their home countries. This is *not* aid.' NZUSA was 'also concerned at the precedent it sets for introducing full-cost education for all New Zealand students'.

The submission began with practicalities. How much demand would there be if full-cost fees were charged? Traditionally Australia and New Zealand attracted students from 'modest financial backgrounds. Moreover, into the act first, Australia would compete with New Zealand, nearer, with a wider range of courses, possibly cheaper. Nor were there spare places in courses they were likely to prefer. Cutting the OSAC places was unacceptable. 'Furthermore, how does the Government propose to decide which students should come in under OSAC quotas and which should be full-fee students?'

Admitting overseas full-fee students might create a precedent. '[I]f an overseas student can gain entry to an engineering course by paying $10 000 or more', NZUSA asked, 'why shouldn't a New Zealand student also want to do the same?' That prospect was 'a compelling reason' for the government to reject the proposal. 'Access to tertiary institutions on the ability to pay would make a total mockery of the Labour Government's education policy of access to education for all New Zealanders and especially to improve access for disadvantaged groups.'

NZUSA noted, however, differences within the government. The Minister of Finance offered assurance that user-pays would not apply to education. The Minister of Education warned that the Treasury and certain sections of the Government were 'very much in favour of it'. NZUSA was 'very much aware that the Government is now proposing a change for overseas students which would mark the beginning of applying these principles *throughout* the system'.

NZUSA also argued that introducing a full-fee system would encourage the universities to drop their academic standards both for admission and for continuation. The tendency to drop entry standards had been noticed in Britain, and it might happen in Australia, given the proliferation of proposals for private universities.

It argued, too, that, while the proposal might help in the short term with the universities' funding problems, it would further undermine their financial position in the long term. There was no guarantee that, if full-fee students were introduced, the government would maintain its current level of funding. '[A]ll it will do is allow the mindframe where universities will become totally "user-pay" and therefore subject to all the fluctuations and demands of the market place.'[44]

Meanwhile officials had visited Australia – where the government, following the Goldring and Jackson reports, was moving towards full-cost fees – but they had been unable to reach agreement on the report to the government. 'One of the disagreements has been about the insertion of a warning that the capacity of universities to respond to a request to produce a reasonable number of cost recovery student places is very limited', Caldwell told UGC in October. He had managed to include a statement to the effect that the subject areas for which the Australians found a demand in Malaysia were just those restricted in New Zealand. There was scope, however, in English as a second language, agriculture, horticulture, and in postgraduate subjects, 'all of which could be negotiated as a package offering'. Treasury and Trade and Industry were pressing to proceed without further delay. UGC had pointed out 'that as the universities would have to take a major part in implementing this policy, it would be foolish not to consult them on the guidelines which will apply'.[45]

The report, completed in December, indicated that the market was 'very large and probably growing'. Australia's response had been slow. Domestic demand meant that there was little spare capacity for subsidised students.

---

[44]   NZUSA submission, 9.86. AU.
[45]   UGC 158/8. UGC Box 93.

Provision for full fee students was introduced only in 1985. 'The response ... has been slow because of philosophical doubts, conservative attitudes, opposition from interest groups and a lack of Government encouragement in marketing.' In New Zealand, 'policy objectives hitherto have been solely in terms of foreign policy. They have not included commercial objectives.' Officials thought New Zealand could compete and that there was 'scope for new investment' and, some departments thought, for job creation.

In general, they concluded, 'institutions should have maximum flexibility to assess the potential market for their own services and to determine their own response'. They were, however, 'strongly divided' on a number of issues: first, 'whether secondary schools should be opened up to private overseas students before there are places for them at tertiary level'; whether private investors should be allowed to set up separate tertiary institutions; and whether private institutions should be required to meet academic and other criteria determined by the State. Education and UGC thought that, in order to ensure cooperation, consultation was required before decisions were taken. They also thought that the question of full-fee domestic students required public discussion. Treasury, Labour and Trade and Industry thought the consultation should be confined to questions of implementation.[46]

These issues were put to the Committee in the New Year. The paper added further questions: whether UGC and DOE should set criteria for private institutions, or whether they should be incorporated in validation procedures now being developed for domestic providers; whether the capital cost component in state institutions should go to the institution or to UGC; whether staff employed to teach full-fee students in state institutions should be on the same terms as other state employees.[47] Meeting on 4 February 1987, the committee noted the officials' view that a full-fees policy framework was required, but it declined to make substantive decisions at that time.[48] The reason, Wendy Cook suggests, was that the differences among its members touched on the very nature of the education sysem, and were not to be raised in election year.[49]

Marshall and his Department – which now, rather than Labour, provided the chair of IDC – had fended off the policy that National had started and some of his colleagues wished to continue. He had not, however, won the battle, and he had made some concessions. The debate

---

[46]   DOE Memorandum to Committee Chairman, 18.12.86. 38/8/1. UGC Box 93.
[47]   Recommendation by Minister of Education to Cabinet Committee, 21.1.87. ER (87) 1. UGC Box 93.
[48]   ER (87) 1 and ER (87) M 1/1, 4.2.87. ibid.
[49]   Cook, pp. 89-90.

on full-cost fees had been confused by the strategy with which National had begun it. It had been presented – if not conceived – in terms of 'spare capacity'. That raised the flag – hitherto more or less furled – of 'New Zealanders First', and it also stumbled on the growth in participation that more or less took up whatever spare capacity there might have been. It is surprising that it took so long before even Treasury began to talk plainly of creating 'new' capacity through full-cost fees, which would set limits on the number of places only in terms of available capital and 'human resources'. Possibly, if that had been done earlier, the idea might have been better received. Moving towards it by starting with 'spare capacity' had probably been counter-productive. But there was sure to be strong opposition to it anyway. The 'aid' approach, enjoined by earlier governments, had a strong hold on public opinion and on the opinion of university students as well as staff. And it was clear that the market-approach Treasury was in a better position to advocate with Muldoon's departure implied that full-cost fees for overseas students might mean higher fees for domestic students who sought the 'private good' of tertiary education.

Marshall stood against that approach. 'I guess my view of what a good education system is differs from some of those young men across the road' in Treasury. 'Leaving aside the arguments about the merits of the whole market economy approach, it is to my mind not an appropriate approach to take for tertiary education.'[50] Again – in the larger sphere of education as well as in the specific case of overseas students, he sought to fend it off while making what he hoped were limited concessions and seeking public and institutional support. He had mixed success. Treasury offered a minority report to the Cabinet on the questions it had raised in December 1984. He dropped the idea of a major enquiry, but welcomed the VCC's decision to commission the Watts report in 1986. After the election he was shifted to Foreign Affairs and the Prime Minister himself took the Education portfolio. Major change was to ensue.

Even before that, however, the Minister of Overseas Trade and Marketing had seized the initiative on overseas students. Mike Moore had watched with annoyance as Australia launched a policy while New Zealand discussed a framework: 'the Australians have yet again stolen one of my policies and are achieving the results we should be achieving were it not for the inertia within our system.'[51] He commissioned a report through the Market Development Board.

[50]   q. Butterworth and Tarling, p. 86.

[51]   Moore/Marshall, 28.8.85. q. Cook, p. 62n.

CHAPTER SEVEN

MDB

The so-called Hugo Report[1] was prepared for the MDB by the Hugo Consulting Group Limited, of which D.F. Quigley, a former National minister who had broken with Muldoon in 1982, was managing director. Sir Frank Holmes was the project leader, and the other members of the team who worked on the project were G.H. Datson, A.R. Kirk, Dr R.S. Deane and Quigley. Their appointment represented the growing practice of using consultants. If that was an attempt to escape the control of officialdom, it did not guarantee independent advice. Consultants tend to give acceptable advice. They want to be used again. Certainly the Hugo group offered what Moore wanted to hear and what he hoped to persuade his colleagues to adopt. Its report offered an overall policy, though not an entirely coherent or well-researched one.

It was presented in the context of earning foreign exchange through the sale of 'educational services', one of the aims of 1981-2. 'The fastest growing sector in world trade is services', wrote Peter Shirtcliffe, chairman of the MDB, in his foreword. By 2088 some predictions suggested it might have risen from 30% to 65% of world trade. The sector offered an opportunity to increase New Zealand's foreign exchange earnings. 'For many New Zealanders the concept of earning foreign exchange from services such as education or health is a new one.' There were, however, factors in New Zealand's favour 'if present constraints are lifted. Our educational system is based on the English language, our educators have a high international reputation, we are close to important potential

---

[1] *Directions in Foreign Exchange Earnings: Educational Services*, Wellington: New Zealand Market Development Board, n.d.

markets, and New Zealand is viewed as politically stable and safe.' There were opportunities in English language education, agricultural and horticultural education, other technical subjects and 'university courses in subjects where there is spare capacity'.

'New Zealand's education system is for New Zealanders first and foremost', Shirtcliffe wrote, 'and this must be a guiding principle in the development of any educational services industry.' Earning foreign exchange by exporting educational services was 'a separate issue' from the current debate on the education system, 'but it is related and does present a number of opportunities to enhance that system'. The key policy objective was 'the promotion of increased foreign exchange earnings from educational services on a basis that is not subsidised by domestic taxpayers and does not conflict with access by New Zealanders to education or policies on overseas aid.' To that end institutions had to be empowered to charge full-cost fees and 'control over the institutions must become more decentralized'. By 'reinvesting' the earnings from foreign students, institutions could 'improve facilities available for all students'. In 'all successful marketing initiatives, entrepreneurship and innovation are key ingredients, and these must be encouraged in New Zealand's educational institutions'.

'Increasing the number of foreign students receiving education through New Zealand institutions has a bridge-building effect too, enhancing mutual understanding of and affinities between our various countries.' New Zealanders would all benefit 'from educational institutions which look outward and are quickly responsive to demand', Shirtcliffe added. To become 'a successful international supplier', it would have to have the best available staff and facilities.[2]

Shirtcliffe's words made a number of connexions that depended more on ideology than logic. Even if the basic premise – that education is a service or a commodity rather than sui generis – is accepted – and that definition foreshortens a debate – it is not clear why that should require that control must be 'decentralized'. Nor is it clear why, or among whom, 'entrepreneurship and innovation' must be encouraged in New Zealand's educational institutions, even supposing that it was part of the terms of reference. The 'New Zealanders First' doctrine is reinterpreted. They would benefit from 'reinvestment' of the earnings. That could happen only if there were not merely cost-recovery but a profit. The preface was, however, in accordance with the spirit of the new age. The consultants themselves used a number of fashionable phrases but their logic was also less than clear, and they interpreted their terms of reference in expansive rhetoric.

In the introduction they argued that the export of educational services

---

[2] Preface, ibid.

was not only 'consistent with the objective of ensuring that all New Zealanders should have access to good education and training, regardless of their means', but that it was 'only ... one element of a more general policy for the radical improvement of New Zealand's educational services', itself vital to 'the improvement of life in New Zealand' and 'the development of the knowledge-based economy' it required.

'The future shape of education policy will be ultimately decided on political, social and economic grounds. Whatever the outcome, there is a strong case for policies designed to make New Zealand a centre of excellence in education and training. An essential element of that policy is the provision of an increasing range of services to foreigners, from which the revenue would contribute to the development of education, training and the economy generally.'[3] How you could assume a 'case' for full fee students if the future shape of policy were yet to be decided the consultants did not explain, nor why or how 'servicing' foreigners was essential to making New Zealand 'a centre of excellence'. It might have the reverse effect. The only logic in the connection that is made is in terms of revenue. But there is no cost-benefit analysis – such as Treasury might have sought – to show whether New Zealand might profit more by using its education system in another way.

The restrictions on institutions that prevented or deterred their responding to 'unsatisfied demands for service by both New Zealanders and foreigners' seriously impeded 'the achievement of economic and social goals'. Knowledge and skill were fundamental to developing 'internationally competitive activities' crucial to New Zealand's 'future growth and prosperity'. Education was not concerned only with preparation for work. 'Its fundamental aim is to assist New Zealanders to 'find satisfaction and joy'; but work was 'an important element of life', and 'economic wellbeing determines the extent of social and cultural improvement', the consultants declared.[4] Their 'argument' here is more about the reform in general and its 'philosophy' than about international students. Indeed – so far as it made sense – it did not need to involve them, except in respect of revenue. Arguably that has remained the focus of policy.

New Zealand education was 'relatively open and accessible' and 'of good overall standard', but there was 'considerable room for improvement', the consultants continued. Too many pupils, especially from minority groups, were 'turned off' at school. Too few continued after school. Many could not obtain the education and training they sought. 'There should be an urgent drive to remove the constraints which are

---

[3]   p. 7.
[4]   ibid.

inhibiting both public and private educational agencies from responding to the growing and changing demand for educational services, both from within New Zealand and overseas.'[5] The argument about New Zealand minority groups really had nothing to do with the case: no one was going to sell education to them. The only connexion – aside from profit – might be the notion that you would break up the alleged complacency of the institutions.

Education services could earn foreign exchange. The 'key issue' was 'how to make them more efficient and effective, and maximise their economic contribution, consistently with their other non-economic purposes'. The government could 'set conditions to ensure that expansion of commercial services to foreigners does not frustrate New Zealand's educational goals'. They should not be subsidised, except as an element of aid.

'Exporting educational services ... will help New Zealand education and educationists. It will widen the market for their services, improve their capacity to take advantage of economies of scale where they exist, improve their financial strength, enhance their capacity to attract and retain staff of quality, and keep them and their students in closer touch with educational and other developments overseas. In short, opening up opportunities for more service to foreigners, here and abroad, should be a significant element of a policy which is designed to enhance the quality, the relevance, and the responsiveness of New Zealand education and training generally.'[6]

The body of the report began with a survey of the current situation. In September 1986 some 3 500 private students had student visas. 917 were at state schools and 122 at private schools, 86 in vocational training, 408 at technical institutes, 1598 were undergraduates, and 364 postgraduates. Most came from the South Pacific (1635) and ASEAN countries (1526), including 1064 from Malaysia, 842 from Fiji, 414 from Western Samoa, 304 from Tonga, 210 from Singapore, and 193 from Indonesia. 88 came from Hong Kong and 27 from the Middle East. There were 479 Science undergraduates (166 Malaysia, 148 Fiji, 40 Indonesia); 468 Commerce (312 Malaysia, 58 Fiji); 225 Arts (64 Malaysia, 50 Fiji); 176 Law (113 Malaysia, 50 Fiji); 175 Engineering (118 Malaysia), and 75 others. 73 of the postgraduates were from Malaysia. In addition there were 589 government and Commonwealth funded students at New Zealand universities. The grand total of overseas students at university was 2551.[7]

---

[5]   ibid.

[6]   pp. 7-8.

[7]   The total internal roll in 1986 was 49 365. John Gould, *The University Grants Committee 1961-1986 A History,* Wellington: UGC, 1988, p. 189.

At technical institutes 267 of the students were from Fiji. Engineering and Business Studies were the main courses sought. The vocational students were mostly either training as pilots or engaged in religious studies.[8]

The total cost of the 'subsidy' that resulted from charging private overseas students domestic fees at state schools and universities was estimated at $23m. Private schools and institutions were allowed to charge fees, but there were 'numerous constraints'. They had to be 'approved' and preference normally went to state schools under the quota system. Their courses had to be approved by Ministers on the recommendation of the IDC, which had to be satisfied the content was worthwhile and the qualification useful. Normally the course had to be completed in two years. Bible colleges, an art School, several English language schools, some aviation colleges, a commerce college and a nautical school had had courses approved.

The report drew attention, too, to other restrictions: the limits on the number of places in some university courses; the 'country of origin' restrictions on undergraduates, taken only from ASEAN, China, Hong Kong, Iran and Iraq, and the South Pacific; the restriction on students who had already attended a university, i. e. on transfers with credit. Yet the demand had been growing again after falling away in the early 1980s. For Commerce and Engineering it had grown from 279 in 1983 to 657 in 1987. 'Despite some special Government assistance to expand places available in commerce at VUW, only 184 or just over 40% of the applicants in commerce, and 56 or about 26% of the applicants for engineering, were admitted.'[9] The report also outlined the restrictions on admissions to secondary schools and technical institutes.

'Current Government policy does not encourage educational institutions to view themselves as potential earners of overseas exchange.' Generally, 'the provision of educational services to foreigners has been as overseas aid, partly through selection of individual students under sponsorship or scholarship programmes, and partly by permitting a restricted number of private students, mainly fom the South Pacific and ASEAN, to enter New Zealand educational institutions on heavily subsidised terms'. Even 'preferred foreigners' found it difficult to access certain courses in heavy domestic demand. 'Preference has been given to developing countries in our neighbourhood and to a few others at some distance from New Zealand. It is presumably on foreign policy grounds that China, Hong Kong, Iran and Iraq have been chosen', and not other developing countries. 'The right to charge full fees has been restricted to a few approved institutions in the private sector. It has been regarded as

---

[8]   Hugo, p. 9.
[9]   ibid., p. 10.

inappropriate so far to charge even affluent individuals or individuals from affluent countries for services rendered by most of our educational institutions.' The report aimed to explore the suitability of such policies and discuss 'alternative approaches' which might take advantage of the potential to earn foreign exchange, while sustaining an aid programme and improving access for qualified New Zealanders.[10]

The report then discussed demand. That could be met in a variety of ways: by sending educators to home countries; by providing distance courses by correspondence or tapes 'or even more sophisticated electronic means'; by joint ventures; or by bringing students from their home countries for part or all of their course. It was not, the report said, merely a matter for tertiary institutions, but for schools, not merely a matter for public institutions, but private, too. There was opportunity, but there was also competition.

Providing education to foreigners was 'a growth industry', and a growing proportion of the students were paying fees. Some of the undergraduate growth was from students in 'more affluent countries', seeking broader experience, wanting credit towards a domestic qualification, seeking language training among native speakers. New Zealand was doing little to attract students of that type. Students had been coming from developing countries since the war. Their numbers continued to grow, even though institutions in those countries were now better developed. Both in the UK and the US, however, there had been moves towards 'greater fee recovery'.[11]

The report pointed out that fees were not the only factor in demand. Another was 'judgment of the quality of the service offered'. The decline in foreign student numbers in Britain since fees were raised was arguably 'due in large part to a perceived deterioration of the quality of some British universities'. Others increased their intake. 'The "quality" that matters', the report continued, 'is that perceived by the students and their sponsors i.e. by the customer. This may not necessarily be based on objective comparison, but will be influenced for example by established connections, by the marketing effort put in by different institutions and Governments, and by knowledge of the opportunities available.' Much also depended on the attitude of governments, for example 'how liberal their attitudes to exit or entry of students are'. The recognition of qualifications was also important.[12] So, too, surely were non-fee costs, though the report did not discuss them: they were elements that a student might trade off against quality or reputation.

---

[10]   p. 11.

[11]   pp. 19-20.

[12]   p. 21.

The difficulties were likely to be 'more on the supply side than on the demand side'. Indications from Australia were certainly 'most encouraging'. Demand from Malaysia – which had 65 000 students abroad – increased, as did demand fom Indonesia, Singapore, Thailand, Korea, Taiwan, Japan and Hong Kong. 'The Australian embassy in Beijing has felt obliged to stop Australian institutions holding seminars there because the number of would-be students was too great to cope with. The demand for Australian-based intensive English-language courses is estimated to be over 100,000.' There were advantages in entering the market sooner rather than later, 'because recommendations of satisfied students or graduates, and their families and friends, play an important part in the recruitment of students'.[13]

Quality and recognition came first, but New Zealand had additional points in its favour: it was English-speaking, its climate equable, its environment 'relatively secure'. VCC did not, however, think that the universities could 'offer much in the way of commercial services with their present staff and facilities', though individual Vice-Chancellors were 'more positive. ... Each identified niches which his university could cater for to some extent within present staff and facilities. With varying degrees of enthusiasm, each felt that his university could and should do a good deal more over time, as part of a general policy of capacity and flexibility of operation.'[14]

The report also discussed the courses for which demand was greatest, but which were declining New Zealand students. '[I]s there any point in contemplating the expansion of services to foreigners, outside the aid programme, until New Zealand's own problems are corrected? We agree with several Vice-Chancellors that it is best to address both issues simultaneously and as a matter of urgency.' The private sector might provide if the public could or would not. The infusion of overseas capital, and the prospect of a flow of fees income, might make private institutions more viable. It would be essential to remove 'unnecessary restraints, not only on private provision of services, but also on the public institutions'.[15]

The report turned to the costs that public institutions incurred and the charges they might levy. 'Institutions should be expected to recover in their charges the full direct and indirect costs of tuition, or of other services provided, including departmental and general overheads, and any accommodation supplied. They should not be required to recover costs not directly related to the services rendered, such as research which should

[13] pp, 21, 22.
[14] pp. 25, 26.
[15] p. 28.

be separately costed. However, there should be no objection if the profit margins for particular courses are such as to enable a contribution to be made to research or to other developments in the institution.'[16] The report was touching on an issue that was being and continued to be much debated: should teaching and research be separately funded, even though a university was commonly characterised by the linking of the two? If students were to attend universities of repute, and receive teaching from those engaged in research, it was not clear why funding it should not be included in the full-cost fee. Not doing so, indeed, implied cross-subsidisation. If the 'profit margin' ruled it out, then it might mean, to deploy a Treasury argument, that New Zealand had no competitive edge after all.

The sale of services overseas was 'one element of a strategy to make New Zealand's total education system more effective and responsive'. If it succeeded, 'the system should be capable of attracting significant numbers on a profitable basis'. If the universities could attract on commercial terms the same number as came on an assisted basis – some 2 500 – and fees were pitched at $8 000-10 000, the annual earnings would be NZ$ 20-25m. The students would number less than 5% of the student body or about 6% of EFTS. 'With numbers and enterprise, these numbers could ... be substantially increased over time with academic, cultural and financial advantage to the universities.' The report made a brief reference to living expenses here, only a brief one, though it was ostensibly about earning foreign exchange, rather than about the wider reforms of which it frequently spoke. Each student would bring into New Zealand another $6 000.[17]

In a further section of their report, the Hugo consultants considered the courses on which there were currently restrictions on New Zealanders' access. Those, they suggested, took two forms. In one – Medicine was an example – a limit was imposed in order to prevent over-supply in New Zealand. Government should reconsider that kind of approach, hardly compatible with its emphasis on 'freedom of choice'. In any case the admission of full fee students, required to leave on New Zealand on completion, would not undermine the objectives of the policy.[18]

'Excluded New Zealanders who are prepared to pay', the report went on, 'ought to be able to enjoy the same options as are accorded to the foreigners.' Such New Zealanders could seek a qualification overseas and return to use it. Why should they not be able to seek it at home? The government could limit the numbers of those it was prepared to subsidise,

---

[16] p. 37.
[17] p. 38.
[18] p. 39.

but allow institutions to provide places open to New Zealanders on an unsubsidised basis.[19] Here the consultants again shifted from their terms of reference, urging a case that, whether practical or not, would run up against political obstacles which even a 'reform' government could not face.

The other kind of limitation on New Zealand students derived, not from manpower planning, but from shortages of staff, buildings and equipment. Some overseas students had nevertheless been admitted 'in accordance with Government aid policy'. Government, the consultants thought, should fully meet their costs, and the income should be 'earmarked' to provide additional facilities and overcome shortages. But 'a more positive approach would be to overcome the domestic problems which lie behind the restrictions'.[20]

'The emphasis should be placed first on dealing with inflexibilities of personnel policy and administration which aggravate staff shortages, and on appropriate extensions of cross-crediting from technical institutes courses to university courses and vice versa.' Some of the problems might, however, 'stem from Government's unwillingness to extend the provision of funds sufficiently to permit unrestricted access by all New Zealand students on the prevailing subsidised conditions'. If so, the government should not 'obstruct private institutions from offering unsubsidised courses which are in excess demand, open to both New Zealanders and foreigners. And it should also permit public institutions to charge higher fees in areas, such as advanced courses in business administration, accountancy and law, where students will derive early private benefit from their training, and where extensive financial support for students can be expected from private and public employers or other sources. Foreign students can then be admitted to these courses on a full cost basis.'

Additional fees would increase the ability to increase staff. 'The fundamental issue is why shortages of staff persist in certain courses. One cause may be the inflexibility of salary structures and other conditions of employment in the educational institutions. ... Another may be the inflexibility of the administration and other arrangements of the institutions, and of the controlling authorities under which they operate, which inhibits their capacity and willingness to reallocate funds towards courses in excess demand and away from those less favoured. These may of course be elements aggravating a more general staffing problem arising from almost exclusive reliance on Government for funds, during a period of expenditure restraint.'[21]

---

[19] ibid.

[20] pp. 39-40.

[21] p. 40.

The report mentioned some of the changes in Australia, such as salary loadings and provision 'within judicious constraints' for outside earnings. Such flexibility was 'important not only to facilitate the expansion of services to foreigners, but to improve the New Zealand educational system generally'. If such measures were insufficient, 'we should not rule out other methods of financing access by both New Zealanders and foreigners to courses which are in demand'. The report referred to 'user pays' and to private enterprise.

The report then noted that the government was 'currently reviewing education on a wide front, including issues of pay, administration and funding of the kind mentioned'. Perhaps somewhat inconsistently, it recommended 'that the proposal for a self-fundng expansion of educational services to foreigners be considered in its own right, in terms of the net benefits which it seems likely to provide to our economy and education system. The means of staffing the expansion should be considered simultaneously with the issue of dealing with staff shortages in catering for domestic users.' It suggested that '[a] successful overseas drive' should 'alleviate the domestic problems' by 'making more resources available for education', 'providing more opportunities for qualified and enterprising New Zealanders now working overseas to base their careers here', and 'increasing the numbers of New Zealanders interested in making a full-time or part-time career in the educational services, by widening the opportunities for staff development and overseas experience'.[22]

In some cases 'an infusion of foreign students' would make for better utilisation of existing resources, through, for example, the provision of short courses in the vacations. Foreign investment might facilitate expansion. 'Fees should provide for a contribution to the capital development needed.' The liberalisation of government policy would assist in planning, 'provided it was clear that the liberalisation would endure'.[23] That, presumably, the consultants believed would assure investors and institutions that there was a long-term prospect of returns. Continuity had certainly not been a feature of overseas student policy.

That 'liberalisation' would involve repealing Section 9A of the Education Act – the 1979 bit – and amending other parts of it and possibly the individual university acts so as 'to empower institutions to offer full-fee courses outside quotas'. Private enterprise was constrained by the quota policy and by the fact that public institutions offered heavily subsidised courses to foreign students admitted under quota. Several required the approval of the Director-General. 'We favour a policy which would give

---

[22] pp. 40-1.
[23] p. 41.

private enterprises equal opportunities with public institutions in seeking to cater for the demand.'[24]

The report again alluded to the current review of New Zealand's education and training. Some might argue that it was not a good time to introduce an additional challenge. 'However, just as our major political parties have concluded that our relatively poor economic performance could be lifted through greater openness to overseas influences, so do we contend that the stimulus to be derived from the removal of constraints on entrepreneurial responses to overseas requirements in education will speed up some changes which should be made here in our own interests.'[25]

The consultants argued that, aside from staffing and salary policies, there were other areas 'where change is essential if institutions are to be enabled to respond with adequate flexibility to opportunities overseas'. The Department of Education's control over the technical institutes should be 'more decentralised and less intrusive'. There should be 'incentives for institutions to become more responsive and effective in meeting the educational, social and economic objectives at which public funding is aimed'. Funding systems could 'try to ensure a more effective division of labour among staff in respect of teaching and research'. UGC should pay 'more attention to obliging institutions to move more quickly to reallocate resources to courses where staff and facilities are deficient. The possibilities of promoting more competition among institutions, public and private, should be explored.'[26] Like Shirtcliffe, the consultants again associated their project with a larger agenda. The specific connexions are not obvious, but they may have been concerned lest the revenue they proffered proved an insulation against change, rather than a concomitant of it.

Potential customers had to be satisfied that the qualifications offered were 'of competitive quality' and would be 'recognised by those who may offer them employment in the future'. In general, the consultants believed – despite all their criticisms – that 'those graduating from New Zealand educational institutions bear favourable comparison with their counterparts in the other advanced countries which would be our major competitors'. Some feared 'that competition among institutions to secure income from overseas students will lead to deterioration of the quality of courses and/or that competition from private enterprise will weaken public institutons'. The Department of Education favoured a policy framework that would allow institutions to offer full fee courses, but wanted 'a system of licensing ... to protect quality and the interests of both overseas and

[24]   ibid.
[25]   p. 42.
[26]   p. 43.

New Zealand students'.[27] The consultants did not favour placing such authority in the hands of the Department or UGC 'because they might be unduly conservative in their decisions'. A more independent authority was required, and it might also decide whether some technical institute qualifications should lead to degrees.

Besides cost and quality, there was marketing. MDB could help institutions to explore the options, such as building on existing commercial arms, creating new organisations, or employing private enterprise. The institutions would also need to consider co-ordinating their efforts, along the lines, perhaps, of IDP in Australia. The government might offer 'some special assistance' in the early stages.

The report also considered some 'social and ethical concerns'. Some feared 'an undesirable extension of commercial principles', and argued that education should be free. Others thought that a system largely monpolised by publicly-owned institutions was 'unduly subject to the interests of the providers' and favoured more competition. They also favoured a greater element of 'user-pays'. 'Reducing restrictions on public and private agencies' capacity to respond to unsatisfied demand would make a positive contribution to economic development and to social and cultural improvement.' It was for the government to decide. But if New Zealand wanted to be 'a centre of excellence in education and training', it 'should be encouraging the widest possible range of institutions to provide what the market wants'.[28] The logic, it seems, was again ideological. There was no obvious connexion between the two ideas.

To claims that New Zealand would be 'pandering' to a wealthy elite in developing countries the consultants responded, rather cynically, (i) that '[t]he rich will always be able to look after themselves; they are in the market for educational services; and if New Zealand does not provide them then other countries will. The real issue is therefore should New Zealand forego oportunities on a vague moral stance that will then be taken up by richer countries anyway?' (ii) that '[p]roviding such services to the wealthy for fees does not reduce the potentiality to assist poorer students in low income countries but probably enhances it'. The consultants also responded to NZUSA's suggestion that full fees for foreign students were 'the thin end of the wedge'. In fact it would remain for the government of the day to decide what proportion of educational services would be financed by taxpayers. 'Successful sales to foreigners would strengthen the financial capacity of New Zealand educational institutions and enhance their potential to serve New Zealanders better.'[29]

---

[27]   ibid.

[28]   pp. 45-6.

[29]   pp. 46-7.

The government would need to assure institutions 'not only that they may retain earnings from their services to foreigners, but also that decisions on grants and subsidies for domestic educational purposes will not be affected by their success'. Nor need there be any reduction in aid, either in terms of scholarships offered or in terms of the quota of private students.[30]

At about the same time as the Watts report appeared, Treasury's advice to the new government was published, *Government Management*. Its section on tertiary education emphasised the 'private good' concept of its 1984 advice and the notion of a market. '[A]ny government interpolation between consumers and suppliers is liable to have very substantial costs ... because government decision makers cannot possibly reflect the range of needs and choices that would occur were customers and providers to contract directly with each other.'[31] That kind of argument paralleled the ideology in the more general parts of the Hugo report. Treasury also included a whole section on Private Overseas Student Policy, the proposals in which were more or less identical with those of the report.[32] It thus fell on fertile ground, and there was no longer any Marshall aid for an alternative view.

The MDB report Caldwell considered 'very comprehensive'. Its recommendations 'closely' followed those the officials made in the report of December 1986, deferred by the External Relations and Security Committee, and 'presumably pigeonholed since that time'.[33] In fact, of course, the officials had been divided on a number of issues. The MDB report, commissioned out of frustration, offered a way out of the impasse by advocating the boldest options. Caldwell recognised that, if the government wished to proceed with the report – 'and it is not a matter which could easily be shelved' – then the various problems in the approval of a framework needed to be dealt with. He did not favour setting up a separate authority for approving qualifications: UGC could work with private institutions. He cautioned against free entry in secondary schools before tertiary capacity was increased. A measure of licensing would be desirable, given the failure of two business colleges in Auckland in the 1970s.[34]

Moore had sent the report to the Cabinet Development and Marketing Committee on 19 November. The Minister of Education and the Associate Minister, Phil Goff, had, he said, endorsed its thrust. A survey quoted by

---

[30] p. 47.
[31] *Government Management*, Wellington: Treasury, 1987, p. 179.
[32] ibid., pp. 255-68.
[33] Memorandum, 20.11.87. UGC Box 93.
[34] ibid.

the report suggested that three out of four New Zealanders would support earning foreign exchange from educational services. Moore recommended that the Committee should endorse the statement that the education system was first and foremost for New Zealanders, and also endorse the statement that a key policy was the promotion of exchange earnings from educational services on a basis that was not subsidised by taxpayers and did not conflict with access by New Zealanders or with aid policies. Officials should report back on the steps necessary to implement the report, and on the implications of doing so, by 1 March 1988.[35] Meeting on 25 November 1987, the Cabinet Committtee accepted the recommendations. The committee of officials was to be chaired by a representative from Education [B. Ashton].[36]

The officials recommended that the Committee should adopt a number of resolutions. Inter alia, it should agree that state educational institutions should be empowered to charge full fees to overseas students entering on a non-quota basis, such fees to include direct and indirect costs, and at the discretion of the institutions 'a margin of profit'. The Department of Education and UGC should set out how full fees should be calculated 'so as to avoid cross-subsidisation from taxpayer funds'. The proceeds should be retained by the institutions 'for their own purposes', and Government should give an assurance 'that public funding of subsidised courses will not be reduced by income derived from full-fee courses'. Foreign Affairs, in consultation with Education, UGC and Treasury, should report on the implications for ODA and 'implications of the introduction of a full-fees non-quota overseas student policy for the existing student aid programme which could involve changes in present provisional quota targets'.

Officials were divided over secondary schools. Should they be allowed, as Treasury, MDB and Trade and Industry thought, to start without delay? or should they be allowed, as Education and the UGC thought, to start 'only after admission to tertiary institutions has been operational for sufficient time to ensure that upon leaving school there will be a sufficient number of places at tertiary level for overseas students'?

The officials also considered that 'quality control facilities' were 'desirable to assist providers in marketing their services and to provide a degree of protection for overseas students'. An independent validation authority was being considered. Officials differed as to whether private institutions should be compulsorily subject to quality control or merely encouraged to seek approval. Some kind of coordinating body or bodies was desirable for marketing 'with voluntary membership'. UGC and

---

[35] Memorandum, 19.11.87. ibid.; also Box 97.
[36] DM (87) M 33/1, 25.11.87. UGC Box 97.

Education were to have a 'watchdog' role, drawing attention to misleading advertising and unfair trading. In such comments, officials were reflecting different views of the market and its 'discipline', and, implicitly, their relevance to education.

The report agreed that 'where supply difficulties arise from inflexibility of administration or in conditions of service, then these inflexibilities should be tackled rather than simply declining to admit more overseas students'. Supply constraints imposed in the interest of preventing 'over-supply' in some categories should not prevent the admission of full-fee overseas or New Zealand students. State universities and polytechnics 'should continue to use the discretion they already have over the level of their fees in order to be able to accept user-paying domestic students into courses with considerable private benefits where such students would otherwise be excluded because of resource constraints'. An annex to the officials' report [B] did not suggest there was much discretion, however: 'At present regulations prevent publicly financed institutions from charging fees to cover costs except for some special continuing education courses.' A state institution wishing to restrict the entry of New Zealand students to particular courses should obtain the assent of UGC or the Department before admitting full-fee students. Where New Zealand students were excluded because of resource constraints, UGC or Education should consult with the institution and the Government 'to ascertain what can be done to remedy the situation and to avoid, if at all possible, denying entry to full-fee overseas students'.[37]

Another annex [G] suggested that the Hugo report was not clear on the integration of ODA and full fees policies. A review of quota arrangements would be needed. In placing ODA students, MFA – which would now have to buy at full-cost rather than receive the benefit of imputed cost – would seek the best possible arrangements, public or private. It identified five areas of concern. a. a consequent reduction of private students from the South Pacific would not be in 'New Zealand's self-interest'. Some additional ODA funding would be needed. b. 'ASEAN Governments (Malaysia and Singapore) will not welcome elimination of current subsidies for private students, but their replacement by unrestricted entry on a full fees basis would have some long term benefits. ... Early consultations emphasising the longer term benefits should minimise the reaction of ASEAN Governments.' c. priority access for ODA students would have to continue. d. 'additional funding for ODA-funded students may be needed to meet full-fee costs not covered in calculations for imputation e.g. market development costs, return on investment'. e. transitional

---

[37]   Report, sent to D and M Committee, 9.5.88. UGC Box 94; also AU.

arrangements were needed for those students already in the system. Education considered that the Government's provisional commitment on a subsidised policy should be maintained. The issue had been much discussed in Commonwealth circles, and New Zealand's abolition of the $1500/1000 fee held up as a model for removing barriers to mobility.

The Hugo report may be read as proposing still to retain the quota of Pacific/ASEAN students who came for domestic fees, previously for $1500/1000; but officials evidently did not take that view. A supplementary note from MFA makes that plain. 'The current system of concessional/subsidised entry from South Pacific and ASEAN countries would be abolished.' Either students would come on ODA scholarships or under the full-fee regime. MFA raised other questions. Would New Zealand admit paying students from Libya or South Africa? How could the flow of students from the South Pacific be maintained, given that there were few wealthy families, that their governments were financially constrained, and that the students might face competition from better qualified students from other countries? 'We would not necessarily replicate existing arrangements for South Pacific students if starting now from scratch.' But access increased New Zealand's influence in the region, 'a principal foreign policy objective', and 'given the prominence private student access has in government-to-government relations (in terms of both numbers and the status of many of the students)' abrupt change would provoke an adverse reaction from South Pacific governments. Some way of funding access was necessary. At present some 1552 were in NZ.

Limits on access had long been 'a source of contention in our relations with Malaysia and Singapore', MFA continued. It thought that 'the extra cost they would face under a full-fee system should be balanced by the greater access they would enjoy in the longer term to the New Zealand education system', though it would be some time before places could be created especially in the subjects most in demand. MFA considered the fees would be affordable in ASEAN and competitive with Australia and North America. But governments that sponsored significant numbers of students were likely to express concern, though transitional arrangements for students already in the system would help. Other Commonwealth governments were unlikely to exert 'significant pressure' against a full-fee regime, but New Zealand's commitment to intra-Commonwealth mobility might be cited by Commonwealth ASEAN and South Pacific governments.

ODA students would need still to enjoy a preference, since many of those from the South Pacific were less well qualified. The new system would offer MFA greater transparency than the imputed cost system, but it would be more costly. If a full economic fee were now charged, MFA would need additional funding if it was to provide the same number of

ODA awards. 'Provided the present allocation for imputed costs remains within the ODA programme, it should be possible in the longer term to use funds not needed for ASEAN private students to pay full fees for ODA students, and still have funds available to subsidise some South Pacific students, but probably not at current levels for private students.' In the short term, however, additional funding might be needed to support private students already in the system.

'The introduction of the full-fee regime has the potential over time to solve problems of limited capacity and eliminate the need for restrictive quotas, while removing the New Zealand Government from the funding of private overseas students. It should produce foreign policy benefits in the form of New Zealand-educated constituencies overseas in greater numbers and from a wider range of countries than is possible under the present quota system.'

In Annex H, officials noted the larger changes Hugo proposed. Several reviews were already or about to get under way, including Picot on education administration, Watts, and the Hawke report on PCET. The larger changes should be considered in reponse to them: 'the bulk of the state education system should not be changed simply in order to accommodate commercial courses for overseas students. However it seems very probable that greater flexibility, decentralisation, and better incentive structures would serve the interests of domestic students as well as allowing state institutions to compete more effectively in the overseas student market.'

If full-fee entry into secondary schools were allowed, 'overseas students could well be leaving school before a sufficient number of spaces have become available at tertiary institutions to allow them entry'. UGC and Education pointed out that under the National government's policy of open entry at private schools, 'there were 500 Malaysian students who would have sought university places which were not available', and Labour had withdrawn the policy as a result. Treasury, MDB, and Labour disagreed: 'some secondary students would come to New Zealand seeking a safe, English speaking environment for secondary schooling before proceeding elsewhere ... for tertiary education.' Overseas students could be 'removed' if ineligible for further study. The notion was somewhat unrealistic. Students had looked for pathways and were to continue to do so.

Another annex [J] provided a fuller account of the ways in which officials were in dispute over quality control. MDB, they agreed, was 'not very specific' about the 'watchdog authority'. Where they differed was over recourse to the proposed validation authority: was it, as the report proposed, to be voluntary, or was it to be compulsory? All agreed that it was 'vital to a successful export drive that quality control facilities are available. Such facilities would serve a two-fold purpose: they would provide providers which do not have an established reputation with a status that would assist them in marketing their services and they would assure potential students that courses and awards have met the standards of a reliable authority.' Education, UGC, and Tourist and Publicity thought quality control should be compulsory for private as well as public providers. First, they considered that a student visa conferred an element of official recognition. Second, they were concerned lest substandard courses should be offered, and undermine the reputation of the rest. 'They consider that the imperatives of the market place could lead to lowering of entry standards and the devaluation of qualifications – such developments would not only jeopardise the export business generally but also lead to adverse political reaction.'

Labour and Treasury, on the other hand, agreed with Hugo that voluntary procedures were preferable. 'Compulsory controls could restrict the ability of institutions to respond rapidly to the changing overseas student market. The competitiveness of that market should encourage the maintenance of standards. They would expect that many institutions would seek external quality control either with the body responsible for funding providers in the domestic market or with a validation authority. Providers and government departments would need to prepare documentation on quality control procedures, and indicate clearly where validation of a course has been given by the relevant national authority. Overseas posts would have an important role in disseminating this documentation.'

The officials' report was considered by the Development and Marketing Committee at a meeting on 18 May, the agenda for which also covered the Rotorua Geothermal Management Programme, the direct marketing of synthetic gasoline, and a review of the glassware industry development plan.[38] Officials did not get in, nor did ministers reveal the outcome on leaving.[39] The Committee had in fact accepted the agreed recommendations. It decided that the full-fees policy should apply to secondary schools without delay. Courses in institutions not already subject to some form of state quality monitoring would be subject to quality control by UGC or Education or the validation authority being considered by the Ministers of Education and Labour. It directed that MFA, in consultation with Education, UGC and Treasury should report to the Domestic and External Security Committee on the implications for foreign policy and ODA of introducing a full-fee non-quota system.[40]

Considering this on 24 May, Cabinet added a directive: officials should

[38] D & M (87) A 15, 16.5.88. UGC Box 97.
[39] Note by Wills fo Caldwell, 18.5.88. ibid.
[40] Minutes, 18.5.88. D & M (88) M 15/1. ibid.

report also on the practicability and implications of retaining 'the present level of non-fee paying places for private students as a continuing category'.[41] In other words, should there be a two-tier [ODA and full-fee] or a three-tier system [ODA, full-fee, and subsidised fee]? Foreign Affairs had assumed that the last category had disappeared. Treasury had indeed argued against funding for 1988 the extra places to which the government had committed itself in 1986.[42]

MFA reiterated its view. ASEAN students would pay a full fee. 'Concerns have been expressed that a full-fee system would make it much more difficult for the poorer students from South East Asia to come to New Zealand. The evidence is, though, that ASEAN students who have achieved highly enough in their own education system to qualify for entry to a New Zealand course or a state institution are not likely to be in the poorest category. Their sponsors (parents, or employers) already do meet the cost of their airfares, accommodation and living costs.' ASEAN countries might complain at first, but 'in the longer term the removal of quota restrictions would meet the concerns they have frequently expressed. At first they would see themselves simply as having to pay for what they were formerly given free of charge with no immediate increase in the number of places available to them (but in time fees revenue would fund the creation of extra places). In the longer term, though, the greater access this extra capacity would provide, should bring positive foreign policy benefits.' Transitional arrangements would be needed for those who started 3-year courses in 1988.

The costs would not be affordable in South Pacific countries. Moving to full-cost would reduce the number of private students drastically and result in 'a political backlash against New Zealand'. Some support should be offered, perhaps in the form of fees scholarships for development-related courses. Alternatively the South Pacific governments could use the funds to make their own institutions 'more self-sufficient'.

Foreign Affairs argued against a three-tier system. It would involve the commitment of 'a growing proportion of the ODA allocation to subsidised students enrolled in courses of no developmental relevance and in many cases from countries to which New Zealand would not otherwise choose to divert such a large volume of ODA funding (Malaysia)'. In 1988-9 $28.445m would be needed to meet the cost of overseas students: only $5.263m, 18.5%, was for the tuition costs of ODA students. 'The continued presence of subsidised students at the present levels would leave little surplus capacity in the State institutions for generating full-fee

---

[41]   CM 88/18/9. ibid.
[42]   Cf Memorandum, 29.1.88. ibid.

revenue and hence the resources for future expansion. Such a dominant subsidy mechanism would also produce price distortions.'

UGC did not support the 3-tier system which had 'worked inequitably'. It would welcome a 2-tier system if that meant that the universities would recover actual expenditure for government sponsored or scholarship students and charging the rest full fees. 'The savings thus made would provide a healthy input towards implementing the current "Kiwis first" policy, as the availability of places built specially for fully funded overseas students becomes available, [and] frees the places held by them at present.' The two-tier system would also put a brake on 'the ever increasing flood of applications'.

The Department of Education was more concerned about the reaction in the Commonwealth, where Ministers and Heads of Government had supported the principle that fees should be less than full cost. Treasury questioned whether, 'in the light of the pressing need for fiscal restraint', the funds released by the new policy should all be committed to aid. In any case, the amount available was unclear, and it would have to be decided annually. That MFA contested.[43]

A UGC paper summarised the policy decisions and circulated them to the VCs. It spoke of 'registering' the courses to be offered to overseas students, including details of content and assessment, fees, numbers, and sufficient information to make it clear that no cross-subsidisation was involved. University courses were to be registered with UGC, given its statutory responsibility to advise the government on the need for university education and research. 'The registering of courses and numbers will provide publicity material which should act as an incentive for other institutions to emulate.' The memorandum also covered the legislative changes required, in particular allowing universities to charge differential fees for foreign students or for domestic students in a closed course.[44]

The Standing Committee on Overseas Students that VCC had finally set up, under Tarling's chairmanship, had met on 29 January 1988 to draft comments on the Hugo report. The VCs themselves thought its report insufficiently positive,[45] though they did not amend it very much. It was sent on to UGC, with an indication that VCC took 'no firm position' on its recommendations, but would be interested in any comment.[46]

The comments began by reiterating that universities welcomed the contribution and goodwill of foreign students, and by endorsing their

---

[43]   Memorandum, 28.6.88. UGC Box 94. Sent to Committee as DES (18) 15. ibid.
[44]   Memorandum by Caldwell, 17.6.88. AU.
[45]   Cf Tarling/Malcolm, 15.2.88; Taiaroa/Tarling, 31.3.88; Tarling/Ross, 8.4.88. AU.
[46]   Taiaroa/Caldwell, 11.5.88. UGC Box 97.

further diversification. The Standing Committee also believed that there were opportunities for marketing educational services which the universities could take up. But it questioned whether Hugo had correctly identified them. It doubted whether the main emphasis should be 'on providing for undergraduate courses in high demand in New Zealand as elsewhere'. It also doubted the potential financial rewards. It was by no means certain that those who could not secure places before would now wish to take up places on a full-cost basis. There was, moreover, little spare capacity in the fields most in demand. 'As a result, not only staff, but buildings would have to be provided, and their costs met by the overseas students concerned. Indeed the costs might be amplified by the need to make provision for counselling and other support services of which overseas students are in need.' But, if immediate demand was uncertain, there was also 'little to show that the demand would be persistent enough to justify the venture'. By investing in it, universities might find that they had depleted their resources rather than increased them.

'In addition universities could not accept that the full-cost should exclude a research component. Universities are distinguished by their association by their association of research and teaching. If research is to be met out of the profit ..., one or the other will be eliminated.' Quality might be sacrificed, too, 'particularly if the numbers of those well qualified fall away before the investment is recouped'. The quality controls Hugo proposed were too weak. 'If New Zealand universities are attractive overseas, it is partly because of the reputation they have built up, as a result of the taxpayers' investment and the efforts of staff and students. It would be no service to them, or even to a marketing venture, if standards were allowed to fall.'

The Standing Committee offered an alternative approach, building in part on some earlier ideas. There were 'other opportunities ... probably more appropriate for New Zealand than entering the international market for large-scale undergraduate courses in currently popular subjects, or the intensely competitive market for less popular subjects'. They involved 'exploring the niches in the market which New Zealand could fill'. Those might be in fields where, 'at least temporarily', there was spare capacity, and places could thus be offered at marginal cost. 'Places in appropriate areas of study or research might also be found or created by developing specific projects or entering contracts or undertaking joint ventures with overseas institutions. This would use and expand New Zealand expertise and add to our critical mass in research, without over-extending our capacity in terms of staffing or accommodation.'

The alternative approach, the Committee thought, had 'another advantage'. Universities in New Zealand would be able to build links with universities and other institutions overseas. 'It seems likely, indeed, that the future should not be seen in terms of the movement of masses of undergraduate students across the globe. Rather there will be [a] need to support the development of local and regional institutions by assisting them to upgrade staffing and enhancing the research experience of their students and junior staff. In some cases, of course, it would still be important to stress undergraduate training. But more of that might be in terms of taking students in-course for a limited period in New Zealand rather than offering them a whole undergraduate degree.'

The Standing Committee suggested that, by adopting its suggestions, New Zealand might 'move ahead of others', while also doing what was within its capacities. Even with the aid of MDB, however, the universities could not activate such a policy on their own. 'It requires, within the university system, a government-supported agency that will coordinate activities, analyse projects, help to secure funding, monitor results, and assist in administration.' Success, it added, would also depend on 'consistency of policy'. The field had been marked by a variety of policies. 'Once a viable and acceptable policy is agreed, it should be sustained. Otherwise planning may be wasted, programmes disrupted, and students misled.'

'In our view', the Standing Committee concluded, 'the interests of New Zealand and of overseas countries may indeed be complementary, but not in the sense the Report for the most part appears to contemplate. The increasing capacity of developing countries to provide their own undergraduate education encourages New Zealand to concentrate on helping them to upgrade it, by providing opportunity for their staff and research students on a basis of mutual benefit. This would be a proper field of academic enterprise. In the longer run it would help us to consolidate centres of excellence based on our universities which would be of national and international significance, particularly in the Pacific region.'[47]

The Watts report – the NZVCC-commissioned report, *New Zealand's Universities: Partners in National Development* – had appeared in October 1987. It made some reference to overseas students, and its suggestions seem to have influenced the Standing Committee's report in January 1988. User-pays might be more appropriate for them than for domestic students, since their families paid no income tax, and given the pressure on space, the fees ought to be full-cost. New Zealand and its universities could gain from their international marketing as 'providers of high quality education, but given the degree of international competition specific market "niches"

---

47 Memorandum, 'Hugo Report', faxed 20.4.88. AU.

would need to be identified'. Several factors had to be considered: the requirement not to disadvantage New Zealand students; the need to be competitive; the 'credit and goodwill' gained by offering some places at concessionary rates; and the contribution overseas graduate students made to research that benefited New Zealand. 'On balance, it would appear appropriate to levy a significant portion of the real cost from foreign students, but to supplement this with scholarships, bursaries or grants for those to whom it is wished to give access as part of the New Zealand aid programme to Third World countries and for foreign research students whose presence contributes to the critical mass necessary for effective research within the universities.'[48]

The Hawke report – which appeared in September 1988 – proposed a radical restructuring of Post Compulsory Education and Training, including the abolition of UGC, the 'chartering' of public and private institutions, the creation of a special agency to disburse research funding within PCET, the establishment of a qualifications authority, and the introduction of fees and loans. It made no explicit recommendations on overseas students, but noted the officials' report on Hugo. That required establishing and monitoring guidelines on fee calculations to ensure that there was no cross-subsidisation from taxpayer funds, and under the proposed reform, that would be task of the new Ministry of Education. It also required the provision of quality control, and there the principal agency would be the new Qualifications Authority. Third, it would require the protection of New Zealanders' access to courses, which could be covered in the charter negotiations between Ministry and institutions. The Hawke group endorsed MDB's view 'that exporting educational services should not be allowed to disrupt provision in New Zealand's aid programme for supporting overseas students, especially those from the South Pacific'.[49]

The Hugo report had seen the overseas student policy it proposed as a contribution towards changes in university policy in general. In fact, though its recommendations were largely endorsed, their implementation became entangled with, and to some extent delayed by, the changes in education policy that were promoted by the Picot report, *Administering for Excellence*, and the Hawke committee. The Cabinet meeting on 24 May sought a report on the legislative amendments that would be required to implement the changes in overseas student policy on which it resolved.

---

[48] pp. 87-8.

[49] Report of the Working Group on Post Compulsory Education and Training [aka Hawke Reprt], prepared for the Cabinet Socila Equity Committee, 31.3.88, p. 67.

Those, the Minister of Education reported on 22 July, would be 'lengthy and complex', and would be better formulated in the light of the Government's decisions on the recommendations of Picot and Hawke. In the meantime, polytechnics could be allowed to offer full-fee courses to overseas students, particularly in English as a foreign language, and, with DOE approval, in some other subjects. The universities had identified some opportunities in English language and subjects not in high demand. A small amendment to the fees section in the Acts was needed: without it, the Human Rights Commission thought that 'a case could succeed on the grounds of racial discrimination'. The universities, it was expected, could develop a formula 'which could be satisfactorily used in the interim'.[50]

Early in September DOE officials outlined, at the Minister's request, the legislation that would be needed to allow the enrolment of full fee students. Given their complexity, and the fact that the amendments would affect a number of acts, 'the Statutes Amendment Bill is not a suitable vehicle for the changes. In fact, the legislation … is likely to be contentious and the Select Committee is likely to be used as a forum for criticism and possible attack of [sic] the changes proposed following decisions on the Picot and Hawke reports.' Introduced now, the amendments would have to fit 'the existing tightly regulated system'. A different set of provisions would be needed under the 'freer' system of the post-Picot post-Hawke legislation.[51]

The UGC by contrast told the Associate Minister that it thought barriers to admission of full fee foreign students could be removed so that entry could begin in 1989. Not to do would 'certainly cause a great deal of frustration in the universities'. The amendment suggested 'seems to be of the kind which could gain opposition concurrence and have a place in the Statutes Amendment Bill'.[52]

At its meeting on 19 September Cabinet agreed that universities should have the power to enrol full-fee paying foreign students in the 1989 academic year. The amendment could be included in the Law Reform (Miscellaneous) Bill, or, if that were not practicable, in a separate Education Amendment Bill. The legislation for entry into polytechnics and schools would be enacted in the context of the legislation for reform and allow entry in 1990.[53] But the amendment was delayed, apparently by a recurrence to the notion of 'three tiers'.

[50] Lange Memorandum for Cabinet, 22.7.88. UGC Box 94.
[51] Memorandum by Egan for Minister, n.d., sent Edginton/Caldwell, FAX, 2.9.89. UGC Box 97.
[52] Memorandum, 5.9.88. ibid.
[53] CM 88/35/13A. ibid.

The same Cabinet meeting had also dealt with the transition to a full-fee regime. That, it agreed in principle, would start in 1990, and cover students who started that year, and also those who started in 1989 and 'were therefore forewarned of the new regime before their applications were accepted'. Tuition costs would be met for those currently completing a basic undergraduate, teachers college or polytechnic course for the mimimum period required for completion, and, from existing funds, merit scholarships could be offered to overseas secondary and postgraduate university students. A subcommittee comprising the Minister of Overseas Trade and Marketing, the Minister of Foreign Affairs, the Associate Minister of Education, and the Deputy Minister of Finance, David Caygill, was 'to determine the level and manner of the distribution of sponsored assistance to overseas students'. It should work on the basis that aid funding, at present $28.8m, should continue at that level, giving first priority to the grandparenting, second to assistance to Bilateral Aid Programme [BAP] students, third to Government sponsored and private students from the South Pacific, and fourth to those from ASEAN, determining which ASEAN countries and students should have priority. The costs were to be calculated so as to include operating costs, a share of capital costs, 'in some instances marketing costs, and also the margin for profit built in by the educational institutions', the last being negotiated with the government so far as aid students were concerned. Officials were to report to the subcommittee by 17 October on implementing these decisions and on any problems they foresaw.[54]

Following a meeting of the sub-committee of ministers, Marshall, Caygill and Goff, Goff asked for a revised paper for Cabinet. Their idea was that there should be three categories, New Zealand students, Quota students, who would be treated like New Zealand students and number perhaps some 4200 in all, and full fee students, unlimited, provided they were not enrolled at the expense of New Zealand students. Three advantages were listed. '1. There would be no need for any transition. 2. Opposition to the proposal would be extremely hard to sustain. 3. It would be more difficult in future for Government to cut back on aid assistance as an easy option for budget cuts.' Some areas needed clarification, however. It would cost over the $28.8m. If the Hawke proposals were adopted, there would, however, be savings, inasmuch as Quota students would pay the increased domestic fees. 4200 might still be 'unrealistic'.[55]

The idea received little support. UGC argued strongly for the full fee

[54] CM 88/35/13B. ibid.
[55] Memorandum by Anna Sharman, 11.11.88. ibid.

scheme. Finance would become available to erect new buildings and create new courses. More foreign exchange would be earned. Universities would be encouraged to be 'innovative' and 'cost effective', so as to compete with the UK, USA and Australia. They had a low cost base, and that would enable them to compete effectively. '[D]ropping the subsidised private overseas programme will create a strong initial base to launch the full fee programme.' The subsidised programme had disadvantages. '[U]nder the New Zealand first and foremost policy, increased domestic demand will squeeze out overseas students.' Given that universities had to find resources out of block grants, 'maintaining present intake levels will become increasingly difficult'. University rolls were increasing, and that would reduce the quotas they could offer. The aid programme was intended to support students who would return to their own countries, but in the year ended September 1987 1047 were given permanent residence. '[B]ecause full fee students can be accepted only when the existing subsidised programme is satisfied, the capacity of the full fee programme will be too limited to become economically important for universities.'[56]

In another memo, Caldwell had told MDB that MFA, UGC, institutions and New Zealand students all saw the full-cost scheme as 'desirable/ inevitable'. The alternative proposal would 'find little favour with the providers'. The New Zealand taxpayer was subsidising students from countries 'hardly "underdeveloped"'. Malaysia wanted places, not necessarily subsidised places. Treasury wanted to restrain education expenditure. MFA would prefer to pay for 'aid' only. MDB had convinced NZUSA that the programme was no threat to them. 'The academics saw an increased Government vote for university education as unlikely.' The UK scheme – government funding for local or aid students and user-pays for the rest – they saw as 'the best solution in the current economic climate'.[57] Never an enthusiast for the 'subsidised' scheme, Caldwell recognised that the universities would, especially in a UGC-less future, need all the revenue they could find.

Foreign Affairs offered its own views. It had, it maintained, consistently supported the full fee proposal and believed the proposal for a quota should be rejected. 'The continued presence of subsidised students at, or around, present levels would leave little surplus capacity in the State institutions for generating full-fee revenue and hence the resources for future expansion.' The retention of a subsidised quota system would 'seriously undermine' a full fees policy. A full fees policy would serve New

---

[56] Foreign Student Programmes UGC View, sent by Caldwell, 17.11.88: 'My bit for Ministerial memo'. ibid.

[57] Caldwell/Farrelly, 16.11.88. ibi.

Zealand's foreign interests, opening up places for students from Asia, while retaining money in the aid vote for the South Pacific and other developing countries. Malaysia wanted fee concessions, but if there were a quota it would want a significant share for those it sponsored, and 'it would be difficult to target much of the quota to Malaysian Chinese students if that were desired'. Under the current arrangement a large part of the aid was outside the control of its managers. 'While the imputed student cost item has a development outcome it is not necessarily the best outcome which could be achieved using these funds.' A dual system would be difficult to administer and possibly politically damaging.[58]

At its meeting on 5 December Cabinet rescinded the decisions of 19 September, but without taking up the notion of a quota. There would be four categories of students: 1. New Zealand; 2. ODA students; 3. privately sponsored or own Government students whose tuition costs were paid by Vote Foreign Affairs; and 4. private overseas students who themselves paid full costs. The money appropriated for imputed student costs would be retained in Vote Foreign Affairs, and used initially for grandparenting, and later for awards. Full fees would be required from 1990 for those in the fourth category, including those enrolled for their first year in 1989.[59]

The Hawke recommendations did not have an easy passage, though much of their substance was finally embodied in the Education Amendment Act 1990. The decisions on overseas students went ahead along their 'separate' path, but not without some government apprehensions about public controversy. Those were, it seems, to be minimised by timing. The essential decision was taken by Cabinet on 5 December 1988. The announcement was embargoed till midnight on Boxing Day, three weeks later. 'I wanted to make the announcement before Christmas but we ran into time delays', the Associate Minister of Education said.[60]

OSAC had in fact advised overseas students who were being offered a place for the first time in 1989 before the Boxing night announcement was made. The letter warned students that, while in 1989 they would pay the domestic fee [now $516], they would from 1989 pay the full cost fee, expected to be, it was added, $8 000 for Arts, Commerce, Law, and Humanities, and $14 000 for Science, Computer Science, Engineering, Agriculture and other applied subjects. 'The introduction of a full fees regime is regretted, but the rapid increase in enrolments by New Zealand students has led to such a shortage of resources that only two options are available: either to stop enrolling overseas students; or to charge full costs

58   Memorandum by Hannah for Minister FA, n.d. ibid.
59   CM 88/4/19. ibid.
60   Star, 27.12.88.
61   Memorandum by Murtagh, 19.12.88. AU.

so that new facilities could be put in place for them in future.'[61]

Hugo was victor: the rhetoric of the report, rather than its research, carried the day. That success – sweeping earlier reservations aside – derived, however, in part from its association with other education reforms for which it had argued and which were put through by the re-elected government. Insofar as there was public consultation, it tended to focus on those reforms. The changes they envisaged, moreover, made it ever more clear that the universities would need the money. That UGC emphasised, while MFAT argued that current 'aid' could be better used. In the sudden rush to a decision, the notion that New Zealand might focus on 'niche' markets, though put up, was sidelined.

CHAPTER EIGHT

LEGISLATION

'The Government has reversed its longstanding opposition to high fees for overseas students in a bid to earn export income from New Zealand's educational services', as the *New Zealand Herald* put it. The election manifesto had boasted that the fee had been abolished. Now Marshall's policy had been abandoned. P'ng Sim Guan, president of the union of Malaysian students in New Zealand, said it would mean that students from poorer families could no longer afford to study in New Zealand. Those that did come would have to limit their cultural input, as they would be trying to complete in the shortest possible time. 'He believed that the imposition of full fees would make overseas students look elsewhere. Universities in Australia, the United States and Britain would be the first choice, because they were considered superior institutions.' The contribution already made – through student expenditure in New Zealand – had been overlooked. Andrew Little, then president of NZUSA, said standards could decline, as had happened in Britain. 'He also warned that the policy could be a first step towards charging full fees for New Zealand students.' The government had not done 'enough homework. ... Widespread doubts existed whether in fact there was a big demand for overseas students to get degrees in New Zealand.'[1] The government had abolished the $1000 as discriminatory, Little said. 'If $1000 is discriminatory, I can't imagine what $14 000 is.'[2] He seemed less convinced by MDB than Caldwell had suggested.

Goff described Little's comments as 'absolute nonsense'. ODA students

---

[1]   NZH, 27.12.88.
[2]   Star, 27.12.88.

would not be affected by the changes, he said. 'A large portion of the market was likely to be teaching English to Japanese students... "Why should the New Zealand taxpayer subsidise students from Japan, Taiwan and Brunei?"'[3] Jim Anderton, rebel backbencher, claimed the government had breached a promise to consult the party over non-manifesto initiatives. Two members of the party's policy committee, Kate Boanas and Chris Tremewan, said they were 'angry' that Goff's announcement had not been 'referred to the party's consultative process'.[4]

Had there been sufficient research? Louise Callan asked in the *Auckland Star*. No one, she noted, seemed to be talking, as they had when fees were first imposed, of the 'gratitude principle'. Maybe there was 'no room for such an emotionally based form of repayment in an increasingly competitive and pragmatic world'. Nothing was said either of the friendships and personal knowledge formed on campus. Those, she thought, would continue. Was the government too optimistic? Would standards be lowered? Once the system was in place, she pointed out, it would be difficult to displace, for it would become 'a basic financial ingredient of institutions' budgets and operating systems, and the education vote'.[5]

Lamenting the lack of consultation, the Deputy Vice-Chancellor at Auckland, Tarling, also expressed concern about lowering standards. His university would ensure, however, that it did not happen. It would after all 'provide only short-lived gains. Once the students returned home the reputation of the institution would be damaged, thus attracting fewer students in the future.' He also drew attention to overseas research students. Those who started in 1989 would have to pay full costs in 1990, as would any who started that year. 'I can't see why they'd keep coming.' Yet many of their topics were New Zealand-related and they helped to provide critical mass in the research schools. A spokesman for Goff told the *Star* that the government would 'look into the matter'.[6] Goff himself subsequently suggested that universities could use some of their 'profits' – from short courses for Japanese, for example – to subsidise overseas research students. 'We're supposed to be doing an awful lot with the purported profits ..., including providing better facilities for New Zealand students', Tarling said.[7]

The current VCC chairman, Wilf Malcolm, Vice-Chancellor of Waikato, was reportedly more positive. Initially, the *Herald* wrote, the universities

---

[3]   ibid.
[4]   NZH, 29.12.88.
[5]   Star, 29.12.88.
[6]   ibid.
[7]   Star, 17.1.89.

had seen full-cost fees as 'a threat to New Zealanders struggling to get into popular courses', but the new policy was now welcomed 'as a source of much-needed income'. Dr Malcolm 'said the universities had changed their minds after the Government gave a commitment to increasing access for New Zealand students, and after they realised that the extra money from foreign students' fees would help to expand existing courses'.[8] The universities had 'already got together to back a private company called Consult New Zealand Education', the *Herald* reported. Chaired by Sir Frank Holmes, project leader for the Hugo report, it had already begun to promote New Zealand's educational services in Japan.

MDB had called a meeting with university representatives in June. They had been told that the Cabinet Social Equity Committee had approved full-cost fees in principle, that the delay in introducing legislation arose from opposition in caucus, that it was nevertheless expected that it would be introduced in July/August, and that full-cost fees would start in 1989. They would have to include all costs, including capital costs, and could not be based on marginal costs. The university representatives emphasised that they were 'financially and physically stretched and could not contemplate full-cost students in areas of currently high popularity such as Computer Science and Commerce'. Niche-marketing was seen as 'the sensible way to proceed'.[9]

In November Sir Frank Holmes offered the VCs advance notice of the formation of Consult New Zealand Education Limited [CNZEL]. It was to be 'a marketing company, promoting and facilitating foreign exchange earnings through the sale of educational services (courses, resources, skills and expertise) to foreign students, institutions and governments and through international organisations'. It would not itself be a provider. Its main functions would be '[t]o promote the sale of quality educational services to and within the target market countries and through international organisations', and '[t]o facilitate the process of recruitment of full fee paying students for study at any of New Zealand's wide range of quality educational establishments'.

The formation of the company, Sir Frank explained, had been initiated by 'a consortium consisting of six educational institutions with a particular interest in distance education' – VUW, OU, MU, Correspondence School, Technical Correspondence Institute, DSIR[10] – the New Zealand Trade Development Board, and the Hugo Consulting Group. It was 'particularly fortunate to have the strong support and backing of the Trade Develop-

---

8   NZH, 27.12.89.
9   Notes from meeting by R. Geddes, 14.6.88. AU.
10   *Dominion,* 19.6.89.

ment Board, an official agency with offices in the major potential market places, in this venture'. It also appreciated 'positive encouragement' from Government minsters and opposition spokesmen. It had received a 'very positive' response in its briefing sessions with 'potential shareholders and clients'. To succeed, however, the company needed support and backing from New Zealand's 'established educational organisations'. Now was the time for them to provide that support and backing by taking shares in the company. By becoming a shareholder at that stage, an organisation could influence the policies, priorities and character of the company. In addition shareholders would receive market intelligence and priority attention in the marketing programme.[11]

When the government announcement was at last made, Sir Frank wrote again. It was, he said, 'very good news', enabling CNZEL to plan ahead. Meantime, he had found 'strong support among educational providers' for adopting a 'New Zealand Incorporated' approach to marketing educational services. 'The only reservation expressed ... related to whether a commercial entity was the best form of association for that purpose.' CNZEL had been set up in its present form, Sir Frank explained, for two reasons: 'To provide an operating entity so that we could start trading even while discussing the objectives, policies and character of the company with potential shareholders and clients'; and 'To register the name ... so that the company is seen as a companion to Consult New Zealand Health Services'. The articles and memorandum of association were set out in general terms, in the expectation they would be changed over time to reflect the interests of a wider group of shareholders. More information, it transpired, was needed. What was now called for, therefore, was 'a general indication of your level of interest in the company, along with any further comments you may have regarding the role, functions, objectives and structure'. But 'don't send us any money at this stage'.[12]

Anxious to get going, the promoters had somewhat botched their opening move: calling for shareholders was tantamount to issuing an unauthorised prospectus. Perhaps it could be argued in mitigation that they were breaking new ground. Certainly the mix of public and private was unusual, if not unprecedented, though itself a comment on Treasury ideology. Holding out the prospect of privileged marketing for shareholders was itself at odds with an all-New Zealand image.

In an ad hoc meeting chaired by Brian Springett of MU on 15 December university representatives had discussed both the expected change in policy and the CNZEL approach. On the general issue, members felt that niche

---

[11]   Holmes/Maiden, 22.11.88. AU.
[12]   Holmes/Maide, 29.12.88. Dated in another hand. AU.

marketing was 'still appropriate': the universities were 'interested in the high quality end of the market, not just attracting fee-paying students to provide a quick cash-flow'. They should be 'endeavouring to retain high quality graduate students and sustain their reputation as providers of high quality education'. Members agreed that the 'servicing' of the needs of overseas students had to be 'comprehensive'. They surmised that the possibility of permanent residence might be more important than the level of fees. New Zealand universities, it was generally agreed, should enter the market 'with the aim of maximising quality over the long term'.

The CNZEL approach was considered in this context. Was it 'the appropriate vehicle (or part of the appropriate vehicle) to act for the universities in the sale of educational services overseas'? Members agreed that 'there was a great deal of effectiveness and efficiency in an integrated approach to marketing educational services', and that the institutions themselves lacked marketing expertise. '[T]he big opportunities in the sale of educational expertise offered by such organisations as the World Bank and the Asian Development Bank could require a consortium of skills from a range of institutions, including some Government endorsement.'

A private company with shareholding was one way of solving the immediate problem of funding, but several concerns were raised. Why should universities be shareholders? It might be better if they were fee-paying clients. 'A better structure could be a two-tier one. First a non-profit organisation comprising the tertiary educational institutions concerned with policy and academic quality control. Second, a marketing and servicing organisation like CNZEL operating on commercial lines. Use of such a marketing company should be voluntary. It was desirable to have a single desk marketer but the organisation should attain that position through performance.' The CNZEL approach put profit-making up front and gave the shareholders only a limited policy role. 'Another more favoured approach would be to adapt the objectives and to make CNZEL more in the nature of a cooperative than a company.'

In conclusion, the meeting felt that the proposal 'needed to be related to a broader non-profit body representative of the tertiary institutional providers of education. This non-profit organisation would be concerned to establish and maintain standards in tuition and general care of fee paying students during their studies in New Zealand in order to enhance New Zealand's reputation as a provider of high quality educational expertise.' The university group would be a VCC standing committee, but the technical institutes and teachers colleges would have to be sounded out. The meeting suggested that the VCC should meet Sir Frank, explain the position of the universities on the proposal, and explore ways of carrying it forward.[13] That was done in February, when both Springett and Sir Frank attended on the regular VCC meeting.

The Springett group was clearly unhappy with too 'commercial' an approach, nervous, too, over the preservation of 'quality'. There was a risk that, starting late, New Zealand would take on just anything. Though the universities were expected to be CNZEL's main supporters, they did not wish their hard-earned reputation used but possibly damaged by others. If you start at the bottom of a market, it is hard to climb up, and the image of the better is damaged by the worse. Parallel with this debate was one about the universities' internal operation. At AU, for example, it was at first thought that the operation, even in respect of regular students, would be one for the university's commercial arm. In the event dealing with them became the task of a division of the Registry and later of an International Office.

At AU, the Deans Committee saw value in working with such an organisation as CNZEL, provided it not preclude 'ventures of our own', and provided that the courses it promoted were 'associated with a tertiary institution that can provide quality control'. The emphasis should be on 'courses of quality that, while not insensitive to shifts in demand, would be envisaged as being in place for some years, so that the necessary structures and infrastructures can be developed', and would be staffed so as to ensure high quality. The role of a restructured CNZEL would be 'the orderly marketing of the offerings developed by Universities and Polytechnics and possibly other institutions', the object being, not to preclude competition, but to avoid presenting 'a fragmented image overseas'. CNZEL could assist in marketing, though that should not preclude direct cooperation between institutions in NZ and institutions overseas. It should be a small organisation, using consultants from the universities to help determine market needs.[14]

Meeting in May 1989, the VCC's Standing Committee on overseas students, augmented to include representatives of all the universities, commented on both market and structures. It still considered that full-fee students offered 'no bonanza' for the universities, 'especially given the high cost, and the high level of competition'. It looked to niches, though suggesting that a market might be developed in Korea. Each country needed an appropriate approach, it argued. Agents would be needed in Korea. A sister university approach would be better in Japan. US universities offered credit for study abroad over a term or semester.

Most universities, though not all, favoured taking shares in CNZEL,

---

13   Report of a meeting held at VUW, 15.12.88. AU; also UGC Box 97.
14   Memorandum for Deans Committee, 5.4.89. AU.

the Committee noted. It would have no monopoly, but could be useful in supplying information both to the universities and to potential students, 'in helping to discover niches', and 'in promoting a New Zealand-wide approach'. A VCC role was conditional on quality control. Some of the language schools were the subject of criticism, but might find CNZEL too costly anyway. That might in some measure resolve the problem, though also limiting CNZEL's commercial future, and it would still not remove 'a more general concern about quality'. Some enterprises might already be letting New Zealand down by reducing quality or overcharging. Perhaps the proposed qualifications authority would find here an appropriate role.

The Committee reiterated concern over the impact of the new policies on research students. The number of ODA students would fall by 50%: of the 825 currently in New Zealand, 382 were undergraduates, 264 graduates. It seemed certain that the number of private overseas research students would also fall: at OU currently overseas students formed 3% of the total roll, 10% of the graduates. 'There is little chance that profits from full cost enterprises could be an effective source of scholarships for overseas students. Funds must be sought from Vote Science (DSIR) and elsewhere.' UGC – perhaps with the disposal of its assets in mind – had suggested a trust fund. Students given UGC postgraduate or other New Zealand scholarships might be treated as New Zealand students for fees purposes, the Committee suggested. 'A further step would be to provide, American-style, for more employment for graduate students, though not all overseas students would be suitable for university teaching tasks.' 'Student visas should allow students and their dependants to earn at the university and outside it. ... Dependants were known to be currently working covertly at exploitative rates. It would be better to regularise their employment.'[15]

ODA had itself been the subject of an enquiry by Parliament's Foreign Affairs and Defence Committee, to which the VCC Standing Committee had made a submission on behalf of VCC early in 1988. 'ODA in respect of education and training', it had argued, 'is cost effective and has long term benefits.' Significant progress had been made. 'But, as the developing countries improve their high school and general tertiary education, their needs change. Specialised undergraduate and technical education will remain important in the medium term, as will postgraduate education in specialised areas, and, more particularly, the training of university teachers of specialist subjects at lower levels.' The Standing Committee recommended a reevaluation of activities in the area 'with a view to redefining

---

[15] Minutes, 12.5.89. AU.

the opportunities and possibly increasing the aid made available'.

New Zealand now had 'significant experience educating people from developing countries in New Zealand', the Standing Committee continued. 'It has less experience in linking its universities and technical institutes with institutions and consortia overseas. But this should now increasingly be the thrust of the programme.' It recommended 'establishing a specific programme for the linking of New Zealand universities with universities in developing countries to provide ODA, including in the programme the establishment of an office in the university system to research, coordinate and develop appropriate activities'.

'The potential long-term importance of providing educational assistance to some of the larger developing countries, such as China and Indonesia, should be taken into account.' The submission saw the priority areas as the South Pacific, ASEAN, China, and Africa. Specific programmes were needed for China and the South Pacific. 'In the case of the PRC that is necessary in particular because the vast size of the country suggests the need for focusing ODA. In the case of the South Pacific, the problem is the reverse. But the area is diverse and there are tertiary institutions to work with that are of differing scope and potential.'

'Opportunity should remain available to establish special purpose initiatives', like the Geothermal Institute at AU, the English Language Institute at VUW, the Crop Agronomy Institute at Lincoln, and the Centre for Seed Technology at Massey. There were precedents, too, for linking institutions and discipline-based groups in New Zealand and in developing countries – such as MU's association with the Academic Centre for Food Technology in Thailand and the Visayas College of Agriculture – and that was a means of providing ODA. A properly funded programme could provide opportunities for financing significant activities on a project-by-project basis, and also finance a university-based programme that would enable New Zealand universities to take their own initiatives, 'a modified AUIDP'.[16]

The submission was completed at the same meeting as the comments on Hugo. Though VCC liked the submission more than the comments,[17] the views the Committee developed on niches and inter-university relationships in responding to Hugo were closely related to its suggestions for the future of ODA, that developing countries were developing further, and that New Zealand should not merely be supplying basic degree training. ODA-type aid and the growth in private students had earlier gone along together. That, it seemed, would or could still occur, the Committee may have thought, whereas the line the government was

---

[16]   Submission, 29.1.88. AU.

pursuing post-Hugo really pulled the two apart: MFA would in effect be buying places for ODA students more or less at full-cost prices. That would enable it to specify its aid objectives, but not necessarily make the best use of the aid it offered. The all-New Zealand approach seemed to extend only to marketing full-cost places.

The Standing Committee reverted to its earlier ideas at its meeting in May 1989, in particular when it made some structural proposals. The universities believed that the VCC should take on some of the tasks of the doomed UGC. VCC, the Standing Committee thought, should at least stand in the same role as the UGC in respect of the officials committee, the former IDC. It should take on OSAC-type activities. By contract with MERT, the VCC's office might also take on the functions of the ODA office suggested in the submission to the Select Committee. The Qualifications Authority could play a role in establishing a data base on overseas equivalences at entry level, and, in liaison with the officials committee, in 'checking the standards, academic and other, of private institutions offering English and other courses to overseas visitors'.

'Immigration would still deal with visas, but it is essential that the system should be clearer, simpler and fairer. There seems to be no provision in the "reformed" system for the current appeal procedure, but it will be all the more necessary given the decentralisation of the Labour Department.' The new Ministry of Education would presumably not be the appropriate location for an appeal body. Perhaps it could be established under the officials' committee – where it had been originally, the Standing Committee failed to note – and include, at least in university cases, a VCC representative.[18]

At its meeting on 5 December the Cabinet had instructed officials to report to its Social Equity Committee on the proposed fees only scholarships and on the cost of the proposals it had approved. They proposed that 'tuition only scholarships including those relating to post-graduates' should be awarded, first, to South Pacific students at current numbers, 'taking into account candidates' academic qualifications and relevance of courses sought to each country's agreed social and economic development needs', and then to others 'on the basis of open competition on academic merit. A reasonable geographic spread would be sought and preference would be given to the poorer ASEAN countries but should include some students from Latin America and Africa'.

The allocation for ODA and subsidised students, $28.8m, had been reassessed at $32.2m, owing to price changes and an increase in overseas

---

[17]   Taiaroa/Tarling, 31.3.88. AU.

[18]   Minutes, 12.5.89. AU.

student numbers. That was based on imputed costs, capital cost being met from Vote Education. To avoid cross-subsidisation from taxpayer funds and to provide transparency, the costing for subsequent years, other than for grandparented students, was based on full cost, with a margin of profit as well. Treasury, however, did not support additional funding for that.[19]

A MERT representative, Geoff Lawson, outlined its position on full fees at a forum at VUW on 17 May 1989. Currently – for 'several years now' – the Aid Programme refunded the full recurrent costs of tuition for overseas students to the education system. In 1988 it paid the Department of Education $8500 for every student from a developing country at a New Zealand university, and that was passed on 'in the form of block grants'. In 1989 the amount was expected to be some $30m. There were currently some 4000 overseas students in state institutions – not including Australians, treated as Kiwis – almost all from developing countries.

'With the advent of full fees from 1990, Ministers have announced that the goal is to maintain the same number of assisted students as have up till now been admitted under the subsidised quotas. This will be done by awarding fees scholarships to be awarded on the basis of academic merit to allow private students from qualifying countries to come here without paying full fees. These scholarships will particularly benefit the countries of the South Pacific.' The government had also stated that students enrolled before 1989 would not have to pay full fees from 1990. 'Full fees will not bring a reduction in the level of assisted students. The distribution of the awards will, however, differ from the former quota system in order to focus this assistance on poorer countries with low economic growth.'[20]

There would be five categories of students, Lawson told VCC. Those would include a. students on full ODA awards, with MERT meeting fees, travel, accommodation and susbistence costs; b. students from developing countries who would have their full fees paid by MERT under the new category of Fees Scholarships; c. 'Transitional' students, those enrolled before 1989, whose tuition costs would be met by MERT's imputed student cost payments to the Department of Education 'to reimburse the education system for that portion of the block grants which are attributable to these students'. d. Full fee overseas students whose fees are met from their own resources or by other sponsors. e. overseas students on recognised reciprocal exchange programmes. 'They will not pay full fees, nor will Australians, or others with New Zealand permanent resident status.'

Hitherto, as Lawson put it, all overseas students, whether directly

[19] Memorandum for Committee, 3.2.89. UGC Box 97.
[20] Comments by Lawson, 17.5.89. AU.

funded by MERT (the holders of ODA study awards), or indirectly (the private students from developing countries whose 'imputed costs' MERT had paid to Education 'to fund such students' share of block grants'), had been allocated places by OSAC. That body would function during 1990, but another means would be needed to handle ODA award holders and fees scholars in subsequent years. 'We understand the Vice Chancellors' Committee has been considering absorbing some of the functions of OSAC post 1990.'

In 1990 full ODA awards would continue to go through MERT. Taking into account the home country's training needs and academic merit, MERT's overseas posts would award the fees scholarships, 'subject to candidates being accepted for a place in an academic institution, up to a volume to be approved by ministers'. Then the students would apply to OSAC or direct to the institution 'as the case may be. After 1990 MERT envisaged commissioning a body to administer the placements and scholarships on its behalf, either a new body or an existing body under contract. It might also monitor the academic progress of fees scholars, and perhaps take over that role from the MERT student support unit in respect of ODA awardees.

In May Cabinet had decided that fees charged to MERT would be calculated on the basis of full cost recovery, including recurrent costs, capital share and a return on investment or profit. 'We see this as desirable in terms of providing an incentive to enrol MERT funded students, and to allow us to deal with institutions on a commercial footing.' Lawson recognised that there might be additional costs, in order to ensure that the students were provided with the additional services and support that MERT believed they needed.[21]

On 28 August 1989 the Ministers of Education [Goff] and External Relations and Trade [Moore] announced details of the full-fee scheme, to be covered in legislation shortly to be introduced. '[A]n entirely new category of foreign student has been created by the new policy. Students in this category will come from countries such as Japan, Hong Kong, Korea or from Europe or North America, and will meet the full costs of their education here', Goff said. 'This is an exciting time for educational institutions because they will now be able to profit from marketing courses to full-fee students. The commercial profits they make can be ploughed back into resources that will benefit New Zealand students.' The injection of funds would 'allow for the expansion of learning institutions in New Zealand, their research capacity and teaching staff. That must be to the benefit of New Zealand students.' Goff found 'great interest' in Japanese

---

[21] Lawson/Taiaroa, 26.5.89. AU.

institutions. Moore spoke of 'many enquiries' from Europe and South America, which represented 'totally new markets for New Zealand educational services', and supplemented increased interest in Asian and Pacific countries. He thought private English language schools could work with [public] tertiary institutions to provide 'complete packages' for foreign students.[22] The press release made no reference to the cultural or intellectual benefits the change might bring.

It introduced a statement on 'Foreign Student Policy'. That set out four objectives: '1. To provide assistance for the social and economic development of countries in the South Pacific, Asia, Latin America and Africa. 2. To contribute to international understanding and cultural exchange through reciprocal exchange programmes. 3. To promote increased foreign exchange earnings from educational services. 4. To enhance the effectiveness and quality of New Zealand educational services to the benefit of New Zealand and overseeas students.'

The statement yet again redefined the categories of students involved. First it put the 'full scholarship students' whose tuition, travel and living costs were met from ODA funds in the MERT vote. Second came the foreign students for whom ODA met only tuition costs, 'fees scholarship students'. Those two categories were collectively referred to as 'MERT Scholars'. Third there were foreign students studying under reciprocal schemes approved by the Minister of Education, 'exchange students'. Fourth were those who met their full tuition costs, 'full-fee students'.

Financial provision at the 1989/90 level – $34 093 000 – would be retained in ODA Vote: Foreign Affairs to meet the cost of the MERT students and the cost of transitional 'grandparented' students. The sum was 'based on current numbers without an element of profit'.

Foreign students could enrol, if accepted, in all categories of state and state integrated and private primary and secondary schools from the age of 5 years; polytechnics; teachers colleges; state and private universities; private colleges; and institutions offering courses through distance education. Students granted visas for secondary education were not guaranteed an entitlement to enrol subsequently in a tertiary course.

'The full, direct and indirect costs of tuition will be included in the fees charged for full scholarship and fees scholarship and full-fee students. Institutions may, at their discretion, include a margin for profit.' They were 'required to charge fees at a level which will not result in any cross-subsidisation from State funds'. The Ministry of Education would issue guidelines. It would have the power to require the reimbursement of state funding if it was used to cross-subsidise MERT or full-fee students. Those

---

[22] PR, 28.8.89.

guidelines ruled out charging at marginal rates.[23]

Institutions would be required to declare that neither New Zealand students nor MERT students had been excluded because of the enrolment of full-fee students, the statement continued. That clause – originating at a time when the talk was of selling 'spare' places – was hardly relevant now that creating new places was clearly in question. But it may have politically necessary, just in case an institution or the government was accused of making places spare so as to sell them.

State tertiary institutions would be required to sight evidence of NZ / Australian citizenship or immigration status. Permanent residents would have to produce a valid permanent resident's permit, stamped in the passport. Foreign students would need a student visa, but for courses lasting less than three months a visitor's visa would suffice, and none would be needed if a visa abolition agreement applied. That arrangement had been decided at Cabinet Economic Development and Employment Committe in March.[24] It also decided that the registration of such courses would be voluntary, despite MOE's doubts about maintaining quality.[25] Institutions would make the students an offer of place, and the visa would specify the institution and course. On arrival students would be issued with a student permit, stamped in their passport.

Foreign students enrolled before 1989 would continue to have their fees met from ODA funds either in full or at domestic levels for the mimimum time required to complete their qualification. The cost was to be met as imputed costs, calculated as at present and transferred from Vote: External Relations to Vote Education. Foreign students first enrolled in 1989 would be liable for full fees from 1990 onwards, unless they held full or tuition fees scholarships, provided by MERT.

An advisory body was to report to Cabinet at least once a year on the range, quality and pricing of full-fee courses, on marketing practices, on the effects of introducing the courses on the provision for New Zealand and ODA students, and on the workload in government offices overseas and in New Zealand. The body was to include representatives of Education, UGC, MERT, Labour (Immigration), Tourist and Publicity, and Trade Development Board.[26]

Bruce Ross, the Principal at Lincoln, now VCC chairman, said that the universities welcomed the announcement of the details of government policy. 'He cautioned, however, that while there will be a number of

---

[23] Guidelines in Caldwell/VC, 19.9.89. AU.

[24] 21.3.89. DEV (89) M 6/3. UGC Box 97.

[25] Memorandum, 28.2.89. ibid.

[26] Foreign Student Policy, attached to PR, 28.8.89.

opportunities for marketing courses overseas there would be no immediate money-making bonanza from the scheme.' The courses most in demand were also those most in demand from New Zealand students. Overseas students were 'very important members of the university community'. They provided 'an extra dimension to the learning experience of New Zealand students', contributed to the research effort, and enhanced interaction on their return home. There had, he said, been particular concern about foreign postgraduate students: they were needed, but would not be able to afford full fees. 'The universities therefore welcomed the assurance of the Minister of Education that the importance of the contribution by overseas postgraduate students to research in New Zealand is recognised, and that steps will be taken to ensure that the numbers of overseas research students will be maintained.'[27] Goff had been reported as saying that postgraduate students would be exempted[28]

The question had been raised earlier in the year. Waiving the fee, David Hall, the UGC chairman, had suggested, could be justified on the basis that overseas students made 'a valuable contribution to research', but doing that, or granting a scholarship out of the block grant, was ruled out as cross-subsidisation. Among the options were including the fee in the cost of applied research projects; securing aid funding where appropriate; and setting up a trust fund.[29]

Now the Minister suggested to the VCs that, while research students from developing countries could apply for scholarships or fees scholarships, and students from Malaysia, Singapore and Hong Kong were grandparented, non full fee research students from developed countries, in future to include those three countries, could be enrolled within a ceiling set at current numbers, about 150 across the system. The funding would be 'within existing bulk grants'.[30] It could be considered as additional targeted funding, not funding for New Zealand students diverted to overseas research students.[31]

In December 1989 the Minister approved a new scheme. Their funding would be tagged in the block grant, and the students could pay the same fee as domestic research students, $500 in 1990. The tagged funding amounted to $2m in 1990, allocated to universities on the basis of their 1989 numbers. Universities could set their own level of concessionary fee, including, at their discretion, the $500 paid by domestic research

27 PR, 28.8.89.
28 *Straits Times*, 30.8.89.
29 Memorandum, 2.89. UGC 173/6A. UGC Box 97.
30 Memorandum to VCs, n.d., received 5.9.89. ibid.
31 Caldwell comment on Memorandum from Moore, 7.9.89. ibid.

students.[32] In the event the sum was 1.42m [AU 440k; WU 180k, MU 40k; VUW 260k; CU 340k; L; 40k; OU 120k.[33]

In 1990 OSAC students would pay $8k for humanities, $14k for science, and $24k for Vet Sci, fees as earlier 'set' by UGC. Postgraduate [research] students would be eligible for a concessionary fee which could be set at $500. Students from Malaysia and Singapore who entered in 1989 were eligible for a MERT fees scholarship, which would cover two-thirds of the OSAC fee. MERT had extended the provision to cover postgraduate students also. Malaysia and Singapore were now regarded as 'developed'. MERT might give a postgraduate student from Malaysia or Singapore a MERT fees scholarship, in which case the students would absorb less of the tagged funding. Grandparented and other transitional students would pay the domestic rate. Foreign students were 'exempt' if under an approved exchange programme.[34] That meant they paid fees to their home institution.[35]

In 1990, OSAC reported, 707 places were available; 523 applied; 350 places were offered. It continued the pattern of decline in applications,1155 in 1989, 1782 in 1988.[36] Did it also suggest that full fees were discouraging? or that uncertainty prevailed?

The necessary legislation had been passed in December 1989. Earlier in the year a new Education Act, No. 80, had been passed, covering the Picot 'reforms'. The Education Amendment Act, No 156, amended that in respect of schools, and amended the Education Act 1964 and the University Acts in respect of tertiary institutions. No. 80, S 2, had defined a foreign student as a person who was not a New Zealand citizen, and to whom S 7 of the Immigration Act 1987 applied. S 3 of the amending act added three further definitions: 'assisted student', a foreign student studying under a programme administered by the New Zealand Government; 'domestic student', a person who is not a foreign student; and 'exempt student', a person studying under an approved exchange scheme. Ss 4 and 5 covered the enrolment of foreign students in state schools and their fees. S 20 applied similar definitions in respect of tertiary institutions, and required Councils to levy a fee 'not less than the sum of – (i) The council's best estimate of the cost to the council (including the appropriate proportion of the council's administrative and other general costs) of

32 Memorandum to Minister, n.d. 38/8/5 FF. Preddy memorandum to Minister, 30.11.90 [lapsus calami for 89]. Barker/VCs, Registrars, 14.12.89. AU.
33 Hutson, Pretty/VCs, 24.1.90. AU.
34 Memorandum from Caldwell, 19.1.90. AU.
35 Wills/Metcalfe, 25.1.90. AU.
36 Wall/Barker, 14.2.90. AU.

providing tuition in the subject, course, or programme for 1 student; and (ii) An amount that is in the council's opinion an appropriate reflection of the use made by 1 student receiving tuition in the subject, course, or programme of the council's capital facilities'.[37]

No foreign student not an exempt student could be enrolled at a tertiary institution or in a course if that meant that a domestic or exempt student who was entitled to enrol and had applied was unable to enrol as a result. To that there was an exception: a foreign student could enrol, even if domestic and exempt students could not, if the enrolment were in 'a vacant place – (a) That the council established for foreign students; and (b) Whose continued availability is dependent on the fees payable by foreign students enrolled in it.'[38] Similar provisions were put into the individual University Acts.[39]

The 1990 Amendment Act [23.7.90], comprising the major reforms of the tertiary sector post-Hawke, amended the definitions in the 1989 Amendment Act. A domestic student is a person who is a New Zealand citizen, or who holds a residence permit under the Immigration Act 1987, or is exempted from holding a permit by Ss 11 or 12 of that Act, or who is a person of a class or description of persons required by the Minister by Gazette notice to be treated as if they were not foreign students. Foreign student meant anyone who was not a domestic student [S 2, pp. 5-6]. In respect of tertiary students S 35 inserted these definitions in the amendment act 1989, and also the definitions of assisted and exempt students [S 159, pp 27-8]. S 38 inserted Ss 224 and 228 into the principal act to cover foreign student enrolment and fees [pp. 81-2, 84]. The University Acts were eviscerated.

The legislation had at last spelled out that a full-fee student would in effect be creating a new place. That provision was coupled with the injunction that there could be no cross-subsidisation, and that Kiwis and New Zealand-aided students had priority in restricted courses. Such issues had been, purposely or not, obscured in earlier discussions of 'spare' capacity. That existed mainly in courses that were not first choice among overseas students. Even in later phases of this long debate, there seemed to be some confusion, and there continued to be some. The fact was that there was no capital to invest in creating places. Their provision could be cranked up only gradually, by finding a few in the existing system, by denying or reducing the aided, or by transferring internal funds from courses not in demand – though that might still produce places that Kiwis

---

[37] pp. 2499-500.
[38] pp. 2501-02.
[39] pp. 2505ff.

could readily fill. Setting a high fee, moreover, made it difficult to enter the market. MFA had earlier suggested starting with a marginal one, and Goff had been advised in November 1988 that 'it may be appropriate for consideration to be given to waiving the capital component, initially at least, to establish a reasonable market share.'[40] But ideology – if not greed – prevailed. Undergraduate numbers were indeed to expand only slowly: and if there were a scarcely anticipated 'bonanza' in English language teaching, it revealed the speculative nature of the business.

Early in 1990 Treasury told its Minister that 'this "export industry" will fall short of its potential unless changes were made'. The number of full-fee paying students was lower than expected because of exemptions, grandfathered and graduate. Those exemptions would diminish in the short term, and Treasury was more concerned, it seems, with the Kiwis first policy. That, it said, worked against the development of an export industry, and in fact deprived Kiwi students of the improved services that increased numbers would make possible. It would 'generally retard expansion and stymie the ability of institutions to meet demand for places in popular programmes in the medium term. The most sensible solution may be to squeeze in some of the overseas applicants in order to generate the funds to hire extra staff and to finance capital works. A continuation of the "Kiwis first" rule may prevent such developments.' The restrictions were 'an anomaly in the post *Learning for Life* [post-Picot, post-Hawke] environment of devolving responsibility to the institutional level where there is likely to be greater familiarity with the trade-offs inherent in many decisions'. The legislative provision that gave absolute preference to New Zealanders should be revoked. The institutions' charter should contain 'a neutral provision' for 'access for New Zealanders to be at least as favourable as for foreigners, based on academic merit; no cross-subsidies to full-fee paying foreign students'.[41]

Grant Wills of UGC thought the Treasury's paper as flawed as it claimed the legislation was. He pointed out that funding was not the only constraint: in Law, for example, it was impossible to recruit staff. 'Changing legislation won't correct this.' The 'profit' factor made New Zealand fees uncompetitive: 'we mightn't be losing much anyway'. The Treasury recommendation would 'scrap positive action initiatives' and deprive the Pacific of educational opportunities.[42] It seems likely that Treasury was trying to find a way to get it all started in the absence of

---

40 Simpson/Goff, ?2.11.88. UGC Box 97.
41 Memorandum by Greig, 7.2.90. ibid.
42 Memorandum, 7.2.90. ibid.
43 Caldwell/McEniff, 9.2.90. ibid.

places or capital, but its own recipe ran up against the prohibition on cross-subsidisation. Caldwell's line differed from his colleague's. The exemptions had removed all incentive from the institutions. Kiwis first was not the problem. MERT was funding developing country students; Education funding postgraduates; and Australians were treated as domestic. 'The only market remaining is undergraduate entry from developed countries eg Malaysia Singapore in future Canada USA etc. Mike Moore's $100m won't happen.'[43]

It was, of course, to happen, but much later than expected, and as a result of unanticipated demand. In the meantime growth was slow, and quality was put in question. Despite the long gestation of the changes, they had finally been introduced in a rather poorly-researched way.

CHAPTER NINE

IMPLEMENTATION

The legislation of 1989-90 and associated decisions put in place the framework for a new approach towards foreign students. The tentative and contested moves towards full-cost tuition over the preceding decade culminated in the creation of a full-cost regime, the removal after a transitional period of the concessionary treatment of private under-graduate students from Malaysia and Singapore, and other ASEAN countries as well, and the focusing of aid even more on the South Pacific. The old regime had been worked out in various ways over the years. To some extent it had grown like topsy, and the policies involved had been ad hoc, influenced by practice abroad and politics at home, reacting to shifts overseas, affected by domestic changes. Indeed few years were marked by a stable or consistent approach. The new regime sought to achieve that, and the basic framework has since remained in place. Within it – and indeed at times modifying it – there has, however, been a great deal of change, and there may now be a need for more.

Change has derived from a number of sources. Some are international. The context in which New Zealand sought to implement its policy was, of course, an international one, itself subject to change. The movement of students continued and indeed expanded, despite the emergence of new forms of distance teaching. The numbers involved in 'Study Abroad' and exchange programmes increased. They came above all from relatively wealthy developed countries, usually either English-speaking or with high levels of English competence, and tended to be interested in a wide range of subjects, though, partly because of the time limits on them, mainly in the arts and humanities. The bulk of students came from Asian countries, by the end of the decade increasingly from the PRC. The 'globalisation' of the 1990s had elevated the importance of learning English still further, and many travelled for that purpose. Those that had further qualifications in mind, however, remained focused on the fields that had become important in the 1980s, business and computing. What changed was the numbers involved. The extent of the Hugo research had been limited by its use of informal data-gathering, and the publicity surrounding New Zealand's change in policy had been exaggerated. But it is doubtful that even a more thoughtful and informed presentation could have envisaged quite what was to happen.

What was to happen in New Zealand itself was, of course, another source of change. The new policy was, after all, only a small part of a great range of reforms, affecting not only education, but almost every aspect of New Zealand society. What happened in this field – and the reaction to what happened – was affected by what happened in other fields – and the reaction to that. In large measure, it might be hazarded, New Zealanders have accepted Labour's reforms of the 1980s and much of the ideology that backed them, reinforced, as they were, by the succeeding National government, then somewhat moderated by the Coalition and Labour governments. It is not clear, however, that they have seen, let alone accepted, the full implications of the policies. Immigration is very much a contested area. The contest reacts upon the temporary immigration involved in the substantial expansion in the numbers of foreign students, particularly from Asia and from the PRC.

Educational institutions are a third source of change within the 1989-90 policy framework. That could hardly be unexpected, inasmuch as they had themselves undergone major reforms following the Picot and Hawke reports, sometimes encapsulated in the phrase the government uninspiredly used, Learning for Life. The framework in which foreign students were to be treated was set within a larger framework of educational reforms which themselves had to be made to work. That framework itself, moreover, envisaged change, intended as it was both to encourage private 'provision' and to encourage state 'providers' to act in a more entrepreneurial manner. The bywords, in this field as in others, were after all 'deregulation' and 'market forces', and the challenge was to reconcile profit and quality, the short-term and the long-term.

State institutions came under continued pressure, indeed, not only from 'competition', but from fiscal decisions, ultimately inherited from the ideology and the reforms of the late 1980s. The state could not afford to finance them better, it was claimed: that would involve increasing rather than cutting taxation and discouraging enterprise. Government at once regulated state institutions – more, perhaps, that the stated objectives of autonomy and devolution justified – and reduced its financial contribution to them. That increased the risk, already present in the debate about policy, that foreign students were seen by public as well as private providers mainly as a source of revenue. As a result, it may be suggested, the perhaps over-protective, if not patronising, attitudes towards the overseas students of the 1950s and 1960s were changed too completely, if not reversed, so far as the 'foreign' or 'international' students of the nineties and noughties were concerned. Too little attention was paid, in particular, to what students could bring to New Zealand aside from their cash. Perhaps that was indeed limited by the fact that most came to learn English or to attempt a limited range of courses. Some indeed came at primary level.

The idea that New Zealand universities should look for 'niches', advocated in the 1980s, was not pursued. But it might still be relevant within the new context created by changes over the past decade. As it has developed, the framework of policy and practice now perhaps rests too much on a mass flow of students, on English language teaching, on undergraduates from PRC. If there are to be changes, however, they must not be abrupt. Instead, they should take place by adjustment. The previous regime had too often been affected by sudden or arbitrary policy changes or rumours of them. The possibilities of changes in the external context argue, moreover, for a well-considered policy, rather than a merely reactive or knee-jerk one.

The inauguration of the new system had been accompanied by controversy, then, as in more recent years, focused on the PRC, and accompanied by damaging publicity, some of it indeed justified. 1989 was, of course, the year of Tiananmen. The closure of the New Zealand embassy made it impossible to obtain student visas. John Langdon, director of the Dominion Teaching English School, and president of the Federation of Independent English Language Schools, said in October that some 10 000 were held up. Chris Butler, then Director Northern Asia at MERT, thought that the backlog numbered hundreds rather than thousands, but the ministry was attempting to take the pressure off the situation.[1]

The immigration service was concerned that some Chinese were using language courses 'to enter New Zealand to stay or to earn money to take home'. Australia had introduced retrospective restrictions to cope with the deluge of applications and the high numbers failing to go home, and that had caused angry protests. There were indications 'before June' that 'the same thing was happening here', according to Kevin Cameron. 'Too many of those who came to study English were using their visas to do other things. Some had paid exorbitant sums to agents in China who had promised them work in New Zealand. They had to borrow money to get

---

[1] NZH, 11.10.89.

here.' Charging foreign students full fees was, Cameron said, 'supposed to earn New Zealand foreign exchange. They were not expected to stay here and earn money.' The service was working on a policy, but it was more difficult than expected. 'The need was to have a policy that would allow New Zealand to accept the types of students who would learn English and then go home.'[2]

A few weeks before the 1989 Education Amendment Act was passed in December, the Minister of Immigration, Roger Douglas, duly approved stricter criteria for overseas language students studying in New Zealand. Significant numbers were working illegally instead of attending their language schools. New Zealand's visa system was 'being abused by a large proportion of these students whose main objective in coming to this country is to work and gain residence here', Douglas said. A new policy would take effect immediately. 'Applications for visas to take English-language courses of less than one academic year can now only be approved when the applicant has completed the equivalent of Form 7 and has been accepted and has paid for further tertiary studies in New Zealand. Alternatively, applicants must have successfully completed the equivalent of Form 7 and have a guarantee of re-employment in their resident country.'[3]

Some language schools supported the new rules. Langdon said they had killed 10% of the market.[4] Then a flood of short-term visa applications allegedly forced the embassy in Beijing to call a temporary halt.[5] That contributed to a further crisis.

Early in 1991 International House English College at Chippendale in Sydney, one of Australia's largest overseas students' English colleges, went into liquidation. It was the ninth ELICOS (English Language Intensive Courses for Overseas Students) institution to close over the previous seven months, 'during which changes to student visa regulations have diminished enrolments'. International House had received fees in advance from about 1000 students, mainly from PRC, but also Koreans, Japanese and Thais. A spokesman for Dawkins, the Minister of Education, said they would receive no government assistance unless the college's failure was attributable to the change in visa regulations. 'It's just what we really can't afford to have happen', said the acting co-ordinator of the ELICOS Accreditation Scheme, 'to tarnish the reputation of the industry yet again.'[6]

---

[2] ibid., 4.11.89.
[3] Press, 25.11.89.
[4] NZH, 8.2.90.
[5] NZH, 28.5.90.
[6] *The Australian*, 13.3.91.

Something similar had happened in Auckland. Late in 1990 Sylvester Ko, the manager of New Zealand Language College, based in Wairakei St, Greenlane, left New Zealand, 'telling staff he was seeking finance overseas', but he did not return. Some students were already In New Zealand. Others had paid fees in advance, about $5 000 a head, 'equal', they said, 'to our total income for 10 to 15 years in China and some of the money was borrowed from others'. NZEIL [formerly CNZEL] had helped those in New Zealand to find another school, but could do nothing for those in China. Their representative, Shi Jin of Shanghai, believed that the New Zealand government had a duty to help, since the students were told that the school was registered with it.[7]

NZEIL provided Phlip Burdon, National's Minister for Trade Negotiations, with a report. That proposed that, as a condition of registration with the Qualifications Authority, all schools accepting fees in advance from foreign students should use trust accounts or, if a state institution, guarantees to provide refunds. It also recommended a pre-visa self-assessment guide, similar to that used in Australia. 'If the student decides to proceed with an application, an application fee is paid, but no tuition fees are paid until students have been told whether they are eligible for a visa.'[8]

The report also recommended that the suspension of short-term visas should continue until the new procedures were in place and the backlog – some 1030 visa applications – had been cleared. The language schools complained over the suspension and the backlog. The embassy in Beijing, the *Herald* reported, had one officer on the job for only 15 hours a week. In June 1990 the service had 4000 visa applications from students who had paid in advance. 'At that time it refused to accept further applications, saying they were piling up faster than they could be dealt with.' Since then the service had dealt with 2410 applications, rejecting 1531, with a form reply that did not indicate the grounds for rejection. Immigration cited 'pressure of work' as the reason students were not given a reason if their applications were declined, but it usually occurred 'when the immigration officer was not satisfied the student would abide by conditions of the visa'. The manager of the Globetrotter School of Languages, Stephen Greenfield, complained that 'bureaucratic bungling' had destroyed a deal he had made with the Peking Economic Commission that was to bring 1500 of its workers to New Zealand a year to learn English, then go on to other qualifications: the service had yet to process the first 25 applications.[9]

---

[7] NZH, 3.4.91.
[8] NZH, 20.3.91.
[9] NZH, 21.3.91.

There were other reasons for what the *Auckland Star* termed 'The ABC of Discontent'. Two schools had collapsed, holding $1.5m in paid fees. 'The schools say they banked on fee-paying students being granted visas within reasonable time. They blame their financial difficulties on the Immigration Service, which they say is taking up to two years to process visa applications.' Immigration said that it had to be 'careful to let in only bona fide students'. Many of the applications it received were from 'people who intend to either work here or settle permanently, or use New Zealand as a stepping stone to Canada, the United States and Australia'. Post-Tiananmen many wanted to leave China, and were unlikely to want to return with language skills. In New Zealand 'many people got into the language school business', encouraged by legislative changes and government rhetoric, and targeted 'the huge Chinese market'. Some were soon in financial difficulties. Larger well-established schools with a spread of students were not affected to the same extent.

Ten schools belonged to the Federation of Independent English Language Schools: they handled some 4 000 students, 80% of the total. Its chairman, Maurice Kirby, said that some of those in financial strife were 'commercially naive, to say the least' if they expected to make fortunes. 'He has grave suspicions about the intentions of some schools set up by Chinese living away from New Zealand.' The registration system was too lax, he claimed, though he also claimed the Federation could police its members.

That was now the responsibility of NZQA, together with carrying out inspections to ensure that the schools maintained 'standards similar to those of public educational institutes'. A transition period that had allowed schools operating under the old Education Act until April 1991 might have been abused, Bill Matthew, NZQA's manager of applications, suggested. Under the old regulations, administered by Education, inspections 'amounted to a check on building standards and did not consider commercial viability, business methods or educational standards'. Schools nevertheless presented themselves as 'New Zealand Government approved', which 'apparently carries much weight in some countries'. Matthew wanted registration to be a requirement for all schools, including those providing short courses. So far 44 out of 50 of those providing courses 12 weeks or over, had applied to NZQA. 26 had been approved and inspections were still being completed on the remainder. The registration was for 1-3 years but could be withdrawn at any time. Operating without it carried a maximum fine of $10 000. He thought visas should be issued only to those who had paid to attend NZQA-registered schools.

Matthew had 'little sympathy' for those schools that had financial problems because the Chinese students from whom they accepted fees had difficulty in securing visas. 'They clearly set themselves up with certain expectations that were perhaps hopeful, or naive. If you're in farming, you can suffer from the drought. These people are in a drought.' What he thought of the cattle he did not say. But he suggested that the government was 'right to regard applications from Chinese students with greater caution after Tiananmen Square'.

Another school was blaming its financial difficulties on the tardiness of the Immigration Service. That was the New Zealand International English Foundation, founded by the Manurewa MP, George Hawkins, and partners, and currently based in surplus nursing staff accommodation at Greenlane Hospital. Also Mayor of Papakura, Hawkins helped to set up a flow of students through a sister city relationship with Guangzhou, but ceased his involvement in September 1989. His co-founder, Kathryn Herbert, said it had advance payment from 100 students, but 75% had been refused visas. Students who had come complained that tuition was inadequate and that facilities were not as set out in the 'glossy pamphlet'.[10] According to the Minister, that included a picture of Hawkins 'in his mayoral chains'.[11]

A third school was also criticised, and that involved a public institution, MU. International English College, lodged in downtown Auckland's Southpac Tower, had been founded by a Korean, Juan Kim, but now Massey had a 51% investment. About 40 out of the 50 students were Korean. A spokesman for them said they were boycotting classes until facilities were improved. 'The brochure on which students based their decision to attend the school promises a language laboratory, computers, a student library ... and the opportunity for private study.' None of that was available.[12]

The school came under scrutiny at a hearing in June. Now called Massey University English Language School, it had still not provided the information required if it were to be registered, Giles Brooker of NZQA said. In March a director of studies, Kevin Armstrong, had left after three days following what the University called 'irreconcilable difficulties' and gone to Languages International in Princes Street. Rob Crozier of the Association of University Teachers expressed concern at 'the manner in which publicly funded institutions become involved in entrepreneurial activities related to overseas students'. Massey University English Language Centre claimed to have no relationship with Massey University, he said. 'Students and staff therefore believe that there is a potential case

[10] Star, 20.3.91.
[11] NZH, 20.3.91.
[12] Star, 20.3.91.

of misrepresentation.' Kim, said Professor Graeme Fraser, was a successful businessman who entered New Zealand under the business immigration programme to open a language school in partnership with similar ventures in Australia. MU, he added, 'has had to create a trading arm for it to fulfil the various expectations that have been placed upon it by this and previous Governments'.[13]

The hearing was before an enquiry set up in March by Parliament's foreign affairs and defence committee, chaired by John Robertson, MP for Papakura. It would aim, he had said, 'to find out why parts of the industry are in trouble, and to recommend what role the Government should take to monitor private language schools'. The focus, however, would be on 'the provision of education services to overseas students in general', and the investigation of language schools would be in that context.[14] 38 submissions were received, of which 28 were heard orally. The report emerged later in 1991.

Among the submissions, of course, was one from the NZVCC. That stressed that New Zealand universities had a long-standing interest in internationalisation and its benefits and, to the extent that it was feasible, had welcomed the new opportunities the legislative changes provided. It believed that it would create goodwill, as had the Colombo Plan and other scholarship programmes: 'there is little doubt that even full-fee paying students who have a good experience in another country at a formative stage of their development are likely to feel well disposed towards their host country for the rest of their lives'. The VCs also stressed the benefit New Zealand and its universities gained from overseas research students, and the damage that 'current very high levels of fees' were doing to postgraduate programmes. They were out of line with those in competing countries that offered a subsidy. In addition the US, UK and Canada offered more scholarships and assistantships. The submission endorsed generic marketing by NZEIL, though universities with capacity across the board might engage in more individual marketing activities than others.

Effective marketing required long lead times. Yet universities could not be certain far in advance whether there would be places available. The problem was yet more acute if schools and universities wished to enter agreements that allowed for 'stair-case' arrangements, guaranteeing a place at a university if a certain level of bursary pass was achieved at school. The VCC recommended that universities should be allowed to make such agreements if they had a reasonable expectation that places would be available, and that such agreements would be binding even if it turned

---

[13]   NZH, 13.6.91.
[14]   NZH, 16.3.91.

out that restrictions had to be placed on New Zealanders.[15]

New Zealand, AU's submission suggested, had some advantages, though it entered the market late: its image as a stable society, its use of English, the reputation its institutions and their graduates had built up. To turn them to account, however, needed more care and more realism than had been evident. The emphasis should be on quality, not on quantity. The market was 'no longer one involving the movement of large numbers of undergraduate'. Other opportunities were opening up which, while not piling up millions of dollars, might 'add to New Zealand's reputation, its ties with other countries, and its own capacities'. In this connexion the University drew attention to the unduly high fees it was necessary to charge reseearch students.[16]

The Committee obviously tried to meet the points the universities raised. Overseas students who came to New Zealand injected into the economy 'vital foreign exchange earnings', which, the committee noted, were estimated at $66m in 1990, including fees and other services and products. The sale of services also increased 'an awareness of New Zealand as a destination for educational opportunities and for tourists; as a source of products and services; and as a potential investment target'. Contacts also broadened the relationship between New Zealanders and 'people of different cultures and languages', and the links established often continued after the students left. Such contacts had 'long term benefits in terms of understanding and goodwill for New Zealand's foreign policy'.[17]

An earner of exchange, the industry must be of high quality. In fact, however, problems in the industry had 'done New Zealand harm'. There were problems with marketing, some private sector operators objecting to NZEIL's efforts on behalf of its 'member' clients. There were also problems with quality control. 'The recent problems with backlogs on visa applications and failure to refund fees for students from the People's Republic ..., and the subsequent concern of the Chinese Government', offered 'an example of this potential pitfall.' The Kiwis first policy was also a difficulty. The committee believed 'that if foreign students were accepted into the seventh form of a secondary school they should be able to progress on to tertiary education. Once in the first year of a tertiary course ... students should be able to continue on to all the courses needed to complete their qualification providing they met the academic prerequisites.'[18]

---

[15] Submission, pp. 4, 6-9,11. AU.

[16] Submission in Spalinger/Hill, 26.4.91. AU.

[17] *Report of the Foreign Affairs and Defence Committee On the Inquiry Into the Sale of Educational Services in New Zealand*, Second Session, Forty-Third Parliament, pp. 13-14.

[18] pp. 14-16.

'The Committee recognised the conflict of interest between wanting to make it easy for overseas students to come to New Zealand in order to maximize revenue and the need to investigate and regulate in order to avoid students overstaying.' Delays in the processing of applications had damaged New Zealand's reputation in the PRC as a study destination, but steps had been taken to overcome the backlog, and it was not expected to recur. 'At the same time the Committee recognised the need for proper and thorough scrutiny of all visa applications. Problems with the Chinese market have arisen not because of problems to do with finding students but rather to do with problems in finding genuine students who plan to return to China once they have finished studying in New Zealand.' The Committee supported a pre-visa assessment scheme, which would screen applicants 'and cut down on the considerable time which was spent on processing applicants for whom there was very little chance of a visa being granted'. It recognised 'that the non refund of fees when necessary, and in particular when visa applications had been declined, had created an unfortunate impression in some overseas countries'. It supported the trust account concept that NZQA proposed.[19]

Adequate support services were important in terms of both quality and goodwill. Overseas students should be supplied with as much useful information about New Zealand as possible before they left home. They should be made to feel welcome, met at the airport, given some form of orientation. Their contact with New Zealand students should be increased, and systems put in place 'that would allow overseas students to stay with host New Zealand families on occasions'.[20] The suggestions seem to recall the Holyoake days. But maybe they were now designed to ensure competitiveness and develop the 'industry' rather than to sustain international relations in the free world.

The Committee also discussed NZEIL. One question was the provision of government funding for the generic promotion that it undertook. Some members of the Committee believed that the government should not be involved in such enterprises. Others took the opposite view. The reasons were 'that a number of countries competing with New Zealand in the educational services export market had Government funded organisations to assist their exporters; that there was a need for the industry's overseas marketing to be co-ordinated; and that NZEIL had now acquired much expertise in this task. A supplementary reason was that for New Zealand this export activity was new; i.e. an infant industry.' The Committee concluded that the arrangement should continue for the time being.

---

[19]   pp. 16-17.

[20]   p. 18.

NZEIL should, however, focus on generic marketing. It certainly should not undertake activities exclusively for its 'members' as distinct from other providers.[21]

The Committee offered a business plan for the industry and made it the basis of further recommendations. It proposed a mission statement: the educational services industry should aim to achieve 'Excellence in the marketing and provision of educational services to foreign clients to ensure a profitable return to New Zealand education providers and the enhancement of New Zealand's foreign relations.'[22] That did not mention the earning of foreign exchange, ostensibly the original objective of Hugo and the reforms. Nor, on the other hand, did it refer to any educational objectives, other than the profit of the providers: there was no reference to intellectual gain. Under the heading long-term objectives, the Committee indeed stated that 'the sale of educational services should be seen in a wider context of learning and cultural exchange, designed to improve political, social and cultural links, as well as serve educational and economic objectives'.[23] But it did not make it clear when you would get to the long-term, nor how the prospect of doing so should shape the short-term or be ruled out by it.

The global market, the Committee noted, was large. In 1988 UNESCO had indicated that some 3m international students were studying in developed countries, about half from East Asia. About a third were engaged in formal courses at tertiary institutions, the rest in shorter courses in English and various vocational and recreational subjects. The total global market was NZD2 220 000 000 p.a. New Zealand earned NZD37 000 000, 1.6% of the market. The largest potential target markets were Japan, Malaysia and Korea. 'A number of countries particularly Japan are both affluent and important for trade and political reasons.'[24] The Committee did not include PRC. No one thought very clearly about Japan. It was seen at that time to be prospering, or at least booming. But there was certainly no reason why a large number of undergraduates should come from Japan – very well provided with universities – though English language students might.

In 1990, the Committee noted, 6223 student visas were issued, 2506 for primary and secondary students, 1359 for university students, 679 for students at technical institutes and community colleges, and 1679 for others. The Federation of Independent English Language Schools [FIELSNZ]

---

[21] p. 19.

[22] p. 20.

[23] pp. 25-6.

[24] pp. 21-2.

catered for 3917 students in 1990, a 37% increase on the previous year. The receipts were NZD11m, 80% higher than the previous year.[25]

'The purchase of educational services by overseas students for long courses is a major once in a life time type purchase and an investment in one's future career.' That made quality an important factor, not price alone. Although the same people did not repeatedly purchase the service, 'the Committee noted that its reputation can be affected by the perceptions and experiences of those who have purchased'. It also noted 'that as overseas students have been obtaining tertiary education from New Zealand for 40 years, repurchasers can often be found in the generations succeeding the original purchasers'.[26] Most of the latter, the Committee failed to note, either secured it 'free' or paid highly subsidised rates.

The Committee listed opportunities identified by the Trade Development Board: English language; agricultural and horticultural education where domestic demand had fallen away, and forestry education; distance education; teacher training; courses in technical institutes and community colleges; continuing education; secondary schools, especially private ones; and university courses where spare capacity existed.[27]

Somewhat echoing the VCC's Standing Committee, it suggested that the best strategy was 'to market a range of educational services in those country target markets where New Zealand had clear opportunities and strengths. This would mean developing a range of services for some distinct market segments for a small range of South East and North Asian countries.'[28] Quality was essential. The Committee supported the trust fund mechanism, and believed it should be a requirement for registration by NZQA. That authority, it added, should have 'an ongoing role in monitoring the service provided by private training establishments in order that standards do not drop once an institution has been accredited'. It should have the power to withdraw accreditation where standards no longer met requirements. Student support services should be covered by its regulatory role.

The Committee made some interesting, but probably impractical, recommendations on fees, now being set by institutions. At undergraduate level, it wanted to distinguish between 'secured places', for which full fees would be charged, and 'places surplus to the requirements of New Zealand students', for which the fee would be 'based on the market cost of the foreign student enrolling'.[29] That had never been the intention, it seems.

---

[25] p. 23.

[26] p. 23.

[27] pp. 24-5.

[28] p. 26.

[29] p. 28.

In the Muldoon phase full-cost fees – not necessarily, however, including capital costs – were to be charged for surplus places, though it had not been clear whether the money would go to institution or government. In the 1988-90 discussions and legislation the notion of a surplus place is hardly present. On the contrary all foreign students were to be charged full fees, and cross subsidy and marginal costing were ruled out. Indeed the Committee recognised that it required a legislative change 'to allow public institutions to use variable costing of services and the consequent charging of fees'.[30] A later recommendation sought research into the real costs of funding places and the way they could be met,[31] the object being to provide additional places for foreign students, i.e. 'secured places', presumably, though the report here refers to 'guaranteeing' places to foreign students.

The Committee had 'stressed the importance of distinguishing between overseas postgraduate students and overseas undergraduate students as there could be a positive benefit arising out of the research which is carried out by the latter and should be taken into account when fees are set'.[32] Fee-setting should take account not only of its suggestions on under-graduate fees, but also of the students' contribution to an institution's 'research and educational excellence', and of the value of their research to New Zealand. To assist in the process of setting the fees, the government should 'move with urgency to enable the universities to access research funds allocated to the Science Foundation'.[33] In this way the Committee sought to meet the points the universities had made, but it was not very clear what it had in mind. Were institutions to reduce fees? That seems to be the implication, though what was to make up the costs was not obvious. The funds that might be available from the Science Foundation, if any, could surely be used not to reduce fees in general, but to help individuals meet them by providing subsidy/scholarship.

'A student paying the marginal cost is not being subsidised', the Minister, Lockwood Smith, told the VCC.[34] Despite the guidelines issued under his Labour predecessor, that view he continued to repeat.[35] However, he agreed to clarify the position through an amendment to the Act.[36]

---

[30] p. 29.
[31] p. 29.
[32] p. 17.
[33] p. 28.
[34] q. *Dominion Sunday Times* [DST], 17.2.91.
[35] Smith/Tarling, 29.8.91. AU.
[36] Memorandum by N. Kingsbury to Tertiay Consultative Committee, 31.7.91. AU.

That was included in the Education Amendment Act (No. 4) (1991, no. 136), passed 18 December 1991, which endeavoured to implement some of the Committee's proposals. S25 amended S 228 of the principal Act, as inserted by S 28 of the 1990 Amendment Act, with the object, it seems, of allowing for marginal costings, and subsidising postgraduates. A foreign student would have to pay '(a) An amount fixed by Council that is not less than the Council's best estimate of – (i) The cost to the institution (including the institution's marginal administrative and other general costs, and the appropriate portion of any initial or start-up costs of the course) of providing tuition in the course for 1 student, in the case of a course in which no domestic student is enrolled; (ii) The marginal cost to the institution (including the institution's marginal administrative and other general costs, and any marginal initial or start-up costs of the course) of providing tuition in the course for 1 student in addition to the domestic students receiving tuition in the course, in every other case; and (b) An amount fixed by Council that is not less than an amount that in the Council's opinion is an appropriate reflection of the use by 1 student receiving tuition in the course of the capital facilities (if any) whose provision at the institution is necessary by virtue only of the institution's provision of tuition to foreign students in addition to domestic students.' Notwithstanding such provisions, a Council could accept a sum that was less by any amount by which it had decided to subsidise the student out of the general revenue of the institution not being funds provided by S 199 [i.e. the grants from government], or out of any special supplementary grant made under S 199.[37]

S 27 inserted a new S236A in the principal Act. That required private training establishments to give prospective students full information about fees, costs and course requirements. It allowed for withdrawal within seven days, together with full refunds in respect of the course. It also required the establishment of trust funds.[38]

The crisis over the language schools – originally the main reason for the Select Committee's enquiry – did not conclude without further incidents, particular and general. The first related to the Massey University Language Centre, owned by Juan Kim, in partnership, it was now said, with a Japanese investor, and the University. Early in February 1992 Kim was reported to be facing 'a teacher revolt'. Wages had not been paid on time, 'due to an administrative error', and teachers threatened not to take classes unless they got their money. They declined his personal cheques, and he was 'so angry that he went to several banks to get thousands of

---

[37] pp. 25-6.

[38] pp. 27-8.

dollars in coins, then counted their money out to them'.[39] NZQA refused to accredit the school while it used the protected term 'university' in its title, and it had other concerns as well. Springett said the school would fold, and the students would be given an opportunity to study at Palmerston or in other Auckland language schools.[40] The school had been operating under a provisional registration, extended from the original DOE approval. Under the new legislation, as Rory O'Connor of NZQA said, all private training establishments had to satisfy the authority that they were financially viable. Those accepting pre-paid fees would have to hold the money in a trust account until seven days after a course began: within that period dissatisfied students could withdraw their money.[41]

The general issue was the compensation the New Zealand government paid to students from the PRC. In March 1992 there were protests outside the embassy in Beijing. Similar protests had been held outside the Australian embassy the previous year, and the Australian government had, after pressure from the Chinese government, paid refunds to Chinese students. Only now had protesters turned their attention to New Zealand. Most of 24 March 'about two dozen Chinese students' stood outside the iron gates. 'They held posters reading "what a shame to cheat", "shame on you", and chanted "return the money".' Embassy staff were 'jostled and roughed up as they tried to leave work'. Don McKinnon, Minister for External Relations and Trade, was 'puzzled' over the motive. 'It is rather hard to read it. It just seems rather unusual to just sort of pop out a year after the event.' There were allegations, he said, 'that policemen had stood by doing nothing'.

Though sympathetic, the New Zealand government had, he said, been unable to help the students, 'other than through a decision to make those offering English language courses put student money into trust accounts'. It would not refund money students had lost. Alan Chisholm, secretary of FIELS, said 'that a very unfortunate situation has arisen because of long delays in processing visa applications in Peking for intending students. The students had paid their school fees, perhaps several thousand dollars, but some schools had gone under or spent the money on operating costs before the visa applications were decided.' In the end most visa applications had been declined. In December 1991 'the Government had changed the rules for Chinese students on private courses, maintaining a ban on allowing them in for short-term study and tightening other entry requirements to prevent a flood of applicants'. Experience had shown, said Bill Birch, the Minister of Immigration, 'that entry for short-term

[39] NZH, 7.2.92.
[40] NZH, 20.2.92.
[41] NZH, 21.2.91.

English language courses was being used by Chinese and Iranian students to leave their countries and, in many cases, drop their courses and work unlawfully in New Zealand'.[42]

The protests continued in Beijing. 'Give us our money back', demonstrators called.[43] In New Zealand at a NZEIL conference, language school and polytechnic managers urged McKinnon at least to repay the visa fees and GST. Hamish Hancock, MP for Horowhenua, 'urged high schools with spare capacity to offer places to the students at no cost other than for books and accommodation'. That, however, officials said, would require a change in immigration rules. Existing rules, said Russell Vogtherr, 'ban student visas for Chinese students unless they already speak English as well as an 11-year-old New Zealander, already have the equivalent of a degree or trade certificate, are under the age of 29, and come to New Zealand for at least a year'.[44]

'One of the saddest things about it', said an Auckland couple who had been in Beijing, 'is that these people haven't got access to any recourse. The ones here have no money for lawyers and there's nothing the ones in China can do.' Some were very poor and had borrowed the money: 'they are distraught and suicidal.' Others were better off, 'but the harm to New Zealand's image was done'. The New Zealand government, McKinnon had said, would not, unlike the Australian government, reimburse the students for lost fees 'because the schools were private concerns'. The acting chairman of the Combined Registered English Schools, Tim Cooper, said that the schools that fell over were 'not New Zealand run'. He hoped that '[t]he cowboys and the quick-buck people' were 'mostly gone'. The 30 or schools still doing a good job had been 'hurt by the language collapses', but the industry was growing.[45]

There seems to have been some attempt to blame the weak schools, even to be glad – the market 'working' – they had gone. But whatever their faults – and whether the faults included not being 'New Zealand run' or not – they had surely been hit by the visa policy. Even more clearly the students had been hit, though some of them were perhaps not bona fide, but anxious to get out of post-Tiananmen China and work elsewhere.

Some had indeed 'abused the system', the *Herald* reported. Elizabeth Goldswothy, a director of Total Education Service, said that after each language collapse, 'every legitimate student was offered a place in another school'. Those who did not accept it 'disappeared of their own free will'. There was, she added, 'a loophole in new laws covering entry for overseas

---

[42]   NZH, 26.3.92.

[43]   NZH, 27.3.92.

[44]   NZH, 28.3.92.

[45]   NZH, 30.3.92.

students which allowed them to easily to claim fee refunds then disappear to work illegally'. Some Koreans and Thais had done so, too. She thought refunds should go to other schools or back to the country of origin. 'One student on a student visa', said Judith Collins of AIS, 'had the cheek to write from Napier to say he had found a job so could he have his refund.' Neil Caddie of Immigration pointed to the steps that had been taken in December 1991. They had been taken because surveys had indicated 'an absentee rate of more than 50 per cent among mainland Chinese students'. The service would check to see whether the new rules had fixed the problem, and if not make further recommendations. 'But it's more a matter of ensuring that the visa being issued is bona fide and is complied with.'[46]

The Minister of External Relations and Trade found the Beijing protest 'all a bit inscrutable', the *Herald* editorialised. His 'minions in Peking' had explained that they could not refund the money. 'The protesters, in turn, probably found that quite inscrutable.' The fees had to be paid in advance as a condition for granting a visa. Some applications were declined; 'some money disappeared with the financial collapse of "schools" last winter'. Now fees have to be placed in trusts, but that was 'no solace to the demonstrators'. New Zealand should follow Australia's example. 'The Government's disinclination to reimburse victims of business failure is prudent in principle; in this instance, the state's role seems hardly blameless. What is the Chinese for refund?'[47]

The incident dominated McKinnon's three-day visit in April. 'As he landed in Peking ... the students began their hunger strike and pressure went on from the highest quarters of the Chinese Government.' At an embassy dinner, Qian Qichen, the Foreign Minister, echoed McKinnon's remarks on the good relationship between the countries, but added: 'As we sit here tonight, let us remember those people not far away who are going without food.' In Shanghai McKinnon expressed 'the strongest condemnation' of those 'who set up language schools, took students' money and failed to provide tuition'. From Beijing he announced that NZQA woud undertake an enquiry. Stuart Rose of NZEIL, which had reported on the issue in 1991, was not sure that would 'advance things much further'. He hoped the issue would 'die away, saying it was immigration driven rather than anything to do with education'.[48]

In Wellington in June Qian Qichen made it clear that his government expected New Zealand to take responsibility for the 1050 students who lost money by seeking to further their education in New Zealand.

---

[46]   NZH, 15.5.92.

[47]   NZH, 2.4.92.

[48]   NZH, 28.4.92.

McKinnon told him that he did not consider his government had a responsibility to reimburse them, but it did not wish the issue to be an impediment to the bilateral relationship. Looking into the problem, officials had found that some schools were now in a position to reimburse students. Another possibility was reduced cost language education at polytechnics and [state] schools. New Zealand might send teachers to Beijing to conduct intensive courses. A fourth possibility was a one-off payment to the students affected.[49]

Mark Hamilton, who worked on the Australian refund scheme in Shanghai, believed that the government had a responsibility, since the schools were endorsed by the Department or NZQA. Full refunds were the only option, he believed. He did not favour transferring a few million dollars for the PRC government to administer. 'There is no assurance that the Chinese Government is going to refund a whole lot of students' money.'[50]

That was, however, the option finally adopted. Meeting Qian Qichen at the APEC meeting in Bangkok a week later, McKinnon announced that the basis of a settlement had been reached. Chinese students who signed up to study were owed $13.5m by existing schools. About $10m had been repaid. The New Zealand government would 'continue to remind these schools firmly of their obligations to repay the outstanding debts as quickly as possible'. It was better that they should not be 'driven to the financial brink' but rather 'trade their way out of debt'. The government could accept no legal responsibility in respect of schools that no longer existed, but as it had played a role in promoting the sale of New Zealand educational services, 'a once-only compensation payment would be made to the Chinese Government'. That would be disbursed at its discretion, 'and should go some way towards meeting the plight of these students'.[51]

Somewhat belatedly, perhaps, Immigration had dropped its requirement that it receive evidence that course fees had been paid before it received visa applications, a change 'intended to reduce the problems experienced by many applicants in securing refunds from New Zealand institutions if they are unsuccessful in obtaining a student visa or permit'. Instead there would be an in-principle application, the visa/permit issued after payment.

The tale had been a sorry one. Immigration procedures had indeed not helped, but they were bound up with the larger issues involved in immigration in general. Despite the earlier warning that the 1990 changes might add to the work of the service, foreign posts were insufficently

49 NZH, 17.6.92.
50 NZH, 4.9.92.
51 NZH, 12.9.92.

staffed to cope with the flood of post-Tiananmen applications. The providers were at fault, too: some at least were under-resourced, even speculative, in no position to cope with the unexpected. Perhaps it should also be said that the Government and its consultants had trusted too much to the market, while also failing to give much consideration to the future of English-language teaching. It had also of course failed to give much consideration to the PRC, though it was not alone in that. The tale provided some lessons and prompted some remedies. The re-emergence of the issue ten years later was the more disconcerting. By then, indeed, more was at stake. China had a larger role for universities and other providers as well as language schools, and the attitude of its government and students was even more significant than in the early 1990s.

The role of NZEIL was another issue on which the parliamentary committee had commented. Its position was always likely to be a difficult one, even if the government continued to provide funding through the MDB/TDB or otherwise. Back in 1989, Kevin Hearle, the principal of Bay of Plenty Polytechnic, had pointed to some of the problems that would accompany the implementation of the new policy. 'The last thing we want is a gold rush that spoils the market', he said. 'Sadly, educational bodies in this country do not have a good record of co-operation.' The market was sensitive and competitive, and institutions lacked experience. Consult New Zealand had been set up to 'provide a co-ordinated marketing agency'.[52]

The problems it would face were, however, scarcely recognised at first. If it acted in a generic way, it might be supporting institutions that were below standard, who would ride on the backs of others, and ultimately damage them. If it in addition acted in a particular way, it might be advantaging some at the expense of others, who, while up to standard, wanted to do their own marketing. A concentration on generic marketing was no doubt the less problematic of the two options. But then some institutions would question whether it was worth doing, and whether the larger and better were not supporting others rather than being able to compete with them. That might apply among state institutions. Even more hazardous, perhaps, was the inclusion of an array of private providers, language schools and others. A convincing system of quality control would be the best assurance of harmony among the providers, as well as affording a guarantee to 'consumers'.

The first meeting of a 'revamped' VCC Standing Committee on Overseas Student Policy – chaired by Bruce Ross – discussed CNZEL, its tasks and structure, with Abdul-Razzaq Khan, the CEO, on 8 November

---

[52]   NZH, 30.8.89.

1989. The TDB, he explained, had underwritten the organisation for the next two years, and would invest $250 000 on a dollar-for-dollar basis with providers to form the share capital. He argued that 'a one-New Zealand approach would maximise the effectiveness of international marketing' and 'provide the basis for a co-operative approach rather than straight competition and the denigration of conflicting institutions that could develop'. The discussion emphasised that NEQA and CNZEL would have to protect quality, particularly in the private sector. Given that the universities were 'perceived as the flagships of international marketing endeavours, the point was made that an organization specifically focused on the universities might be better'.[53]

Khan, and the new chairman, Basil Logan, former New Zealand head of IBM, were struggling to get the outfit going, the *Herald* reported early in 1990. Some providers complained that it was in fact too slow in starting, and many had set up their own networks. The 10 schools in FIELS had pulled out, and Langdon was 'totally disillusioned' with CNZEL, 'believing that its attempts to split commissions and monopolise the services of trade commissioners are actually damaging the industry'. Even the institutions that supported CNZEL wanted to be able to sign up students themselves, rather than use the outfit in all cases. The current aim was to offer shares to the university, polytechnic and other sectors according to their size and likely use of the services. Shareholders would get a discount on service fees for each market and priority for consulting projects, along with the right to influence policy and receive a dividend.[54]

The structure of what was renamed NZEIL was hammered out during 1990. Previously a private company, with a paid-up capital of $1 000, 1 000 shares of $1 each, it had been re-registered as an unlisted private company with an authorised capital of $1m. The TDB had agreed to take up 250 000 of the 600 000 shares to be offered, and to underwrite a further 250 000 of the 350 000 to be offered to education institutions. It intended eventually to sell its shares down to them. It had also established an Education Research and Development project.

Meanwhile the company had begun operations, taking part in education fairs in Geneva and Malaysia and setting up an office in KL. Over 600 applications had been vetted and passed on to institutions, to supplement those they had received directly. 1990 was 'a testing time' for all in the sector, including NZEIL. The most difficult question in the learning process, it said, was a fundamental one: 'how the company should operate and balance its efforts between the activities of the general promotion of

---

[53] Minutes, 8.11.89. AU.
[54] NZH, 10.2.90.

New Zealand as a quality education provider and meeting the specific marketing needs of those who do not wish to do their own'. The first, it said, was 'desired by all participants', but provided 'no identifiable return to fund the company operations. The support for the latter, for which returns are directly identifiable, ranges from 100% positive from those institutions who do not wish to invest in their own marketing, to negative from some who feel the company's activities are in competition with them or are stepping between them and the market.' The Directors were, however, certain that, through 'the structuring of our service offerings, service agreement fees and future mode of operation', the 'correct balance' could be struck.[55]

In February 1991 NZEIL decided not to proceed with the share issue, and to refund the monies subscribed with interest. The forecast revenues had been dependent on government policy on the provision of places and on the ability of institutions to make them available at competitive prices. In fact enrolments for 1991 were 'lower than expected and impossible to predict'. Among the factors were 'Government policies regarding Post-graduate fees', its 'clawback of fees from primary and secondary schools, general funding issues, and lack of experience in planning and managing the allocation of space to full-fee students'. The Directors had decided to delay the issue of shares and continue the company as a wholly owned subsidiary of the TDB, while the Research and Development fund would be merged with the company.[56]

The company also planned to attain the 'balance' it had sought – not having shareholders, privileged over non-shareholders, would no doubt help – and reaffirmed that 'the key imperative for us is that a New Zealand institution or company successfully captures the business', not that it came through NZEIL. Tertiary institutions were mostly interested in generic promotion, and they would be charged a service fee, but no fee in respect of any student recruited through NZEIL's CEPROS system. Secondary schools and other providers were more interested in 'contributing from their cash flow, as students are recruited'.[57]

The complaints the parliamentary committee received did not suggest that this ensured the 'balance'. Commenting during the crisis over the language schools in February, Maurice Kirby, chairman of FIELS, saw no need for NZEIL. 'The federation is opposed to what it sees as the Government's attempt to cream off some of its business. It says the industry is quite capable of policing itself, and notes that none of its

---

[55] Logan/Maiden, 9.10.90. AU.
[56] Logan/Maiden, 9.2.91. AU.
[57] Logan/Maiden, 9.2.91, a second letter. AU.

members is in financial trouble, or the subject of complaints to the qualifying authority over quality of courses.'[58] The Committee, as the Minister of External Affairs later put it, recommended that NZEIL 'should have its wings clipped', and sell New Zealand 'as an education source, without getting into the hands-on sale of specific institutions and courses'.[59] But then it could survive only by subsidy or levy.

On 24 October 1991 TDB announced that it would transfer ownership to participating institutions by July 1992. Its chief executive, Rick Christie, 'stressed that the TDB would continue to fund significant levels of generic promotion of the education industry overseas and TDB's generic support will continue to include the use of TDB's overseas posts to represent industry in overseas markets'. The change would put TDB's relationship with 'the education industry' on the same basis as other industries.[60] The NZEIL newsletter reported in November 1991 that there were 64 service agreements, including 6 universities, 15 polytechnicss, 27 secondary schools, and 13 private English Language schools. 'Across both private and public English Language Schools, NZEIL encompasses 28 providers.'[61]

TRADENZ was likely still to provide some funding – say $200-300k as against $800k – and some support at overseas posts, NZEIL said in May 1992. That would not meet the needs of the industry. At present it contributed $0.4m, in fact a similar rate per student compared with that in the UK or Australia, but, since there were still relatively few overseas students in New Zealand – 1865 formal full fee students, as against 24k and 30k respectively – the sum spent per student on facilitation was higher. 'New Zealand has not yet reached a viable number of students.' The government's revenue in 1991, NZEIL noted, included $3.9m from GST on tuition, and another $3.9m from GST on general spending, $7.8m. It needed continued government support to survive. Self-funding – based on a voluntary levy of 2% of tuition fees – would not be possible for 4 or 5 years.[62]

NZEIL members met on 27 April and favoured the continuation of generic marketing. They also favoured the idea of a trust, wth NZEIL as its operating arm. 'In the formal sectors there is support in principle for a level of financial commitment proportional to the number of students in the country and the size of institution.' Government funding would be sought for the shortfall expected until 1996/7.[63] Subsequently NZEIL

[58] NZH, 20.3.91.
[59] Speech to NZIIA, Auckland Branch, 13.3.91.
[60] PR, 24.10.91.
[61] *NZEIL News*, 11.91.
[62] NZEIL paper, 27.3.92. AU.
[63] Logan/Maiden, 8.5.92. AU.

secured a financial commitment from the government, shared 50/50 by Education and Tradenz, taking the form of a suspensory loan, its amount diminishing in each subsequent year.[64]

The universities agreed to join as a committee, the VCC, working out a formula for each university.[65] An ad hoc meeting of managers and others on 27 January 1993 recommended to VCC a flat rate per institution, plus 1.5% of actual income.[66] The relationship did not prove a smooth one. NZEIL argued that the tertiary sector, especially the universities, had to take a leadership role, as they did in IDP, a subsidiary of AVCC, and in the ECS division of the British Council. It was not unreasonable for them to bear a substantial part of the funding burden. It would encourage more schools to become involved and help schools recruit more students of high quality. That would have flow-on effects. The English language schools argued that they were in the market before NZEIL, and were almost 100% dependent on agents. There was something in their arguments, but NZEIL thought the private operators would need to increase their contribution.[67]

Some felt the universities were paying too much for the generic marketing, and benefiting from it too little. In 1995 the sum was \$422 612 [AU 77 410; WU 45 703; MU 56 667; VUW 50 268; CU 36 494; LU 71 611; OU 84 459].[68] The VC at OU, G. Fogelberg, questioned whether NZEIL was delivering value for money. Only 222 of its 900 overseas students had not been recruited by the University itself or sent by MERT. The maximum annual total of recruits might be 50.[69]

The government asked the State Services Commission to establish a study team on international education and NZEIL's role. *Campus News* carried a report in April 1994 pointing out that the Australian government spent far more on promotion than the New Zealand government. New Zealand could have earned more than it had. Government should not phase out the subsidies.[70] Nor did it, though in early 1996 it was providing 25% and the 'members' 75%.[71]

Developing the new arrangements – difficult enough in itself – had been made more difficult by exaggerated hopes and impatience, by differences of interest, by the Tiananmen crisis. Amid all this the institutions themselves had to work out not only how they would organise the new

---

64 Logan/Irvine, 29.9.92. AU.
65 DST, 13.12.92.
66 Minutes, s.d. AU.
67 NZEIL Funding Regime and Sector Representation, 12.92. AU.
68 Taiaroa/Rose, 9.5.95. AU.
69 Memorandum, n.d., attached to VCC (M 5) 95. AU.
70 *Campus News*, 4.14, 14.4.94.
71 *Campus Review*, 6.3, 1.2.96.

activity – generally they opted for a dedicated section of the administration rather than for a company or commercial arm – but, crucially, what they would charge. The 1990 fees had been set – somewhat arbitrarily – by UGC. After that it was the task of the institutions, first under the un-amended legislation, which seemed to rule out marginal costing, and then under the 1991 amendment, designed to allow it.

The 1991 fee-setting brought home the reality of the 1990 legislation. Goff's earmarked funding, never popular with the VCs, was dropped. Lockwood Smith, his successor, did not take up the idea of a 60% reduction for 100 students per year.[72] Postgraduate Massey Horticultural students would be charged $28k, for example. Yet 25% of the enrolments were postgraduate and of those 55% or 189 were not New Zealand residents. That made MU non-competitive, even though many of the students were working on topics of direct relevance to New Zealand.[73] New Zealand could be pricing itself out of the market, said Craig Ross, the president of the Institute of Agricultural Science. No consideration had been given to the contribution the students made to research, not to the long-term commercial contacts that 'flowed from having the overseas students trained to a high standard in New Zealand'.[74]

In the Arts most universities had settled for 1991 on fees of approxi-mately $14k at the postgraduate level and $8k at the undergraduate level. In Science the fees were generally around $24k and $10-14k. In Engineering $29k and $14-17.6k. In Business $13.1.-15k and $7.3-12.5k.[75] At AU the original basis of calculation in the case of graduates was 1990 EFTS funding plus 3% plus $1000 'profit' and in the case of undergraduates 1990 EFTS plus 3% plus $ 1000 capital contri-bution plus 25% 'profit'.[76] There were some modifications to the general rule, and information on the fees in Australia was taken into account.[77]

The fees AU set for postgraduates for 1992 were notably lower, though settled before the Amendment was passed. Commerce undergraduates would pay $11.5k, postgraduates $14k; Engineering $16k, $25k; Science, $13k, $20k. The fees for postgraduates were often lower than those for other universities.[78] For 1993 the VC at AU agreed that for 1993 the postgraduate fee would be the same as the full-cost undergraduate fee, the subsidy being 'in recognition of the valuable contribution which is

[72] NZH, 12.12.90.
[73] Comment by Prof K. Millne, MU Council, 5.10.90. AU.
[74] NZH, 6.10.90.
[75] Memorandum by A. Werren, 28.10.90. AU.
[76] Memorandum by Tarling, 1.8.90. AU.
[77] Cf MacCormick/Tarling, 5.9.90. AU.
[78] Schedule, 28.11.91. AU.

made by a private postgraduate student to university research'. The total subsidy was not to exceed the amount derived by the university from academic fees in any one year.[79] Those fees were derived from non-taxpayer funds, late enrolment fees, for example.

Other structures had been created in the wake of legislative and policy changes, besides NZEIL and the administrative arrangements within the institutions. One was a mechanism for placing and monitoring the progress of students from developing countries assisted by the New Zealand Government under ODA awards and fees scholarships. Neither VCC nor most of the administrators in the individual universities favoured a central structure for admitting full-fee students in general. As it had made clear, MERT was, however, interested in a service which would cover ODA students coming to universities, polytechnics and teachers colleges. A central clearing house would avoid the extra work caused by multiple applications.[80] What it had discussed with the VCC was a contract for services.[81] The service got under way in 1990, but ran at a loss, in part because of the unexpected extent of the monitoring exercise. VCC put up the fee for 1993, but did not expect that to be sufficient. If MERT could not offer a subsidy, it might have to withdraw.[82]

The admission of assisted graduates from developing countries outside the South Pacific was left to the universities, but there were country quotas. The universities wanted to meet the higher demand from China, MERT wanted them to be more 'pro-active' in Southeast Asia.[83] In 1992 it declared that the universities were to allocate 50% of the funds to students from eligible countries in Southeast Asia, and to allocate no more than 25% to students from any one country, in effect meaning China.[84]

Students entering New Zealand under exchange agreements approved by the Minister had been exempted from the foreign student fees since they had been imposed in 1979. That was to continue under the full-fee regime, foreign students paying domestic fees. S20 of the 1989 Amendment Act was, however, revoked from 1.1.91. That meant that there was no legislation for the exemption. A notice in the Gazette, 13.8.92, therefore provided that they should pay domestic fees.[85] There was an emphasis on reciprocity, presumably because the New Zealand taxpayer was assumed

---

[79]   Maien/Tarling, 15.10.92. AU.

[80]   Minutes of Overseas Student Admission Administrators, 6.6.90. AU.

[81]   Standing Committee teleconference, 3.4.90. AU.

[82]   Taiaroa/Lawson, 15.6.92, and report enclosed. AU.

[83]   Farrell/Tairoa, 21.3.91. AU.

[84]   Woods/Taiaroa, 17.8.92. AU.

[85]   Guidelines, 28.10.92, paras. 2,3 . AU.

to be meeting the EFTS value. That reciprocity was, moreover, essentially agreement-by-agreement and year-by-year. The Minister of Education would no longer be involved, but Immigration was.[86]

Implementing the new scheme was not easy, partly because it had not been thought through, partly because of changes that could not have been anticipated even if it had been. The striking features of the phase were the dramatic growth in private English language teaching and the relatively slow growth in university enrolments, even at the undergraduate level.

---

[86] General Requirements for Exchange Schemes, Immigration Department, as Appendix to ibid.

CHAPTER TEN

THE CHINESE

The sometimes controverted arrangements of 1990-4 filled out the structure created by the legislative changes of 1989-90. They provided a framework for the following decade, but were subject to further modifications. Some were designed to remedy deficiencies or fill gaps, some to meet unanticipated contingencies and changed circumstances. The outcome of what New Zealand and New Zealanders did was much affected by the policies and decisions of other countries and their peoples. The major change might be seen as quantitative, but also qualitative. That was the arrival of large numbers of students from the People's Republic of China, both as undergraduate students and as students of private sector English language schools. That happened as a result, not only New Zealand's policies, but of China's. It happened quite late in the decade and quite suddenly, challenging the policies that had developed and indeed the structures that had been set up.

'Nobody, it seems, saw it coming. The seemingly non-stop growth – or more like explosion – of the export education industry has certainly caught short the policy-makers and regulators', Geoff Collett wrote in November 2002. '... Now, politicians and officialdom are playing a rapid game of catch-up, to try to impose a new system of regulation and order on a sector which has so far outpaced anyone's attempts to keep a coherent overview of all that is going on', he added, perhaps with a touch of hyperbole. In the 1990s 'the industry grew quietly, and mostly unremarkably. It received a huge fillip at the end of that decade with the removal of the final barriers to students from China being able to study here without restriction'.[1]

---

[1]   Press, 16.11.02.

THE CHINESE

Despite the hype that had accompanied the change that the MDB report promoted, the number of full-fee paying students indeed grew relatively slowly at first. By 1994 the number of full fee paying students in public tertiary institutions had reached 3199. 2303 of them came from Asia, with Malaysia, at 995, by far the largest source, and China supplying 49. By 1997 the total was 6228, with 5197 from Asia, including 2461 from Malaysia and 75 from China. The Asian financial crisis prompted a fall in overall numbers. That was retrieved by 1999, and in the following years the numbers grew very rapidly. In 2000 the total was 7931, with 6275 from Asia; in 2001 12 649, with 10 543 from Asia; in 2002 20 767, with 17682 from Asia. The numbers from Malaysia fell during the crisis and continued to fall. The numbers from the People's Republic rose dramatically. 89 came in 1998, 457 in 1999, 1696 in 2000, 5236 in 2001, and 11 700 in 2002. In 1994 72% of full fee paying students at public tertiary institutions were from Asia and in 2002 85.1%; in 1994 1.5% were from China and in 2002 56.3%; in 1994 31.1% were from Malaysia and in 2002 4.9%.

Universities and polytechnics showed the greatest increase. Of the 3199 foreign full fee paying students at public tertiary institutions in 1994, 2299 were at universities, 880 at polytechnics, and 20 at colleges of education. In 1997, of the 6228, 4489 were at universities, 1660 at polytechnics, and 79 at colleges. The 20 767 students of 2002 comprised 13 825 at universities, 680 at polytechnics and 139 at colleges of education. The largest proportion of the students were at university, 67% in 2002, the growth emphasised by AIT's securing university status in 1999. While enrolments increased overall, the enrolment of foreign full-fee students increased more rapidly still. In 1990 there were 78 919 university students, in 1995 104 389, in 2002 122 727. Full fee payers students made up 2.3% of total formal enrolments in 1994, 3.9% in 1997, 10.1% in 2002. At polytechnics the comparable percentages were 1%, 2.3%, and 7.1%. There were regional and institutional variants. In 2002 the Auckland region took 8 263 of the 20 767 full fee students at public tertiary institutions, the next largest regions being Manawatu-Wanganui with 3003 and Canterbury with 2 588. At some universities the local roll had slowed. Lincoln had 27% full fee students in 2002 and WU 18%.

The fields of study overseas students chose emphasised literacy and numeracy programmes, commerce and business studies. Their preference for the latter exceeded that of domestic students, emphatically though that had grown since the late 1970s. In 2002 39.9% of full fee students in public tertiary institutions were enrolled in management and commerce programmes, whereas the overall total was 21.4%. At universities, the full fee students were predominantly undergraduate. Of the 13 373 students enrolled in 2002, 8 747 were enrolled at degree level, and 1041 were enrolled at postgraduate level.

At school level, the percentage of full fee students was, of course, far smaller, 0.2% of the total roll at primary level in 2000, and 2.6% of secondary. It was even more predominantly of Asian origin: 86.9% and 91.9%, though not so predominantly Chinese: in 2000 30.6% of Asian primary and secondary students were from China, 23% were from Korea and 19.3% were from Japan. Half of them were in the Auckland region. Half of them were in just ten secondary schools. Schools in the highest socio-economic status communities had significantly more full-fee payers than those in the lowest. At secondary school they were much more likely than local students to be studying Mathematics, Science, Physics and Chemistry, and more also enrolled in the less tradtional school subjects, Economics and Accountancy.

At primary level – where the 'reforms' had reversed an earlier decision not to admit foreign students at all – the majority of students in 2000 came from ROK, 636 out of 1026 in 2000. Auckland accounted annually for 45-60% of all fee-paying primary students. The trend was a greater participation in the market by higher decile schools. At secondary school numbers increased from 1 748 in 1993 – when data were first collected – to 6 254 in 2000, with a slump during the downturn. The main sources were China, Japan and Korea, China becoming the largest single source country in 2000 and providing 31.7% of the students, while Japan provided 19.9% and Korea 13.9%. Students concentrated in Year 12 and 13 [Forms 6 and 7 old-style] – suggesting their tertiary aspirations. Further dramatic increases followed. In 2003 17 448 foreign fee-paying students were attending New Zealand schools, out of a total of 761 755.[2]

The data available in respect of private providers over these years are limited. MOE returns included only from those that receive tuition subsidies or were recognised for student loans and allowances, a minority. It did not cover all the EL providers, which concentrate on foreign students nor in general other providers who cater mainly for foreign students. An annual questionnaire sent to providers registered with NZQA captured only limited information. Statistics New Zealand, however, conducted surveys of EL providers. In 1999 a census of 90 providers returned 15 718 students. In 2000 a census of 49 providers returned 18 054 foreign students. A census of 104 providers in 2003 returned nearly 70 000. An Asia 2000 paper pointed to the boom. It suggested that there were in fact some 122 EL schools, 93 of them registered with NZQA.[3]

---

[2] NZH, 10.12.83.

[3] *The Export Education Industry: Challenges for New Zealand*, Wellington: Asia 2000, ?2003, p. 9.

What the MOE's data on private providers revealed in many respects paralleled the indications of its data on state institutions, used above. Asia provided 89% of foreign students in the PTE sector, and China had rapidly become the largest single source, providing 1.5% of the students in 1997 and 28.9% in 2000. Statistics New Zealand's image of the language sector was rather different. About 80% of the students indeed came from Asia, but Japan was the largest single source, accounting for almost half the students.

Though these changes took place within the 1988-9 framework, they did not entirely accord with the forecasts its progenitors made. Forecasts continued to be conservative: in 2002 Lester Taylor, chief executive of Education New Zealand [NZEIL's successor], said that the 'industry' had generated an income of 1bn the previous year, though that had been the target for 2004.[4] The progenitors had probably expected a more gradual growth, rather than a slow advance followed by a dramatic increase. Nor did they anticipate that China would belatedly but rapidly become the largest single source. That was indeed in some sense a function of New Zealand's late entry into the market, and its difficulty in penetrating new markets – and indeed in retaining old markets like Malaysia – in turn a function of the contorted way in which it had made new policy, and its tendency to rely on a mix of old-fashioned boot-strapping and unsubsidised enterprise. The progenitors of the framework might also respond more generally that their aim was to allow the free market to operate, and that their forecasts could be no more than best guesses as to the way in which it might happen.

Such a discussion, however, risks omitting significant factors that may be regarded either as interventions in the operation of market forces or as part of the market itself. Those must indeed be borne in mind in explaining what happened, and perhaps, too, in any attempt to frame future policies in the light of what happened. They relate both to supply and demand. For such changes to operate, it was essential, on the one hand, that China should develop a middle class that could pay for overseas education and that its government would allow its citizens to go abroad to secure it. In that sense New Zealand's success in export education was dependent on the transformation of Chinese society, economy, government and ideology. The burgeoning middle-class, it was reported in 2002, was ready to spend 15% of the household income on education.[5] There were then 460 000 Chinese students abroad, 305 095 of them in the US, 6.8% supported by the state, 21% by their companies, and the rest private.[6]

---

4 *Dominion*, 22.1.02.
5 Roger Barnard, *The Guardian*, 21.2.02.
6 Mark O'Neill, *South China Morning Post*, 7.10.02.

It was, on the other hand, also essential, if it was to share in this market, for New Zealand to be ready to welcome students from China and to provide them with the opportunities they sought. The 1997 financial crisis led to a drop in enquiries from Asian students, according to Stuart Rose, director of NZEIL.[7] Mark Nixon, director of Southern English Schools, suggested that New Zealand was not making up for the shortfall, as were other countries, by looking to China, less affected by the crisis. It sat on its hands, he said, the Government arguing that such students would try for refugee status or political asylum.[8] The 1991-2 rules indeed made private PRC students ineligible for visas or permits for short-term courses, while for courses of one year or more, they had to have a degree or its equivalent already.[9] But late in 1997 the government agreed to admit 400 Chinese students; in June 1998 it extended the quota to 1000; and in October to 4000.[10]

The change also required an institutional response. That was readily forthcoming, not only, of course, from private providers, but from state providers, particularly because government funding of universities and schools had been curtailed, and domestic fees had not made up for that. Financial starvation complemented a wish to 'internationalise' the universities, but tended to overwhelm it. There was a risk that full fee-paying students would be seen, and come to realise that they were seen, simply as profitable commodities, even in public institutions, let alone in PTEs.

These changes were, moreover, taking place during a larger demographic change. General Asian migration also expanded – particularly but not merely in the Auckland region – and, with the aid of some political and media elements, created a backlash directed indifferently against international students and citizens and permanent residents of Asian origin, damaging not only to the student 'market', but to the relationships with Asia that New Zealand had set out to foster fifty years earlier. '[T]he immigration debate is spilling over into other, unrelated areas', said Ben King, the student president at WU in 1996. '... International students are not immigrants. They are visitors to this country and they bring a lot to us.'[11] Like the growth in private overseas students in the days of subsidy, the growth of the late nineties and early noughties, somewhat haphazard, needed reconsideration, but it needed to be done with much more rather than even less sensitivity, so far as both New Zealand and New Zealanders

---

[7] Press, 10.12.97.
[8] Press, 2.2.98.
[9] Circular 91/9.
[10] NZH, 31.10.97; 18.6.98; 15.10.98.
[11] NZH, 18.4.96.

and 'Asia' and 'Asians' were concerned, and also with respect to the students. Not surprisingly the issue bulked quite large at the 15th NZASIA conference and was discussed at the Seriously Asia conference in November 2003.

In 2002, however, Trevor Mallard, the Minister of Education, had spoken of 'capping' the number of foreign students, in the context of 'the strain being put on the education system and wider community'. Generally, he said, New Zealand offered 'high quality, but we're just at the edge of that'. There were 'concerns about our reputation'.[12] SARS and the rising Kiwi dollar reduced the rate of increase. The concerns about quality continued, particularly in respect of the language schools.[13] Indeed some more collapsed.

Limits were imposed at state schools. In 2002, as well, some universities, such as AU and CU, had begun once more to consider whether a limit should be set on the numbers of full fee students, and if so, whether it should be done by raising the academic level required for entry, already higher than the domestic level, or by stepping up the English language test, TOEFL. Though others, such as LU and WU, went well beyond the limits AU had in mind, the AU approach to some extent echoed the Minister's. His concept had a political context, for the students, though seen as a source of profit, added to the tension created by the presence of large numbers of recent migrants from Asia. But it was also true that both groups needed additional educational support, the latter as much as, if not more than, the former. The same was true at the university, particularly as both groups tended to cluster in a limited number of faculties and subjects. Lecturers found themselves facing a sea of 'Asians', some PR and citizens, some full-fee payers, some with New Zealand qualifications, but without an EL qualification, some with ad eundem or New Zealand qualifications, and with a TOEFL score. The fee-paying students might themselves be surprised to find so few non-Asians in the class and feel that a dimension of their international education was missing. If there were local non-Asian students in the class, they might tend to feel that students who had to struggle with the language or the mode of learning were delaying their completion of a costly course, if not down-grading its quality.[14]

Half or more of the sea might a China sea, considerably more if those from Hong Kong and Taiwan were added to those from the PRC. In the new context, the VC at AU, John Hood, raised the 1970s question of a quota within a quota. The question could indeed be asked on economic if

---

[12] Xinhuanet, 16.7.02.

[13] ibid., 4.9.03.

[14] Bridget Cameron and Phil Meade, 'Supporting the Transition of International Students: Issues and Challenges', OU paper.

not on ethnic grounds: was it desirable to rely so much on one source? If, however, the government had been able to instruct the UGC/OSAC to introduce a quota in 1976 – in the form of a limit of 40% on students from any one country – it was not clear that institutions – or perhaps the government itself – could do so in the early twenty-first century. The Human Rights legislation – passed after the 1976 instruction, but affecting the 1979 fee – stood in the way of such discrimination. So did practical issues. How would it be administered? Could the institutions do without the money? Would the step seem defeatist and worsen race relations? Would it damage the market in China or in general?

One answer was to seek to develop other sources. That, indeed, was a continued endeavour, both on the part of institutions, and on the part of Education New Zealand, set up in 1998 as the generic promoter in succession to NZEIL, and the New Zealand International Marketing Network, which endeavoured to establish a brand, 'The New World Class: Educated in New Zealand'. The venture enjoyed some success, in India, in Latin America, in Africa, but even in the long term other markets were unlikely to surpass the China market. In the meantime that provided so many students so readily and with so little effort and expense that it was tempting for agents and entrepreneurs to take undue advantage of it. Even if the flow out of China was to continue, it did not guarantee a flow into New Zealand. The response was an increasingly formal attempt to ensure 'quality' – though financed by a levy effectively falling on the students – rather than a real attempt to treat the students as a means of learning and a foundation for international relationships in the way that Colombo Plan students and others had been treated in the 1950s and 1960s.

There was another context for the discussion in government and university circles. The framework created in 1988-9 had been filled out not only by publicly-funded schools and tertiary institutions, but by the creation of a large number of 'private providers', even more focused than the public institutions had come to be on the need to realise a financial return. Some of them were offering qualifications at degree or certificate level, others preparing students for entry into universities, and laying no special emphasis on full fee paying foreign students. Others, particularly, of course, the EL schools, relied on the foreign student market, predominantly, though not exclusively, 'Asian'. Early in the 1990s, when the framework was still being elaborated, some of those providers had been shown to be speculative and under-capitalised. That this was still the case ten years later was suggested when a further collapse – that of Planet English[15] – was prompted in part by SARS, and perhaps affected, too, by

---

[15]   NZH, 14.5.03.

the talk of caps and the negative publicity on racialism and violence. The government of the PRC, which had made New Zealand a 'preferred destination', expressed its concern and, later, its wish to list approved providers on its study abroad website.[16] The Minister of Education visited Beijing[17] – just as a further but less foreign student-focused provider, Modern Age Institute of Learning was falling[18] – to offer reassurance. He appeared on Chinese TV in November.[19]

The need to sustain the market had already provided an inducement for introducing a compulsory Code of Practice. That was provided for by the Education Standards Act 2001 No. 88, which secured assent on 24 October, and the proposed code was gazetted in December 2001. It set out requirements in respect of informing and recruiting prospective students and of providing for their welfare, and established an International Education Appeal Authority to investigate and determine complaints from international students about alleged breaches of the code after all internal grievance procedures had been exhausted. An amendment followed in 2002, the Education (Tertiary Reform) Amendment Act 2002, No. 50. That, S 30, replaced the fee that the previous Act had envisaged by a levy, a move controverted by those providers that catered for large numbers of students and for students whose courses extended over several years. 'It punished the successful', said the VUW VC.[20] The amendment also brought under the legislation providers offering courses of less than three months' duration, hitherto excluded from quality control. Regulations made by Order-in-Council on 18 December 2002 specified the levy, which was to comprise a flat fee of $185, plus 0.45% of the total course fees exclusive of GST. An increase to .7% was proposed in December 2003.[21]

Providers had been aware of the need for a code of practice. NZEIL had adopted one, prepared by John Watson, in 1991,[22] and MOE had promoted 'a tough code of ethics', still voluntary, in 1996.[23] What was above all new about the code of practice was its compulsory nature. The progenitors of the framework had opted for the discipline of the market. Providers that offered poor quality or failed to meet the demands of their

---

[16] NZH, 12.1.03.
[17] NXH, 17.9.03.
[18] NZH, 16.9.03.
[19] NZH, 6.11.03.
[20] NZH, 10.5.02.
[21] NZH, 4.12.03.
[22] *NZEIL Newa*, 2.91.
[23] NZER, 15.5.96.

'customers' would go to the wall, and the best would survive. That concept was an unrealistic application of 'free market' concepts to the education field. On the one hand, export education was in some sense a national venture, and had been promoted as such and was seen as such in the market: a poor provider could damage the prospects of good providers, not merely punishing itself but others, too. On the other hand, the student was not a mere one-off purchaser. He or she had to pay in advance, but 'consume' only over time. A 'guarantee' could not be offered, not merely because the 'consumer' was required to be an active participant, but also because the seller, too, had to make a sustained effort. The legislative amendments and regulations were designed to make the 'market' work more effectively, more justly, and more fairly.

No doubt that was necessary, if only to help sustain it. There is, however, a limit to what such regulations can achieve. Even those whose mind is on the 'market' and whose focus is on economic benefit need to adopt a wider and more humane perspective. Not only institutions, but other bodies, too, cities and regions, for example, focus almost exclusively on the size and earnings of the 'business', continuing the rhetoric of the progenitors of the change of policy. The Waikato economy benefited by $100m in 2002, the *Waikato Times* tells us.[24] Even a non-progenitor, Marshall, proclaimed as chair of Education New Zealand: 'It's one of the few industries which is great for every region.'[25] In fact Auckland had half of the 88k students in New Zealand in 2001/2. Their total spending was $650m, or, including flow-on, $1290m.[26] Yet an emphasis only on the financials can only be counter-productive if the students see themselves merely as tradeable commodities.

Meanwhile institutions and other bodies as well make too little of the other benefits that international students offer. Even those who well-meaningly insist that they have a different style of learning may be missing an opportunity. Certainly the universities have made too little of them in their avowed pursuit of internationalisation, while the new over-arching body, TEC, emerged out of discussions that made only the most limited reference to international students.[27] It is far from clear that the full-fee students will remain friends of New Zealand as, it seems, those have who came under the Colombo Plan or through paying domestic fees. They may feel they are charged more and given less. The research which the

---

[24] 25.2.03.

[25] *Dominion*, 18.8.00.

[26] Infometrics {Aolf Strombergen], International Students their impact on Auckland City, 12.03.

[27] Second Report, p. 15; Fourth Report, pp. 141-2.

levy is intended to promote may assist in handling the problem. But it also requires a shift in attitude in institutions and outside as well.

'[W]e entered the market using a price penetration strategy, and competed using the low Kiwi dollar as one of our strongest selling points', Robert Stephens, CEO of the Education New Zealand Trust, told the 12th International Education Conference in Wellington on 12 August 2003. The strategy was appropriate at the time. 'Competing initially in price is a standard strategy for most industries when a new market opens up. We did well by penetrating the market using our comparative cost advantage.' But it could be argued that the medium-term result was 'that New Zealand is not generally perceived as being positioned at the premium end of the market, has students concentrated in a limited range of fields of study and is highly dependent on a few source countries.' It should, Stevens argued, raise quality for students who came to New Zealand, and move into offshore delivery.

In fact, of course, New Zealand had not initially adopted a price penetration strategy so far as fees were concerned, though it had the advantage of low living costs, especially when the dollar was low. Writing in 1992, James Tsui suggested that – not the only, best, or most well-known supplier – New Zealand had to weigh alternatives: 'whether it could offer niche products or whether more competitive prices would work best to attract customers'.[28] He favoured a niche approach, suggesting a focus on Asian secondary students and on distance learning, with tailor-made approaches for different countries, organised by some analogue to the producer boards.[29]

During the discussions that led to the creation of the new framework in 1987-8, an alternative approach was, however, sometimes put forward, including the elements that Tsui advocated, though with different 'niches'. Arriving relatively late on the scene, New Zealand, a small-scale and underfunded operator, would concentrate its effort on what it could best offer and seek to establish a network of connexions based upon its specialities. That option was not pursued: instead New Zealand competed with major players, including its nearest neighbour, in seeking access to the market for undergraduate education, particularly in business and computing, and to the market for English language teaching. Those were fields in which what it offered was generally of sound quality, if not outstanding, but it offered nothing that was special. Any price advantage diminished when the dollar rose, while fees, set at profit-making levels by

---

28 'The development of a foreign student policy in New Zealand', MA (Ed) thesis, VUW, 1992, p. 151.

29 ibid., pp. 158-60.

private providers and cash-strapped state institutions, could not easily be lowered. There was a risk both that its own standards would slip if it continued to rely simply on doing more of the same and that the standard of the students it would feel bound to accept might also slip, particularly if the supply began to fall away because sending countries developed their own facilities, or receiving countries competed yet more effectively.

In that context the concept of a 'niche' approach deserves reconsideration. Seeking to sustain their international standing in a world in which the gap between the best and the worst institutions had expanded, and in which the whole concept of a university as an institution in which teaching and research were necessarily connected was under threat, the New Zealand universities have been anxious to build on the research capacity they had laboriously created during the UGC phase, despite the increasing constraints on their funding. The new fees and loans regime, introduced for domestic students in the early 1990s, reduced the attraction of postgraduate qualifications and of research degrees, particularly if pursued on a full-time basis. The fees for international students were, of course, even higher. Universities felt able in some cases to offer fees concessions, but rarely fees scholarships. Nor were they in a position to offer employment opportunities on the scale of those that sustain foreign graduate students in US universities.

It is clear that a scholarship scheme could not be sustained simply on the current financial and institutional basis, and it would require a new measure of government funding, particularly at the outset. That could well be justified, if focused on research students, since, like the research reported in the late 1970s and early 1980s, it was bound, done in New Zealand, to reflect on New Zealand concerns or discuss New Zealand problems. In addition it would help to build critical mass within research fields at New Zealand universities, within and outside centres of excellence, building staff morale, making them more attractive to staff in other countries or expatriate New Zealanders, and developing relationships with universities in other countries on the basis not merely of undergraduate exchange but of research networks. Such a move would, of course, have to be coupled with a more generous provision for domestic and PR students, in the form, perhaps, of a restoration of the national postgraduate scholarship scheme, abandoned in the early 1990s.

At the same time, such a move might also mitigate the problems New Zealand may face in the market for international students. It cannot, of course, drop its focus on the mass market and abruptly turn to a niche market. The two can and should be combined. If the market shifts, it is surely likely itself to focus less on undergraduate and English language study, and turn rather to second-qualification or higher-level study or even to research-oriented degrees. New Zealand might do well to signal its interest in such provison and demonstrate its capacity to make it. That would open up a new market. But it would also help to sustain the existing market in basic undergraduate and EL education by demonstrating, other than by regulatory means or embarrassing apology, that New Zealand is concerned with high-quality education and able to provide it.

Fifty years ago New Zealand launched its participation in the provision of international education by taking part in the Colombo Plan. That was a successful project, at home as well abroad, and many New Zealanders continue, twenty years after their government stopped using the title, to employ the words almost as a synonym for the funded provision of international education. In some sense the search for a niche in higher-level international education might be conceived, presented and received as a new Colombo Plan. Like that Plan, it would no doubt have unplanned outcomes, including the attraction of other students to New Zealand, and the assurance of a network of connexions of great if incommensurable value. The research funded by the Code levy could include – aside from continued work on pastoral care and learning differentials – a project that would establish the parameters for such a scheme. 'We need to recapture that programme's great qualities', Chris Hawley said in 2002.[30] This may be a way.

It would not, of course, displace the international education that New Zealand has continued to fund under its ODA schemes. Those set up when the new framework was created, partly designed to cover the transition from the old framework, were reviewed in 1993-4. They then included secondary and tertiary fees scholarships, by that time almost exclusively focused on the South Pacific.[31] They also included the MERT postgraduate fees scholarships for students from developing countries outside the South Pacific, 55% going to Southeast Asian students, not more than 25% to students from any one country. In addition, there were ODA study awards, which met other costs as well. In this case, by contrast to the Fees Scholarships, candidates had to be nominated by their own governments, Colombo-Plan style.[32]

The reviews led to the phasing-out of the South Pacific Fees Scholarships. They were replaced by a new equity and merit scheme, the Aotearoa Scholarship scheme. There was to be some provision for non-academic

---

[30] NZH, 21.6.03.
[31] Evaluation of NZODA, 6.93, p. 15. AU.
[32] Fees Scholarships, Policy guidelines and administrative procedures, MERT, 1.93. AU.

costs, and half of the scholarships were to go to women.[33] The post-graduate fees scholarship scheme was also terminated. Though by the end of 1992, some 200 students had either completed their course or were still working on it, it had been difficult to meet the regional criteria – the numbers applying from China far outnumbered those from Southeast Asia – and a number of able students had been unable to take up their awards on financial grounds.[34] Hence the introduction of a new NZODA Postgraduate Scholarships scheme open to direct applicants from developing countries world-wide.[35]

The Aotearoa Awards continued for some years, but are now being phased out. Successors in a sense of the Colombo Plan awards, NZODA Study Awards, offered at undergraduate and graduate levels, require the endorsement of partner governments. The Postgraduate Scholarships scheme attracts a very large number of applicants, but many are unacceptable, and the number of awards is small. For example, in total there were 152 on the roll at AU in 2002. AU itself awarded 6 all-country doctoral awards and 25 fees scholarships. The latter were not well-known nor competitive. Such statistics form a guide for any new scholarship scheme that might be offered. They need not be seen as an argument against it. Arguably they suggest that a bold step may be needed to build New Zealand's reputation.

---

[33] NZODA South Pacific Fees Scholarships. An evaluation, MFAT, 4.94. Shroff/Taiaroa, 17.5.95. AU.

[34] Postgraduate Fees Scholarships to Students from Asia, Africa and the Americas, A Review..., MFAT, 6.93. AU.

SOURCES

The main archival sources used in this work are to be found in three places.

National Archives, Wellington

Archives of the University of New Zealand and University Grants
Committee [Agency AAMJ]:
Accession W 3119, including Boxes 539, 653
Accession W 3601, including Boxes 89-96, 154, 166, 167

New Zealand Vice-Chancellors Committee, Wellington

Boxes 7, 11, 12, 13, 46

The University of Auckland

Overseas Students, six boxes

ABBREVIATIONS

AIS Auckland Institute of Studies
AJHR Appendixes to the Journals of the House of Representatives
ASEAN Association of Southeast Asian States
AU The University of Auckland
AUTNZ Association of University Teachers of New Zealand

BAP Bilateral Aid Programme

CNZEL Consult New Zealand Education Limited
CP Colombo Plan
CU The University of Canterbury

DEA Department of External Affairs
DIT Department of Island Territories
DOE Department of Education
DOL Department of Labour
DSIR Department of Scientific and Industrial Research

EAR External Affairs Review
EG Education Gazette
ELI English Language Institute

FAR Foreign Affairs Review
FIELS Federation of Independent English Language Schools

HSC Higher School Certificate

IDC Interdepartmental Committee

KL Kuala Lumpur

LATOS Language Aptitude Test for Overseas Students
LC Lincoln College

MDB Market Development Board
MERT Ministry of External Affairs and Trade
MFA Ministry of Foreign Affairs
MFAT Ministry of Foreign Affairs and Trade
MU Massey University

NOSAC National Overseas Students Action Committee
NZCE New Zealand Certificate in Engineering
NZCER New Zealand Council for Educational Research
NZEIL New Zealand Education International Limited
NZQA New Zealand Qualifications Authority
NZUSA New Zealand University Students' Association

OSAC Overseas Students Admissions Committee
OU The University of Otago

PGS Postgraduate Scholarship
PI Pacific Island
PR Press Release

TDB Trade Development Board
TEC Tertiary Education Commission
THES Times Higher Education Supplement
TI Technical Institute

UE University Entrance
UEB University Entrance Board
UGC University Grants Committee
USP University of the South Pacific

VC Vice-Chancellor
VCC Vice-Chancellors' Committee
VUW Victoria University of Wellington

WU University of Waikato